Responding to Rising Seas

OECD COUNTRY APPROACHES TO TACKLING COASTAL RISKS

OECD
BETTER POLICIES FOR BETTER LIVES

Please cite this publication as:
OECD (2019), *Responding to Rising Seas: OECD Country Approaches to Tackling Coastal Risks*, OECD Publishing, Paris.
https://doi.org/10.1787/9789264312487-en

ISBN 978-92-64-31247-0 (print)
ISBN 978-92-64-31248-7 (pdf)

Revised version, January 2020
Details of revisions available at:
http://www.oecd.org/about/publishing/Corrigendum_Responding-to-rising-seas.pdf

Photo credits: Cover © RBOZUK/GettyImages

Corrigenda to OECD publications may be found on line at: *www.oecd.org/about/publishing/corrigenda.htm*.

Foreword

Sea-level rise is one of the major challenges identified in the recent Intergovernmental Panel on Climate Change's Special Report "Global Warming of 1.5°C". It is almost certain that we will experience at least one metre of sea level rise, with some models estimating this will happen within the next 80 years. This will have serious implications for damage to infrastructure, loss of land and displacement of communities. Even if we succeeded in limiting the temperature increase to 1.5 degrees, sea levels will continue to rise for centuries to come, due to emissions we have already locked in. While living on the coast has always come with a certain level of flooding and erosion risks, climate change will alter our coastlines and we must prepare for this new reality.

This report, *Responding to Rising Seas: OECD Country Approaches to Tackling Coastal Risks* takes a major step forward in providing policy guidance on how countries can more effectively manage the risks from sea level rise. The report takes stock of what OECD countries are currently doing to prepare for coastal change, and puts forward a policy framework for coastal adaptation that is equipped to meet the challenges of ever-increasing global temperatures. Four case studies – Canada, Germany, New Zealand and the United Kingdom – provide in-depth examples of the challenges and success factors of coastal adaptation strategies under different institutional contexts. This report builds on the body of OECD work on managing climate risks.

It is vital that countries strengthen their ability to understand, plan for and continuously manage climate risks. There is some progress more and more OECD countries are developing national strategies to cope with climate change, and sub-national and private actors are also increasingly tackling this issue. However, there is a pressing need to translate planning into implementation. This OECD report provides lessons learned and guidance for countries in approaching the challenges from climate change that will surely mount over coming years.

Rodolfo Lacy

OECD Environment Director

Acknowledgements

Responding to Rising Seas: OECD Country Approaches to Tackling Coastal Risks is an output of the OECD Environment Directorate.

This report was co-ordinated by Lisa Danielson. Chapters 1 was drafted by Alexander Bisaro, Jochen Hinkel and Daniel Lincke. Lisa Danielson and Michael Mullan drafted Chapter 2, and benefited from contributions from Alexander Bisaro. Lisa Danielson, Aurélien Seawert and Alexander Bisaro drafted Chapter 3. Alexander Bisaro and Jochen Hinkel drafted chapter 4. Kate Sherren, Tony Bowron, Jennifer M. Graham, H.M. Tuihedur Rahman and Danika van Proosdij drafted Chapter 5. Emma Corbett and Simon Bendall drafted Chapter 6. Nick Haigh drafted Chapter 7 and benefited from contributions from Rob Goodliffe and Kellie Fisher.

The authors would also like to thank OECD colleagues Simon Buckle, Xavier Leflaive, Nicolina Lamhauge, Leigh Wolfrom, Catherine Gamper, Teresa Deubelli, Oriana Romano, Kathleen Dominique, Will Symes, Rodney Boyd, Brilé Anderson and Jane Ellis for their input and comments on earlier versions of the report. The authors are are also grateful for the oversight, review and comments by the Working Party on Climate, Investment, and Development (WPCID) and the Environment Policy Committee (EPOC). The production benefited from the assistance of Sama Al Taher Cucci and Anna Rourke.

Financial support from Natural Resources Canada is gratefully acknowledged. The authors would also like to thank the New Zealand Ministry for the Environment and the UK Department for Environment, Food & Rural Affairs for providing case studies. Special thanks is given to the Global Climate Forum for their support on this project.

GCF
Global Climate Forum

Table of contents

Tables

Figures

Boxes

Glossary

Coastal zone: The interface between the land and the sea.

Dike/coastal realignment: The process of changing the line of currently maintained coastal defences, either by shortening defence length, moving defences inland or removing defences altogether. This allows for the creation of intertidal habitat (e.g. salt marshes), which can provide a natural buffer against tides and storm surges.

Ecosystem-based adaptation: Ecosystem-based adaptation is the use of biodiversity and ecosystem services as part of an overall adaptation strategy to help people to adapt to the adverse effects of climate change. It aims to maintain and increase the resilience and reduce the vulnerability of ecosystems and people.

Maladaptation: Actions that may lead to increased risk of adverse climate-related outcomes or increased vulnerability to climate change.

Nature-based solutions: Refers to an umbrella concept for various ecosystem-related approaches. It covers actions to protect, sustainably manage and restore natural or modified ecosystems. Nature-based solutions aim to achieve resilience in ways that enhance the resilience of ecosystems, their capacity for renewal and the provision of services.

Resilience: The ability of households, communities and nations to absorb and recover from shocks, while positively adapting and transforming their structures and means for living in the face of long-term stresses, change and uncertainty.

Risk: The potential for consequences where something of value is at stake and where the outcome is uncertain, recognising the diversity of values. Risk is often represented as probability or likelihood of occurrence of hazardous events or trends multiplied by the impacts if these events or trends occur. In this report, the term risk is often used to refer to the potential, when the outcome is uncertain, for adverse consequences on lives, livelihoods, health, ecosystems and species, economic, social and cultural assets, services (including environmental services), and infrastructure (Intergovernmental Panel on Climate Change, 2014[1]).

Sea-level rise: The change in sea levels caused by global warming (e.g. though thermal expansion of the ocean, melting glaciers and polar ice caps, and ice loss from Greenland and West Antarctica ice sheets). The temporal average for a given location is mean sea level and the spatial average is global mean sea level. Changes in local relative sea level can vary significantly from changes in global mean sea level.

Transformational adaptation: Actions or interventions opened when the limits of incremental adaptation (e.g. actions where the central aim is to maintain an existing system or process) have been reached (Intergovernmental Panel on Climate Change, 2014[1]).

Uncertainty: "A state of incomplete knowledge, resulting from a lack of information or from disagreement about what is known or even knowable. It may have many types of sources, from imprecision in the data to ambiguously defined concepts or terminology, or uncertain projections of human behaviour. Uncertainty can therefore be represented by quantitative measures (e.g. a probability density function) or by qualitative statements e.g. reflecting the judgment of a team of experts)".

Acronyms and abbreviations

CPCFD	Coastal protection and flood defence
DAPP	Dynamic adaptive planning pathways
Defra	Department for Environment, Food & Rural Affairs (United Kingdom)
EU	European Union
FDRP	Flood Damage Reduction Program (Nova Scotia)
GAK	Joint Task for the Improvement of Agricultural Structures and Coastal Protection (Germany)
GCM	General circulation model
GDP	Gross domestic product
ICZM	Integrated coastal zone management
IPCC	International Panel on Climate Change
MCDA	Multi-criteria decision analysis
MSL	Mean sea level
NFIP	National Flood Insurance Program (United States)
NNDC	North Norfolk District Council (United Kingdom)
NRCan	Natural Resources Canada
NSDA	Nova Scotia Department of Agriculture
NSDE	Nova Scotia Department of Environment
NSDNR	Nova Scotia Department of Natural Resources
NSTIR	Nova Scotia Department of Transportation and Infrastructure Renewal
RCP	Representative concentration pathways

ROA	Real options analysis
SLR	Sea-level rise
SMP	Shoreline management plan
SSP	Socio economic pathway

Executive summary

People have long been drawn to the coast by the availability of transport links, amenity value and access to marine resources. Being located on the coast has many benefits, but also exposes people and assets to a range of hazards, such as storm surges. Climate change induced sea-level rise will act as a risk multiplier, affecting the world's coasts by increasing flood and erosion risks, and potentially fully inundating some areas. As risks increase, so will the associated economic and human costs from extreme events and slow-onset changes. New modelling projects that under a high-end sea-level rise scenario, residual damage costs could be between USD 1.7 trillion and USD 5.5 trillion over the 21st century.

Existing institutional arrangements will be put under pressure by increasing risks. For example, in countries where flood insurance is provided on a commercial basis, coverage may become unaffordable or unattainable as premiums increase in line with risks or insurers withdraw from markets. National governments may also be exposed to increasing contingent liabilities given their role in providing relief and compensation for uninsured losses after they happen. Increased exposure and hazards will make it more expensive to protect all properties to a given standard, which will have financial implications for different levels of government, as well as for individuals. Adaptation options, such as protect, accommodate, retreat can reduce the economic and human costs of sea-level rise, and are considered economically rational for most developed coastlines. A combination of these options will be required to address future risks. However, policy misalignments and other barriers can hinder the implementation of cost-effective responses or lead to choices that prove maladaptive over time.

In order to gauge progress and gain insights from countries' coastal adaptation efforts, this study reviews member countries' adaptation plans. While in most OECD countries local governments implement measures that directly manage coastal risks, the enabling framework is set at the national level. The analysis reveals that the implementation of measures to support adaptation to sea-level rise is generally at an early stage, despite the trends of increasing losses. The results additionally find that while many countries are increasing investments in information services, there has been less action in considering regulation, economic instruments, funding and operational monitoring evaluation frameworks.

Four case studies (Canada, Germany, New Zealand and the United Kingdom), provide in-depth examples of the challenges and success factors of coastal adaptation strategies under different institutional contexts. Drawing on these case studies, this report puts forward four principles of a policy framework for coastal adaptation that is equipped to meet the challenges described above, which should be considered by national governments as they further develop their adaptation plans:

- engage stakeholders early and substantively
- plan for the future and prevent lock-in to unsustainable pathways
- align actors' responsibilities, resources and incentives

- explicitly consider distributional and equity implications of policies.

There is robust evidence and a compelling case for further action to address the consequences of sea-level rise. While not all coastal risks can be avoided, well-prepared coastal communities will be better able to adjust to new conditions, at lower cost, and rapidly bounce back from disasters when they do occur.

Chapter 1. Rising risks in coastal zones

This chapter provides an overview of how coastal zones are facing growing risks from sea-level rise, the economic costs associated with this increasing risk and the implications for policy making. The chapter reviews the current scientific understanding of sea-level rise and coastal flood hazards. It then discusses the costs and benefits of adaptation under future sea-level rise, particularly focusing on coastal protection measures. It provides analysis of coastal adaptation from a robust decision-making perspective. Finally, the policy implications of current knowledge on coastal adaptation costs and benefits are discussed, along with priorities for future research to support coastal adaptation policy.

This chapter was written by Alexander Bisaro, Jochen Hinkel and Daniel Lincke, Global Climate Forum, Berlin and Division of Resource Economics, Humboldt University, Berlin.

1.1. Evolution of risks in coastal zones

Climate change-induced sea-level rise (SLR) will affect the world's coasts by increasing flood and erosion risks, and potentially fully inundating some areas. As risks increase, so will the associated economic and human costs from extreme events and slow-onset changes. This will strain society's capacity to maintain an acceptable level of risk at reasonable cost in coastal zones.

The core challenge of coastal adaptation is that decisions need to accommodate ongoing change, which is subject to deep uncertainty, in an area with contested stakeholder priorities. Coastal adaptation choices involve difficult trade-offs between different objectives and interests, and are constrained by existing institutional arrangements and the legacy of past decisions.

This report uses the Intergovernmental Panel on Climate Change (IPCC)'s 5th Assessment Report framework to describe risk[1]. Risks are a function of the range of potential outcomes and the associated likelihoods of those outcomes materialising in a given period. In this context, risks arise from the interaction between hazards, exposure and vulnerability:

- **Hazards** are the potential occurrence of a physical event or trend (flooding, erosion) that may cause loss of life, injury, as well as damage and loss to property, infrastructure, livelihoods, service provision, ecosystems and environmental resources.
- **Exposure** refers to the presence of people, infrastructure, housing and other tangible human assets in hazard-prone areas. A measure of exposure can include the number of people or types of assets in a coastal flood zone.
- **Vulnerability** is the degree to which natural or social systems are susceptible to, and unable to cope with, exposure to hazard.

Figure 1.1. Risk-based conceptual framework

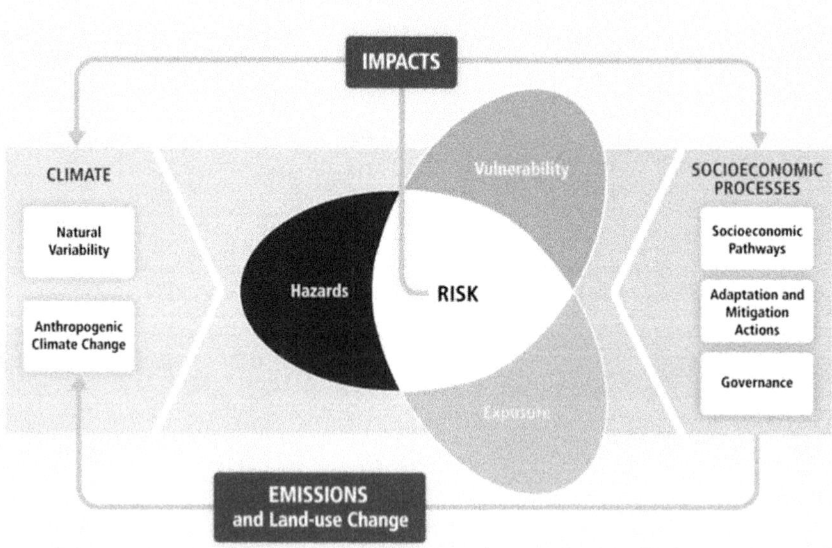

Source: Intergovernmental Panel on Climate Change (2014[1]), "Glossary, acronyms and chemical symbols", https://doi.org/10.1017/CBO9781107415416.023.

Risks from SLR include high-probability, low-consequence events (e.g. nuisance flooding) and high-probability, high-consequence events (e.g. storm surges). There is robust evidence that storm surges are already penetrating farther inland than a few decades ago, with adverse impacts on communities and coastal ecosystems (Hoegh-Guldberg et al., 2018[2]).

1.1.1. Climate change and sea-level rise

Climate change-induced sea-level rise increases coastal risks by raising the likelihood of flooding events, and inducing land loss through inundation. Generally, sea-level increases are driven by changes in global mean temperature, which are in turn driven by atmospheric greenhouse gas concentrations. Projecting future sea levels thus requires developing SLR scenarios based on different greenhouse gas concentration pathways. Representative concentration pathways (RCP) cover a wide range of such potential future concentration pathways out to 2100.

Figure 1.2 illustrates a range of SLR scenarios based on recent global studies of sea-level rise impacts (Hinkel et al., 2014[3]). All SLR values are shown with respect to mean sea-level in the 1985-2005 reference period. SLR projections in the range of 0.3 m to 1.3 m over the 21st century are based on scenarios that span three representative concentration pathways (RCP2.6, RCP4.5 and RCP8.5); four general circulation models (GCMs) (HadGEM2-ES, IPSLCM5A-LR, MIROC-ESM-CHEM and NorESM1-M); and a low, medium and high land-ice scenario (Hinkel et al., 2014[3]; Lincke and Hinkel, 2018[4]). However, future SLR outside of this range is also possible. For instance, Figure 1.2 also includes a scenario of up to 2.0 m of SLR by 2100, based on a high-end SLR scenario (H++) (Nicholls et al., 2013[5]). Such a high-end scenario can be located in the low-probability, high-impact tail of possible 21st century SLR.

Figure 1.2. Sea-level rise scenarios to 2100

All sea-level rise values shown are with respect to mean sea level in the 1985-2005 reference period.

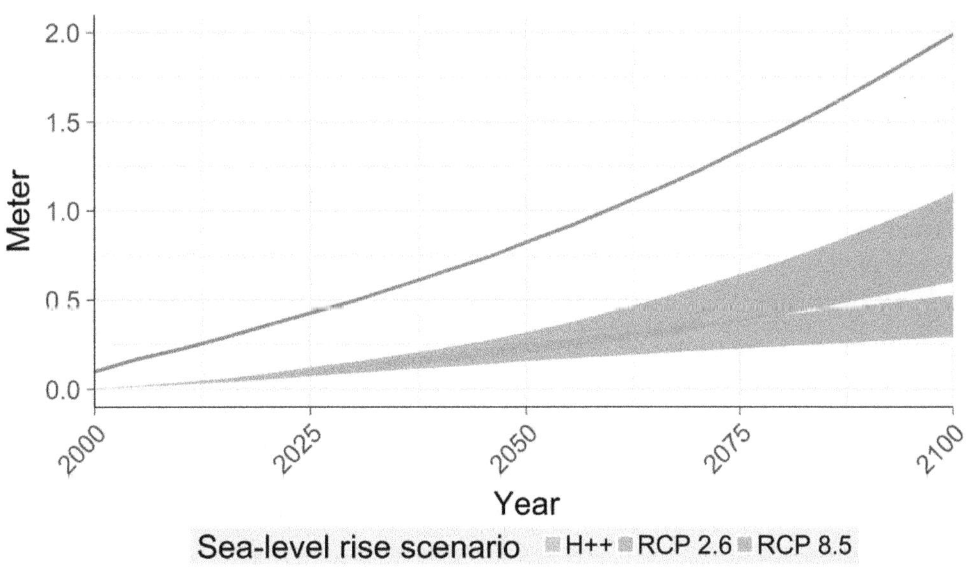

Source: Lincke, D. and J. Hinkel (2018[4]), "Economically robust protection against 21st century sea-level rise", http://dx.doi.org/10.1016/J.GLOENVCHA.2018.05.003.

Different processes drive increases in global mean sea level, with the four main ones being: oceanic thermal expansion (Taylor et al., 2012[6]), melting from glaciers (Marzeion, Jarosch and Hofer, 2012[7]), the Greenland ice sheet (Fettweis et al., 2013[8]) and Antarctic ice sheets (Levermann et al., 2014[9]). Analysis comparing contributions of these components, using different GCMs and concentration pathways, found that the largest single contribution to global mean SLR comes from oceanic thermal expansion. Mountain glaciers and ice caps also contribute substantially, but less than thermal expansion. However, if considered as a whole, the melting of land ice is projected to contribute most to future sea-level rise (Hinkel et al., 2014[3]).

Gravitational and rotational effects from changes in ice masses (Farrell and Clark, 2007[10]) and ocean circulation (Hinkel et al., 2014[3]) additionally influence the regional distribution of sea-level rise. These effects lead to sea-level rise being higher in the tropics than at high latitudes (Perrette et al., 2013[11]).

Uncertainties around the contribution of these processes to SLR are the greatest regarding the melting of ice sheets. The contribution of the Antarctic ice sheet is the most uncertain, and gives rise to a long-tailed risk of very high sea-level rise. Recent studies find that 5th percentile of Antarctic ice sheet contribution is around 2 cm, and the 50th percentile is 10 cm. The 95th percentile of the Antarctic ice sheet contribution is, however, as high as 41 cm in the RCP 8.5 scenario (Hinkel et al., 2014[3]). A further uncertainty arises from model differences. For example, Hinkel et al. (2014[3]) find that median sea-level projections can differ by up to 20 cm by 2100 depending on the GCM used. These various uncertainties arising from physical processes are captured in the probability distributions illustrated in Figure 1.2.

Changes in local relative sea level can, however, vary significantly from changes in global mean sea level. Biophysical and geological processes such as vertical land movement, changes in ocean circulation patterns or natural glacial-isostatic adjustment influence local relative sea level. For instance, on the north coast of Finland and Sweden, the land is currently rising faster than the sea due to post-glacial uplift. Further, local relative sea level is also influenced by human activities, such as extraction of groundwater or oil, mining and changes in sediment supply from rivers due to dam building. In some areas, the contribution of these activities to SLR can be an order of magnitude higher than that from global climate change (Ericson et al., 2006[12]).

Densely populated deltas, which globally have a population of more than 500 million, are particularly susceptible to such human-induced subsidence due to their geological setting (Woodroffe et al., 2006[13]). Many of the world's coastal megacities are also situated in deltas and several metres of human-induced subsidence have been observed during the 20th century (Nicholls, 1995[14]; World Bank, 2010[15]). For instance, in Jakarta, observed subsidence rates over the last three decades have been between 3 cm and 10 cm per year (Abidin et al., 2015[16]). Rural areas are also susceptible, as local subsidence rates of 250 mm per year have been observed in areas where intensive aquaculture activities require groundwater pumping to freshen fishponds (Higgins et al., 2013[17]).

Human-induced local relative changes in sea level can thus be a major source of uncertainty about the risks faced by coastal areas (Hinkel et al., 2014[3]). As such, geographically specific modelling is required to understand the potential impacts in a given area. While global models are available for natural glacial-isostatic adjustment (Douglas, Kearney and Leatherman, 2000[18]), information on annual rates of human-induced subsidence is extremely limited and both the drivers and responses are localised, making modelling extremely difficult (Hanson et al., 2011[19]).

Climate change-induced SLR beyond 2100 will, however, continue for thousands to tens of thousands years, even if greenhouse gas concentrations are stabilised during the 21st century (Levermann et al., 2013[20]). This has been termed commitment to SLR (Church et al., 2001[21]). However, the rate and magnitude of SLR over these long time frames is deeply uncertain and subject to some controversy. For example, IPCC AR5 estimates SLR in 2500 between 1.5 m and 6.6 m under high-concentration scenarios (> 700 ppm CO_2eq). In contrast, (Clark et al., 2016[22]) estimate 25-52 metres within the next 10 000 years under a stipulated equilibrium climate sensitivity of 3.5°C. Levermann et al. (2013[20]) estimate the committed SLR with rising temperature as approximately 2.3 m/°Celsius. Thus, the extent of long-term SLR could range from tens of centimetres up to several metres. Alternatively, a world with SLR much beyond present experience is also possible. These alternatives present radically different situations in future centuries.

1.1.2. Evidence of the reduced resilience of ecosystems, and the link with human activity

Estuarine and coastal ecosystems are some of the most heavily used and threatened natural systems globally, with significant deterioration due to human activities. For example, 50% of salt marshes, 35% of mangroves, 30% of coral reefs and 29% of seagrasses have been either lost or are degraded worldwide (Barbier et al., 2011[23]). Murray et al. (2014[24]) found that 28% of tidal flats bordering the Yellow Sea disappeared between 1980 and the late 2000s, at a rate of 1.2% annually.

Coastal development processes, such as land reclamation or hard coastal protection measures, can degrade coastal ecosystems (Hoegh-Guldberg et al., 2018[2]). Indeed, land reclamation has an extensive history in areas with dense populations and a shortage of land, e.g. southern North Sea countries and the People's Republic of China (hereafter "China") (Bisaro and Hinkel, 2018[25]). Globally, total land area gained from the sea in the last 30 years is approximately 33 700 km^2 (about 50% more than has been lost), with most land reclamation areas occurring in places like Dubai, Singapore and China (Donchyts et al., 2016[26]; Ma et al., 2014[27]). Wetlands loss or degradation due to land reclamation for urban or industrial uses reduces water storage areas. In such cases, high waters from storm surges can reach higher velocities and heights when forced into remaining channels (Wong et al., 2014[28]). Further, land reclamation may disrupt coastal ecosystems, negatively affecting coral reefs, mangroves or seagrass beds (Li et al., 2013[29]), while also disrupting natural morphological processes, leading to coastal erosion and increased flood risk (Murray et al., 2014[24]). Finally, as discussed above, coastal development often leads to increased groundwater extraction, causing land subsidence and increasing coastal risk (Wong et al., 2014[28]).

The loss of biodiversity, ecosystem functions and coastal vegetation has contributed to decreased coastal protection from flooding and storm events (Liquete et al., 2013[30]). Wetlands, mangroves, near-shore coral reefs and dunes can all reduce storm surges and stabilise shorelines (Spalding et al., 2014[31]). This protection has significant value; for example, globally, coral reefs are estimated to protect over 100 million people from wave-induced flooding. Further, it has been estimated that annual expected flood damage reduction from coral reefs exceed USD 400 million for Cuba, Indonesia, Malaysia, Mexico and Philippines alone (Beck et al., 2018[32]). In addition to coastal protection, healthy coastal ecosystems provide a suite of other valuable benefits (e.g. ecosystem services) on which humans depend. These include providing nursery habitat for fish and other marine species, water filtration, carbon storage, and opportunities for recreation (Mehvar et al., 2018[33]).

SLR itself poses a threat to coastal ecosystems, and (Spencer et al., 2016[34]) estimate that up to 78% of the global wetland area could be lost under a high SLR scenario. As coastal ecosystems change under SLR, the benefits that they provide in the form of ecosystem services are likely to decline and negatively impact the people who depend on them (Mehvar et al., 2018[33]).

1.2. The economic cost of sea-level rise

As risks from sea-level rise increase, so too will the associated economic and human costs from extreme events and slow-onset changes. This section uses new modelling to provide economic estimates of the impacts of rising sea levels on coastal assets, as well as the costs of adapting through protection.

Assessments of the costs of SLR must consider flood risk and adaptation costs, i.e. the costs of implementing protection, accommodation or retreat measures (further detailed in Chapter 2). The costs and benefits of adaptation have been assessed on a country level by a first generation of studies considering the gradual loss of land as the main impact of sea-level rise (Fankhauser, 1995[35]; Nicholls, Tol and Vafeidis, 2008[36]; Sugiyama, Nicholls and Vafeidis, 2008[37]; Yohe, Neumann and Ameden, 1995[38]). As mentioned above, these studies generally disregarded the adverse effects of extreme sea-level events that are rising with mean sea levels, and which manifest even before land is lost permanently (Wong et al., 2014[28]). A second generation of studies have addressed this limitation, considering the expected damage caused by extreme sea levels as well as refining the scale of analysis to subnational levels based on segmentations of coastline into units (Diaz, 2016[39]; Hinkel et al., 2014[40]; Nicholls et al., 2011[41]; Vafeidis, 2008[42]).

The DIVA model, a global coastal SLR impact model, offers one of the most comprehensive and advanced representations of relevant processes for assessing coastal flood risk and adaptation costs, and detailed global scale representation of the coastal zone based on 12 148 coastline segments defined in the *DINAS-COAST database* (Vafeidis et al., 2008[43]). By using DIVA, it is possible to assess the costs associated with SLR under different adaptation scenarios for the 21st century. Flood damages are calculated by combining elevation-based population exposure with flood depths caused by extreme events and applying a depth-damage function. Expected annual flood damages are computed as the mathematical expectation of damages based on extreme event distributions, given protection levels (Hinkel et al., 2014[3]). Within DIVA, adaptation costs are assessed in terms of dike investment and additional maintenance costs.

Assessing the impacts of increased coastal flooding on population and assets requires a comprehensive sampling of state-of-the-art socio-economic and sea-level rise scenarios. Thus, a range of scenarios are applied in order to address uncertainties regarding the development of future coastal risk described above. For socio-economic scenarios, five population and gross domestic product (GDP) growth scenarios based on the shared socio-economic pathways (SSPs) (Box 1.1) provide such a sampling.

Box 1.1. Shared socio-economic pathways and future coastal risk

Shared socio-economic pathways (SSPs) are widely used in climate impact assessment to describe future socio-economic development scenarios in a coherent and consistent manner (IIASA, 2012[44]; Lincke and Hinkel, 2018[4])The DIVA results described in this section have been obtained using SSPs 1-5. These can be described as follows:

- SSP 1 (Sustainability) reflects a world progressing towards sustainability with reduced resource intensity and fossil fuel dependency. SSP 1 attains the highest GDP and lowest population numbers.
- SSP 2 (Middle of the Road) reflects a world with medium assumptions.
- SSP 3 (Fragmentation) reflects a world fragmented into poor regions with low resource intensity and moderately wealthy regions with a high fossil fuel dependency. GDP is lowest and population highest in SSP 3.
- SSP 4 (Inequality) reflects a highly unequal world both within and across countries. GDP and population follow a similar, but lower, trend compared to SSP 3.
- SSP 5 (Conventional Development) reflects a world oriented toward rapid, equitable development that is dependent on fossil fuels.

Table 1.1. Global population and GDP in 2050 and 2100 under different shared socio-economic pathways

	Population (millions)		GDP (billion USD/yr)	
	2050	2100	2050	2100
SSP 1	8 400	7 200	295 000	771 000
SSP 2	9 300	9 800	260 000	685 000
SSP 3	10 300	14 100	334 000	667 000
SSP 4	9 400	11 800	242 000	462 000
SSP 5	8 500	7 700	348 000	1 207 000

Source: Hinkel, J. et al. (2014[3]), "Coastal flood damage and adaptation costs under 21st century sea-level rise", https://doi.org/10.1073/pnas.1222469111.

Different adaptation scenarios, which come on top of the main SSP storylines, can be considered in DIVA, and a baseline adaptation scenario is required for assessing sea-level rise impacts and adaptation. Generally, most approaches in the literature have considered a "no adaptation" case where coastal defences are not upgraded while sea levels rise, and socio-economic development in the flood plain continues. In such a constant protection strategy, dikes remain at their current height, so flood risk increases with time as relative sea level rises. In an enhanced protection strategy, dikes are raised following both socio-economic development and relative sea-level rise (Hinkel et al., 2014[3]).

Figure 1.3 shows the coastal flooding costs for SSP 3 and SSP 5 and low and high-end RCPs 2.6 and 8.5 respectively, as analysed by Hinkel et al. (2014[3]). SSP 3 and SSP 5 are illustrative because they represent the low and high extremes respectively of annual flood costs over the 21st century. SSP 3 represents the second-lowest GDP of the SSPs (after SSP 4), distributed to most people, and thus coastal exposure is the lowest under SSP 3. Figure 1.3 illustrates that, without adaptation, flood damage costs will be very high by the end of the century. The median outcome for high-end SLR (1.3 m in RCP8.5) being approximately USD 50 trillion annually or *ca.* 4% of world GDP annually. Adaptation, through enhanced protection, can reduce these costs by two to three orders of magnitude, showing substantial benefits across all combinations of scenarios. Thus, one implication of the analysis is that for large parts of the world, coastal protection is economically attractive regardless of how SLR and socio-economic development proceed (see Section 1.4).

Figure 1.3. Global annual flood costs for different socio-economic and climate scenarios with and without adaptation

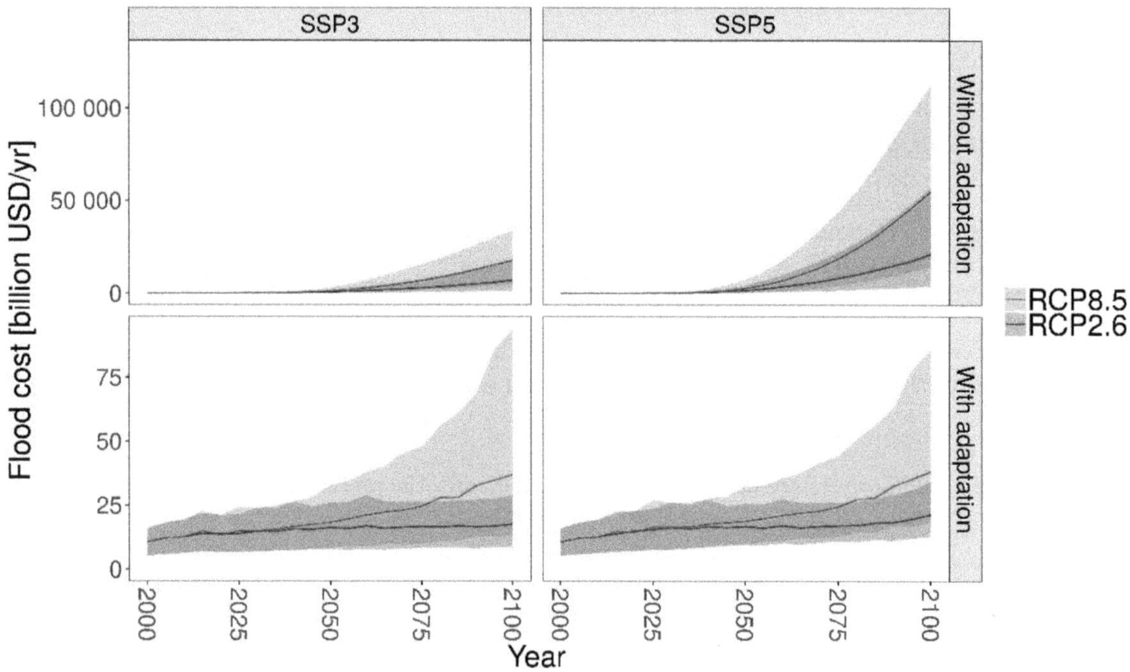

Note: The solid lines represent the median and the shaded area represents the range from the 5th to 95th percentile for a given scenario combination.
Source: Hinkel; J. et al. (2014[40]), "Coastal flood damage and adaptation costs under 21st century sea-level rise", https://doi.org/10.1073/pnas.1222469111.

At the global level, cumulative residual flood damages of USD (2005) 0.3 trillion to USD (2005) 3.9 trillion for the 21st century are reported by Hinkel et al. (2014[3]). Considering high-end sea-level rise increases to this range, as Lincke and Hinkel (2018[4]) report, residual damage costs of USD (2014) 1.7 trillion to USD (2014) 5.5 trillion (undiscounted) over the 21st century. Higher damage costs (for both the low- and high-end of the range) come from the fact that Lincke and Hinkel (2018[4]) consider SLR scenarios up to 2.0 m, while the previous study only considered them up to 1.3 m. For OECD countries only, by 2100, residual flood damages range from USD (2005) 2.5 billion to USD (2005) 29.8 billion. While still significant, the smaller share of overall global damages indicated for OECD countries by these numbers represent the relatively greater ability of OECD countries to invest in coastal protection.

Figure 1.4 shows the global costs of adaptation under an enhanced coastal protection strategy. Generally, protection costs increase significantly under high SLR scenarios regardless of socio-economic development. Further, protection costs are the highest under SSP 5, which represents a rich fossil-intensive world, as growing wealth leads to increasing exposure of assets, and thus increased protection costs. A range of USD (2005) 1.9 trillion to USD (2005) 4.2 trillion for protection considering SLR scenarios up to 1.3 m is reported by Hinkel et al. (2014[3]) over the 21st century. Including high-end SLR scenarios (up to 2.0 m) increases the high costs to USD (2014) 7.8 trillion (not discounted). These results are of the same order of magnitude as those reported in earlier global studies. For example, (Tol, 2002[45]) reports protection costs of USD (1995) 0.6 trillion to USD (1995) 1.06 trillion for 1 metre of SLR, excluding maintenance cost.

Figure 1.4. Global annual costs of adaptation under an enhanced coastal protection strategy for different socio-economic and climate scenarios

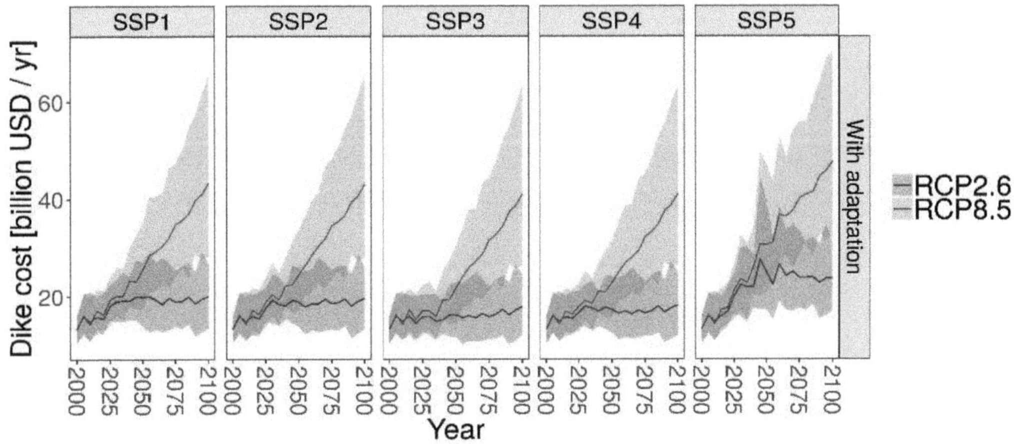

Source: Hinkel, J. et al. (2014[40]), "Coastal flood damage and adaptation costs under 21st century sea-level rise", https://doi.org/10.1073/pnas.1222469111.

The relative costs of SLR are another important consideration because this indicates how significant SLR costs will be for a specific country or region. Relative SLR costs can be defined as the present value of protection and residual damage cost as a percentage of present value of GDP over the 21st century (Lincke and Hinkel, 2018[4]). Relative costs of SLR, provided an optimal protection strategy is pursued, represent a small proportion of GDP at the global level, but will be a significant share of GDP for some individual countries. Globally, under an optimal adaptation strategy, the relative costs of SLR lie between 0.02% of global GDP under the best-case scenario (0.3 m global mean SLR, SSP 5 and not discounted) and 0.07% of global GDP under the worst-case scenario (2.0 m global mean SLR, SSP 3 and 6% discount rate). While generally OECD countries do not experience high relative costs of SLR, there are some countries for which the relative cost of SLR exceeds 1% under the worst-case scenario combination. These are Iceland (2.3%), Korea (1.8%) and Norway (1.1%). Globally, small islands in particular will experience high relative costs of SLR, including the risk of inundation. There are in total 41 countries for which the relative cost of SLR exceeds 1% of GDP under the worst-case scenario combination.

Figure 1.5 shows the global number of people flooded under different socio-economic and climate scenarios under constant protection ("no adaptation") and enhanced protection ("adaptation") scenarios. Under constant levels of flood protection, the number of people flooded will grow throughout the century across all socio-economic scenarios. This is despite the fact that SSP 1 and SSP 5 project decreasing global population from 2050 onwards (Hinkel et al., 2014[3]). The expected annual number of people flooded is the highest under SSP 3 and the lowest under SSP 1, reflecting the highest and lowest population numbers under these scenarios (see Table 1.1).

Figure 1.5. Global annual number of people flooded under constant protection

"No adaptation" and enhanced protection ("adaptation") scenarios

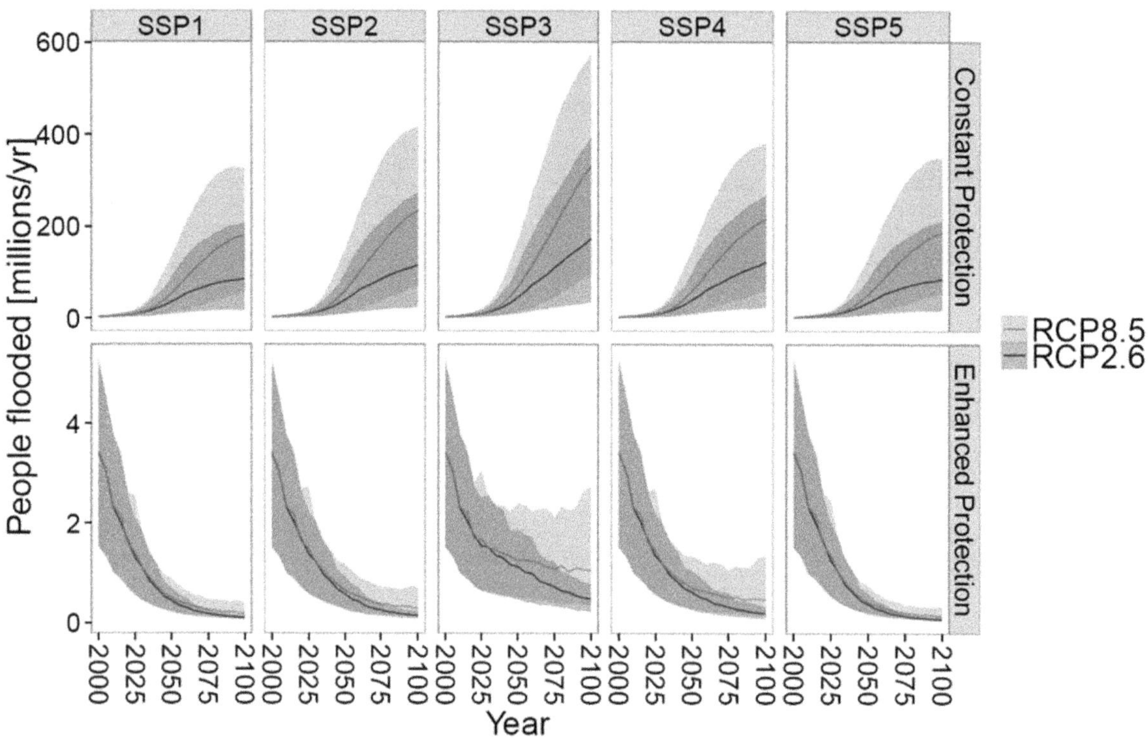

Source: Hinkel, J. et al. (2014[40]), "Coastal flood damage and adaptation costs under 21st century sea-level rise", https://doi.org/10.1073/pnas.1222469111.

In an enhanced protection scenario, the number of people flooded actually falls over the course of the century, as more regions become rich enough to build dikes. Further, the influence of socio-economic development on the number of people flooded is smaller as compared to under constant protection. An exception is the extreme scenario SSP 3, under which population grows fastest, but GDP and hence dike height grow the slowest.

While the modelled relative costs of SLR could represent a small proportion of GDP at the global level if an optimal protection strategy is pursued, there are other elements that should be considered. First, these costs will be unequally distributed, falling particularly heavily in some areas, which may not be well-equipped to adapt. Second, these cost estimates assume that an economically "optimal" protection strategy will be followed: the challenges of achieving this are explored in Chapter 2. Lastly, not all of the potential costs, including non-market impacts, are captured in this model.

1.3. Robust coastal adaptation to 21st century sea-level rise

The global studies reviewed above have applied a range of SLR and socio-economic scenarios. They have, however, all taken the general approach of assessing SLR impacts and thus adaptation decisions within a given SLR and socio-economic scenario. This is indeed appropriate for gaining understanding of the range of possible sea-level rise impacts, and understanding adaptation costs and benefits within a given scenario. However, such an approach does not reflect the actual decision framing for coastal planners at national to subnational levels because such decisions need to consider all scenarios.

The need for decision making to account for all different scenarios is acknowledged by local coastal adaptation studies and substantial literature on coastal adaptation decision making under "deep uncertainty" has emerged. Representative approaches include robust decision making (Lempert and Schlesinger, 2001[46]) and adaptation pathways analysis (Haasnoot et al., 2013[47]). These approaches are characterised by finding options that are robust in the sense that they satisfy given criteria, e.g. a flood safety level, for a sample of scenarios covering all the relevant uncertainties. Indeed, the Thames Estuary 2100 study provides a prominent example of the latter approach further examples are discussed in Chapter 3.

Such an approach to "deep uncertainty" can also be applied globally, and a first study does just this, applying the DIVA model introduced above (Lincke and Hinkel, 2018[4]). Based on the five scenarios of 21st century global mean SLR from 0.3-2.0 m, introduced above, and the five SSPs (see Box 1.1), the study assesses for which parts of the global coastline coastal protection is economically robust. Further details on this method are described in Box 1.2.

Box 1.2. Applying "deep uncertainty" to a global sea-level rise model

The 2018 study by Lincke and Hinkel is based on the five scenarios of 21st century global mean sea-level rise (SLR) from 0.3 m to 2.0 m, and the five shared socio-economic pathways (SSPs). The study assesses for which parts of the global coastline coastal protection is economically robust by considering all 25 combinations of SLR and socio-economic development, in order to account for the whole uncertainty space spanned by these scenarios. However, some combinations of SLR and socio-economic development are less likely to occur (O'Neill et al., 2014[48]). The study also considers a range of five discount rates from 0.0% to 6.0%. Discount rates represent a major uncertainty dimension in flood risk management decisions, particularly over the long term (Hall and Solomatine, 2008[49]; Lempert and Schlesinger, 2001[46]), though they have not been addressed in global studies on sea-level rise impacts.

The optimal protection level for each coastline segment under each scenario combination is determined by minimising the net present value of the sum of protection cost streams and residual damage costs streams (avoided flood damage). Coastal segments are defined as robust to protect when protection is economically desirable (i.e. protection produces a positive net present value) under all scenarios

The principle result is the level of robustness of the decision to protect across all possible combinations of different scenarios for each coastal segment. The study also analyses the length of coastline and coastal plain exposure (area, population, assets) for which it is robust to protect, i.e. where protection is desirable for all scenario combinations.

Source: Lincke, D. and J. Hinkel (2018[4]), "Economically robust protection against 21st century sea-level rise", http://dx.doi.org/10.1016/J.GLOENVCHA.2018.05.003.

The results show that coastal protection is economically robust across all scenario combinations for 13% of the world's coastline. These coastlines account for 90% of the global coastal population and 96% of global assets situated in the 1-in-100-year event floodplain in 2015. Conversely, it is robust not to protect 65% of the world's coastline, which corresponds to a small fraction of global coastal floodplain population (0.2%) and assets (0.2%). For the remaining 22% of the world's coastline, the optimal adaptation strategy varies across scenarios.

Most of the locations for which protection is robust are located on the east coast of the United States, and in Europe. In Asia, China, Korea and Japan also have coastline for which it is robust to protect (Figure 1.6). The reason for this is that these areas have high levels of coastal urbanisation and are located in countries with high levels of existing protection standards. Further, large cities in Australia are also robust to protect due to their high population densities. Conversely, it is robust not to protect most of the coasts of countries with long and uninhabited coastlines such as in Australia, Canada, Chile and Norway.

Figure 1.6. Economic robustness of coastal protection globally

At the level of coastline segments in terms of the percentage of scenarios with benefit-cost ratio (BCR)>1 and countries in terms of the shares of a countries' coast having a BCR > 1 under all scenarios considered

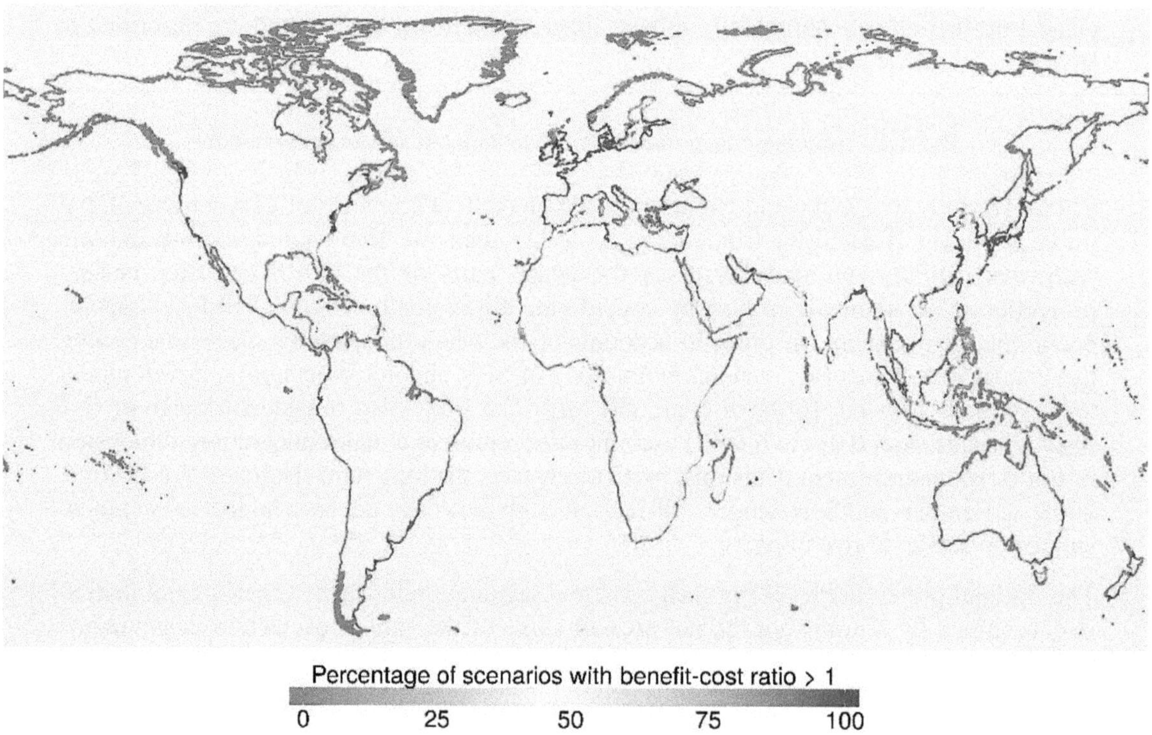

Source: Lincke, D. and J. Hinkel (2018[4]), "Economically robust protection against 21st century sea-level rise", https://doi.org/10.1016/j.gloenvcha.2018.05.003.

Generally, for countries with a very short but densely populated coastline, it may be robust to protect the entire coast. Globally, there are 18 countries for which this modelling suggests that it would be robust to protect the entire coastline. Two of those are OECD countries (Belgium and Poland). Conversely, there are 30 countries for which it is economically robust not to protect any part of the coast.

Considering the different individual scenario combinations, one can observe the share of protected coast grows with higher sea-level rise, higher GDP and lower discount rates.

Hence, the biggest share of protected coast is obtained under the highest SLR scenario (i.e. H++ scenario), the wealthiest socio-economic scenario and a zero discount rate.

Discount rates are clearly a significant factor influencing the level of robustness of protection, in that lower discount rates make it more robust to protect. Protection costs largely occur as upfront investments near the beginning of the century, while damage costs are the greatest at the end of the century due to rising sea levels. High discount rates therefore lower the present value of damage costs more than the present value of protection costs, and decrease the economic attractiveness of protection.

Under higher levels of socio-economic development and for higher SLR, it is economically robust to protect more of the coast. Damage costs are higher for socio-economic development scenarios representing a rich world than for scenarios representing a poor world, as more assets are exposed in the rich-world scenarios. At the same, time, protection costs are not influenced by socio-economic development. It follows then that a larger share of coast will be protected in scenarios representing a rich world because more flood damage can be avoided by protecting is such scenarios, compared to poor-world scenarios. Relatedly, in high SLR scenarios, a larger share of the coast is protected. This is because SLR increases damage costs faster than protection costs. That is, protection costs grow linearly with SLR, while damage costs grow super-linearly with SLR.

Finally, comparing these results to previous studies, it is important to note that the share of protected coastline under the robust cost-benefit adaptation strategy explored by Lincke and Hinkel (2018[4]) is much lower than the ones found in previous studies under alternative protection strategies. For instance, Fankhauser (1995[35]) found that about 80% of the open coast, 98% of harbours and 99% of cities should be protected under a strategy that minimises 21st century costs of land loss, forced migration and protection for 0.2-2.0 m of SLR until 2100. More recently, (Nicholls, Tol and Vafeidis, 2008[50]) provide a global estimate reporting 50-85% of protected coast under 1.0-6.0 m SLR until 2130. In contrast, Lincke and Hinkel (2018[4]) find only 15% of the US coast is protected under all scenario combinations while 66% are not protected under any scenario combination. The earlier studies report much higher lengths of protected coast than Lincke and Hinkel (2018[4]) because they do not provide subnational resolution of exposed people and assets. When protection decisions are evaluated for whole countries or regions, many parts of the coast are protected that would not be protected in approaches with more coastal segmentation, because local differences in exposure are averaged away.

1.4. Implications for future research and policy

To put these results into context, it should again be emphasised that the DIVA studies (Hinkel et al., 2014[3]; Lincke and Hinkel, 2018[4]), similar to other global studies reviewed above, focus on coastal protection and do not explore other forms of adaptation. Future assessment of coastal impacts at all levels should also explore other adaptation options, including accommodate and retreat measures. While including these measures is unlikely to significantly alter the global picture, locally it may be economically more efficient to retreat from the coast. For instance, the countries found by Lincke and Hinkel (2018[4]) to have high relative SLR cost all have sparse, but mainly coastal, population. In such sparsely populated places, though infrastructure and people might be concentrated on the coast, coastal planners and decision makers should explore alternative adaptation options that may be economically more efficient than protection (see Chapter 2).

In particular, the global results shown in Figure 1.6, only consider hard protection, but other adaptation options may be more cost-effective, and better maintain ecosystem health in any given area. These results should not be seen as advocating protection in only those areas where it is economically viable. Rather, at a highly aggregated level, these results show that protection is viable across a range of scenarios in various locations. This provides an entry point for national coastal decision makers and planners, who then must decide on adaptation measures, acknowledging that the timing of adaptation, and adaptation options that are flexible (i.e. which can be reversed or extended), are key to achieving efficient adaptation, given the uncertainties associated with future coastal risk (see Chapter 3).

Turning to policy implications of the above analysis, there are two overarching points to consider. First, the results showing that it is economically robust to protect the vast majority of the world's assets in the coastal zone suggest that the world is likely to see bifurcating coastal futures. On the one hand, the large majority of coastal inhabitants live in densely populated urban coastal areas, and are likely to continue to protect themselves even under high-end sea-level rise due to the high cost-benefit ratios of coastal protection in these areas. Residual risks will remain with possible catastrophic consequences in the case of dike failure, but these can also be reduced by building stronger and wider defences (De Bruijn, Klijn and Knoeff, 2013[51]). A key point in this regard is that the SLR literature needs to account for adaptation to give a realistic picture of the coastal future. Where high concentrations of assets and people are present at the coast, we are likely to see increased protection, rather than large-scale damages. It is also worth mentioning that it will be important to consider alternatives to hard protection, such as nature-based solutions, in order to avoid escalating damage to ecosystems or loss of amenity value through hard protection alone.

A second policy implication concerns financing coastal adaptation. According to the global studies reviewed, it is attractive from an economic point of view to protect around 90% of the world's coastal population (Lincke and Hinkel, 2018[4]). In practice, however, financing and implementing coastal protection gives rise to a number of challenges due to the public-good nature of coastal protection and its benefits being stochastic, long-term and distributed across diverse beneficiaries (Bisaro and Hinkel, 2018[25]; Bisaro and Hinkel, 2016[52]; Moser, Jeffress Williams and Boesch, 2012[53]). The governance and finance issues related to coastal adaptation are discussed in Chapter 2.

Note

[1] As the terminology used in this report is relevant to climate change adaptation, the definitions may differ slightly from other frameworks used to describe risk.

References

Abidin, H. et al. (2015), "On correlation between urban development, land subsidence and flooding phenomena in Jakarta", *Proceedings of the International Association of Hydrological Sciences* 370, pp. 15-20. [16]

Barbier, E. et al. (2011), "The value of estuarine and coastal ecosystem services", *Ecological Monographs*, Vol. 81/2, pp. 169-193, http://dx.doi.org/10.1890/10-1510.1. [23]

Beck, M. et al. (2018), "The global flood protection savings provided by coral reefs", *Nature Communications*, Vol. 9/1, p. 2186, http://dx.doi.org/10.1038/s41467-018-04568-z. [32]

Bisaro, A. and J. Hinkel (2018), "Mobilizing private finance for coastal adaptation: A literature review", *Wiley Interdisciplinary Reviews: Climate Change*, Vol. 9/3, p. e514, http://dx.doi.org/10.1002/wcc.514. [25]

Bisaro, A. and J. Hinkel (2016), "Governance of social dilemmas in climate change adaptation", *Nature Climate Change*, Vol. 6/4, pp. 354-359, http://dx.doi.org/10.1038/nclimate2936. [52]

Church, J. et al. (2001), "Changes in sea level: Contribution of Working Group I to the Third Assessment Report of the Intergovernmental Panel on Climate Change", in J.T., Ding, Y., Griggs, D.J., Noguer, M., Linden, P.J. van der, Dai, X., Maskell, K., Johnson, C. (ed.), *Climate Change 2001: The Scientific Basis*, Cambridge University Press. [21]

Clark, P. et al. (2016), "Consequences of twenty-first-century policy for multi-millennial climate and sea-level change", *Nature Climate Change*, Vol. 6/4, pp. 360-369, http://dx.doi.org/10.1038/nclimate2923. [22]

De Bruijn, K., F. Klijn and J. Knoeff (2013), *Unbreachable embankments? In pursuit of the most effective stretches for reducing fatality risk.* [51]

Diaz, D. (2016), "Estimating global damages from sea level rise with the Coastal Impact and Adaptation Model (CIAM)", *Climatic Change*, Vol. 137/1-2, pp. 143-156, http://dx.doi.org/10.1007/s10584-016-1675-4. [39]

Donchyts, G. et al. (2016), "Earth's surface water change over the past 30 years", *Nature Climate Change*. [26]

Douglas, B., M. Kearney and S. Leatherman (2000), "Sea level rise: History and consequences", Elsevier. [18]

Ericson, J. et al. (2006), "Effective sea-level rise and deltas: Causes of change and human dimension implications", *Global and Planetary Change*, Vol. 50, pp. 63-82, http://dx.doi.org/10.1016/j.gloplacha.2005.07.004. [12]

Fankhauser, S. (1995), "Protection versus retreat: The economic costs of sea-level rise", *Environment and Planning A*, Vol. 27/2, pp. 299-319, http://dx.doi.org/10.1068/a270299. [35]

Farrell, W. and J. Clark (2007), "On Postglacial Sea Level", *Geophysical Journal of the Royal Astronomical Society*, Vol. 46/3, pp. 647-667, http://dx.doi.org/10.1111/j.1365-246X.1976.tb01252.x. [10]

Fettweis, X. et al. (2013), "Estimating the Greenland ice sheet surface mass balance contribution to future sea level rise using the regional atmospheric climate model MAR", *The Cryosphere*, Vol. 7/2, pp. 469-489, http://dx.doi.org/10.5194/tc-7-469-2013. [8]

Haasnoot, M. et al. (2013), "Dynamic adaptive policy pathways: A method for crafting robust decisions for a deeply uncertain world", *Global Environmental Change*, Vol. 23/2, pp. 485-498, http://dx.doi.org/10.1016/J.GLOENVCHA.2012.12.006. [47]

Hall, J. and D. Solomatine (2008), "A framework for uncertainty analysis in flood risk management decisions", *International Journal of River Basin Management*, Vol. 6/2, pp. 85-98, http://dx.doi.org/10.1080/15715124.2008.9635339. [49]

Hanson, S. et al. (2011), "A global ranking of port cities with high exposure to climate extremes", *Climatic Change*, Vol. 104/1, pp. 89-111, http://dx.doi.org/10.1007/s10584-010-9977-4. [19]

Higgins, S. et al. (2013), "Land subsidence at aquaculture facilities in the Yellow River delta, China", *Geophysical Research Letters*, Vol. 40, pp. 3898-3902. [17]

Hinkel, J. et al. (2014), "Coastal flood damage and adaptation costs under 21st century sea-level rise", *Proceedings of the National Academy of Sciences of the United States of America*, Vol. 111/9, pp. 3292-3297, http://dx.doi.org/10.1073/pnas.1222469111. [3]

Hinkel, J. et al. (2014), "Coastal flood damage and adaptation costs under 21st century sea-level rise.", *Proceedings of the National Academy of Sciences of the United States of America*, Vol. 111/9, pp. 3292-7, http://dx.doi.org/10.1073/pnas.1222469111. [40]

IIASA (2012), *SSP Database*.. [44]

Intergovernmental Panel on Climate Change (2014), "Glossary, acronyms and chemical symbols", in *Climate Change 2014 Mitigation of Climate Change*, Cambridge University Press, Cambridge, http://dx.doi.org/10.1017/CBO9781107415416.023. [1]

Lempert, R. and M. Schlesinger (2001), "Climate-change strategy needs to be robust", *Nature*, Vol. 412/6845, pp. 375-375, http://dx.doi.org/10.1038/35086617. [46]

Levermann, A. et al. (2013), "The multimillennial sea-level commitment of global warming.", *Proceedings of the National Academy of Sciences of the United States of America*, Vol. 110/34, pp. 13745-50, http://dx.doi.org/10.1073/pnas.1219414110. [20]

Levermann, A. et al. (2014), "Projecting Antarctic ice discharge using response functions from SeaRISE ice-sheet models", *Earth System Dynamics*, Vol. 5, pp. 271-293, http://dx.doi.org/10.5194/esd-5-271-2014. [9]

Lincke, D. and J. Hinkel (2018), "Economically robust protection against 21st century sea-level rise", *Global Environmental Change*, Vol. 51, pp. 67-73, http://dx.doi.org/10.1016/J.GLOENVCHA.2018.05.003. [4]

Liquete, C. et al. (2013), "Assessment of coastal protection as an ecosystem service in Europe", *Ecological Indicators*, Vol. 30, pp. 205-217, http://dx.doi.org/10.1016/j.ecolind.2013.02.013. [30]

Li, Y. et al. (2013), "Coastal wetland loss and environmental change due to rapid urban expansion in Lianyungang, Jiangsu, China", *Regional Environmental Change*, Vol. 14/3, pp. 1175-1188, http://dx.doi.org/10.1007/s10113-013-0552-1. [29]

Marzeion, B., A. Jarosch and M. Hofer (2012), "Past and future sea-level change from the surface mass balance of glaciers", *The Cryosphere*, Vol. 6, http://dx.doi.org/10.5194/tc-6-1295-2012. [7]

Masson-Delmotte, V. (ed.) (2018), *Impacts of 1.5°C global warming on natural and human systems*, Intergovernmental Panel on CLimate Change, https://www.ipcc.ch/site/assets/uploads/sites/2/2018/11/SR15_Chapter3_Low_Res.pdf (accessed on 10 December 2018). [2]

Ma, Z. et al. (2014), "Rethinking China's new great wall.", *Science*, Vol. 346, pp. 912–914. [27]

Mehvar, S. et al. (2018), "Quantifying economic value of coastal ecosystem services: A review", *Journal of Marine Science and Engineering*, Vol. 6/1, p. 5, http://dx.doi.org/10.3390/jmse6010005. [33]

Moser, S., S. Jeffress Williams and D. Boesch (2012), "Wicked challenges at Land's End: Managing coastal vulnerability under climate change", *Annual Review of Environment and Resources*, Vol. 37/1, pp. 51-78, http://dx.doi.org/10.1146/annurev-environ-021611-135158. [53]

Murray, N. et al. (2014), "Tracking the rapid loss of tidal wetlands in the Yellow Sea", *Frontiers in Ecology and the Environment*, Vol. 12/5, pp. 267-272, http://dx.doi.org/10.1890/130260. [24]

Nicholls, R. (1995), "Coastal mega-cities and climate change.", *GeoJournal*, Vol. 37, pp. 369-379. [14]

Nicholls, R. et al. (2013), "Sea-level scenarios for evaluating coastal impacts", *Wiley Interdisciplinary Reviews: Climate Change*, Vol. 5/1, pp. 129-150, http://dx.doi.org/10.1002/wcc.253. [5]

Nicholls, R. et al. (2011), "Sea-level rise and its possible impacts given a 'beyond 4 C world' in the twenty-first century", *Philosophical Transactions of the Royal Society A: Mathematical, Physical and Engineering Sciences*, Vol. 369/1934, pp. 161-181, http://dx.doi.org/10.1098/rsta.2010.0291. [41]

Nicholls, R., R. Tol and A. Vafeidis (2008), "Global estimates of the impact of a collapse of the West Antarctic ice sheet: an application of FUND", *Climatic Change*, Vol. 91/1-2, pp. 171-191, http://dx.doi.org/10.1007/s10584-008-9424-y. [50]

Nicholls, R., R. Tol and A. Vafeidis (2008), "Global estimates of the impact of a collapse of the West Antarctic ice sheet: An application of FUND", *Climatic Change*, Vol. 91/1-2, pp. 171-191, http://dx.doi.org/10.1007/s10584-008-9424-y. [36]

O'Neill, B. et al. (2014), "A new scenario framework for climate change research: The concept of shared socioeconomic pathways", *Climatic Change*, Vol. 122, pp. 387–400, https://doi.org/10.1007/s10584-013-0905-2. [48]

Perrette, M. et al. (2013), "A scaling approach to project regional sea level rise and its uncertainties", *Earth System Dynamics*, Vol. 4/1, pp. 11-29, http://dx.doi.org/10.5194/esd-4-11-2013. [11]

Spalding, M. et al. (2014), "The role of ecosystems in coastal protection: Adapting to climate change and coastal hazards", *Ocean & Coastal Management*, Vol. 90, pp. 50-57, http://dx.doi.org/10.1016/J.OCECOAMAN.2013.09.007. [31]

Spencer, T. et al. (2016), "Global coastal wetland change under sea-level rise and related stresses: The DIVA Wetland Change Model", *Global and Planetary Change*, Vol. 139, pp. 15-30. [34]

Sugiyama, M., R. Nicholls and A. Vafeidis (2008), "Estimating the economic cost of sea-level rise", *Joint Program on the Science and Policy of Global Change Reports*, Vol. 156, https://dspace.mit.edu/handle/1721.1/41522 (accessed on 29 November 2018). [37]

Taylor, K. et al. (2012), "An overview of CMIP5 and the experiment design", *Bulletin of the American Meteorological Society*, Vol. 93/4, pp. 485-498, http://dx.doi.org/10.1175/BAMS-D-11-00094.1. [6]

Tol, R. (2002), "Estimates of the damage costs of climate change. Part 1: Benchmark estimates", *Environmental and Resource Economics*, Vol. 21/1, pp. 47-72, https://doi.org/10.1023/A:1014500930521. [45]

Vafeidis, A. (2008), "A new global coastal database for impact and vulnerability analysis to sea-level rise", *Journal of Coastal Research*, Vol. 24/4, pp. 917-924, http://dx.doi.org/10.2112/06-0725.1. [42]

Vafeidis, A. et al. (2008), "A new global coastal database for impact and vulnerability analysis to sea-level rise", *Journal of Coastal Research*, Vol. 244/4, pp. 917-924, http://dx.doi.org/10.2112/06-0725.1. [43]

Wong, P. et al. (2014), *Coastal Systems and Low-Lying Areas*, IPCC, https://www.ipcc.ch/pdf/assessment-report/ar5/wg2/WGIIAR5-Chap5_FINAL.pdf (accessed on 17 August 2017). [28]

Woodroffe, C. et al. (2006), "Landscape variability and the response of Asian megadeltas to environmental change", *Global Change and Integrated Coastal Management*, pp. 277-314. [13]

World Bank (2010), "The Global Report on the Economics of Adaptation to Climate Change Study". [15]

Yohe, G., J. Neumann and H. Ameden (1995), "Assessing the economic cost of greenhouse-induced sea level rise: Methods and application in support of a national survey", *Journal of Environmental Economics and Management*, Vol. 29/3, pp. S78-S97, http://dx.doi.org/10.1006/jeem.1995.1062. [38]

Chapter 2. The challenge of coastal adaptation

The trends outlined in Chapter 1 will strain the ability of existing coastal management arrangements to maintain an acceptable level of risk at reasonable cost. This chapter analyses how different adaptation strategies can be used to respond to rising coastal risks and their distributional consequences. It then examines how the misalignment between incentives, capacity and roles in the coastal zone can discourage risk reduction, create policy lock-in and lead to inefficient outcomes overall.

This chapter was written by Lisa Danielson and Michael Mullan, OECD, with contributions from Alexander Bisaro, Global Climate Forum.

2.1. Balancing competing priorities in the context of rising risk

Coastal adaptation aims to maintain an acceptable level of coastal risks for society and the environment, today and into the future. Maintaining an acceptable level of risk is not the same as maintaining the *status quo* at all costs. Indeed, the acceptable level of risk for society and the environment requires balancing the economic, social and environmental consequences of inaction, as well as the costs of risk-reduction measures (OECD, 2013[1]). It is neither technically nor financially feasible to aim to achieve a "zero risk" level, as there are usually competing demands and more productive allocation choices for available resources (OECD, 2014[2]).

Defining what constitutes an acceptable level of risk is the result of a political process, which can be informed by both evidence-based assessments of the risks as well as the financial costs involved (OECD, 2013[1]). Stakeholders' views about what constitutes an acceptable risk level will differ based on risk preferences and context, including level of information. Decision makers, including households, companies, local or national governments, are likely to have different risk thresholds. In some cases, the acceptable level of risk in a given area is the cumulative result of different decisions taken for different reasons, rather than a deliberate choice. For example, allowing an area to be exposed to coastal erosion may not be the result of an explicit risk assessment, but is instead linked to low concentration of assets and population in that area. In other cases, such as the construction of structural flood defences, governments make use of technical decision support tools, such as a cost-benefit analysis, for determining acceptable levels of flood risk. Whether implicit or explicit, the judgement regarding the acceptability of coastal risks strongly influences the response adopted, the role of government, and the current and future cost of risk management (OECD, 2013[3]).

Defining the acceptability of coastal risks allows for proportional policy responses, but coming to a decision on what is acceptable can be challenging in an area that involves multiple stakeholders with different values and expectations (OECD, 2014[2]). Depending on the level of risks faced, continuing with traditional approaches to risk management may be disproportionally costly, and more transformative approaches will need to be adopted. For example, if an area will soon face major flooding, relying on post-disaster emergency management, or small seawall repairs, will eventually become unsustainable. Planning to retreat from the area, while highly disruptive, may be more efficient for some areas over the long term. Yet, without sufficient political will, common understanding of what level of risk is acceptable and tolerable, or increased levels of stakeholder engagement, adopting transformational change may be impossible.

Moving from traditional approaches of increasing protection towards new ways of mobilising risk-reduction behaviour across actors through a "whole-of-society approach" (Box 2.1) can help to build resilience in coastal zones (OECD, 2017[8]). Countries are embracing inclusive approaches to risk reduction in coastal areas, but greater implementation will be needed given the scale of potential risks.

Box 2.1. Embracing a whole-of-society approach to risk management

A whole-of-society approach involves all relevant stakeholders in the policy-making process, including individuals, households, government bodies and businesses. The adoption of an inclusive risk management approach enables the development of a shared vision of the risks and the distribution of responsibilities between stakeholders. With this comes recognition that government efforts cannot be effective if private sector actors and individuals do not contribute their share in terms of risk-adapted behaviour and self-protection investments.

The OECD *Recommendation of the Council on the Governance of Critical Risks* promotes such a whole-of-society approach, and suggests governments facilitate two-way communication with households and businesses to encourage whole-of-society engagement in disaster risk management. This includes:

1. the provision of tailored risk information that is accessible in a manner appropriate to diverse communities, sectors, industries and with international actors
2. the combination of targeted communication with incentives and tools for stakeholders to work together and take responsibility for self-protective and resilience-building measures
3. providing notice to households about different scales of hazards and human-induced threats, and supporting informed debate on the need for prevention, mitigation and preparation measures
4. informing and educating the public in advance of a specific emergency about what measures to take when it occurs, and mobilising public education systems to promote a culture of resilience.

Sources: OECD (2014[4]), Recommendation of the Council on the Governance of Critical Risks, www.oecd.org/gov/risk/Critical-Risks-Recommendation.pdf; OECD (2017[5]), Boosting Disaster Prevention through Innovative Risk Governance: Insights from Austria, France and Switzerland, https://doi.org/10.1787/9789264281370-en.

A key element of coastal adaptation is that policies need to be able to accommodate increasing risk profiles into the future. Planning for future sea-level rise (SLR) is especially challenging due to the "deep uncertainty" of risks themselves, meaning that the range of probabilities and outcomes cannot be known (see Chapter 1). There are inherent uncertainties in projecting the effects of SLR, but also in other drivers of risk. The twin issues of increasing risks over time and deep uncertainty have implications for decisions taken now, as measures implemented now face the possibility of being inappropriate for the future that actually materialises.

Decisions that do not consider the future can lock-in patterns of coastal development and may be impossible to undo without prohibitive expense and effort. An illustrative example of lock-in is the construction of protective infrastructure, either engineered or nature-based, which can create a cycle of coastal development and increased protection, termed "the levee effect". Once structural protection is built, the perception of increased safety can lead to further development in the flood plain, which can have the perverse impact of increasing vulnerability in the longer term (OECD, 2014[6]). If those defences then fail, the results can be catastrophic. In some jurisdictions, the provision of defences can create a responsibility for sustaining them: in Australia and the United States, local governments have come up against legal challenges when trying to cease maintenance of coastal defences (Hino, Field and Mach, 2017[7]).

The following sections review the main coastal strategies, detail their potential distributional impacts and examine how different institutional arrangements can influence the choice of adaptation strategy.

2.2. Strategies to manage rising coastal risks

Coastal adaptation strategies manage risks using a combination of protection, accommodation and retreat (Wong et al., 2014[8]), which are elaborated in Table 2.1 and further described below. Each strategy has implementation costs, and each provides a distribution of benefits based on how they modify coastal flood and erosion risks.

There are no universally appropriate solutions to address SLR risks; the locally appropriate strategy will depend on the nature of the area, the policy and institutional context, and the risks it faces. Each option has limitations. For example, constructing a seawall has high upfront costs, and can lock in increased development. Nature-based options are not always technically possible. Building codes only work for new development and therefore can be a slow mechanism to enact change, and require proper enforcement. Even strategies that pass a cost-benefit test can be blocked in implementation by institutional and political challenges.

The suitability and acceptability of different adaptation strategies depends in part on countries' broader institutional contexts. OECD countries tend to rely on structural coastal defence to manage flood risk in densely populated coastal areas (Tol, Klein and Nicholls, 2008[9]; Harman et al., 2013[10]; Gralepois et al., 2016[11]). This reflects both the existing investment in coastal assets and infrastructure as well as the institutional and political challenges of measures that disrupt the *status quo* and have potentially adverse impacts on individual properties (Harman et al., 2013[10]; Filatova, Mulder and Van der Veen, 2011[12]).

Table 2.1. Strategies to manage coastal risks

Objective	Measure	Benefits	Limitations
Protect (reduce the likelihood of the hazard)	Build/maintain hard defences	• Proven to be effective at preventing damage to infrastructure during extreme events • Well-established engineering guidelines and certainty under certain margins	• Displacement of beach and associated amenities • Maintenance costs once infrastructure is established • Lack of flexibility and the potential for lock-in • Risk of infrastructure failure in the future • Can create a sense of security for communities which inadvertently discourages the adoption of other risk-reduction measures
	Beach nourishment and dune restoration	• Preserves beach amenities and associated tourism activities • Is reversible and can be easily modified to the actual rate of sea-level rise	• Expensive to continue in the long term • In some cases, can be environmentally damaging to continually dredge new sand • Effectiveness is expected to decrease over time as beaches become more unstable
	Replace/reinforce shoreline protection with "living" shorelines – through planting vegetation, etc.	• Reduces negative effects of protective infrastructure (downdrift erosion) • Maintains beach habitat in enclosed areas	• Requires more planning and materials than traditional protection • Not suited for high-wave energy areas such as open beaches • Implementation and monitoring of success is not as advanced as other strategies
Accommodate (reduce vulnerability)	Change building codes and design standards to account for sea-level rise, for example in building elevation and foundation design	• Provides flexibility to manage future coastal inundation and flooding • More incremental change than other options	• Adds upfront development costs • Only applicable for new buildings or refurbishments • Requires a high degree of co-ordination between planning and implementing agencies
	Encourage the use of property-level measures for both new and existing properties	• Flexible and easily combined with other measures • Raises household awareness of risks	• Property-level technology still underdeveloped
	Emergency management	• Mitigate loss of life and assets from coastal flooding	• Uncertainty of storm-surge predictions within early warning systems • Significant financial cost for evacuation of people
Avoidance and planned retreat (reduce exposure)	Prevent new development in areas at risk of flood or erosion through land-use regulation/zoning	• Flexible to address different conditions and needs within a community • Provides opportunity for additional access to waterfront area • Reduces potential for coastal squeeze	• Removing existing zoning rights can be a slow process that requires compensation • Only applicable for new development
	Physical relocation of people and critical assets, including removal of existing hard protection	• Protects existing and creates new intertidal habitats, which are a natural form of flood protection • Can save communities from future costs of flood protection	• Often substantial financial cost if existing property owners need to be compensated • Direct impact on those living in affected properties

Note: Non-exhaustive list.

Sources: Wilby, R.L. and R. Keenan (2012[13]), "Adapting to flood risk under climate change", https://doi.org/10.1177/0309133312438908; Spalding, M.D. et al. (2014[14]), "The role of ecosystems in coastal protection: Adapting to climate change and coastal hazards", http://dx.doi.org/10.1016/J.OCECOAMAN.2013.09.007; Harman, B.P. et al. (2015[15]), "Global lessons for adapting coastal communities to protect against storm surge inundation", https://doi.org/10.2112/JCOASTRES-D-13-00095.1.

The following section describes each strategy in more detail.

2.2.1. Protect

Measures to protect against SLR hazards are typically static, engineered structures designed to reduce wave damage and flooding. They can also be designed to decrease shoreline erosion. Sometimes termed "grey" or "hard" infrastructure, these structures include seawalls, levees/floodwalls and storm surge barriers. Many countries have long histories of using hard defences, such as most of Western Europe and Japan. The technical characteristics of these types of measures is generally well understood and they are projected to play a significant role in reducing the expected damages from sea-level rise across a range of scenarios (see Chapter 1).

While this hard protection has proved to be effective at reducing coastal flood risks, these defences may become financially unsustainable in some locations due to their recurring and costly maintenance to match increasing risk (Driessen et al., 2016[16]; Keeler, McNamara and Irish, 2018[17]). Furthermore, conventional coastal defences can intensify land subsidence and prevent the natural accumulation of sediments by tides, waves and wind (Temmerman et al., 2013[18]), thereby undermining the natural adaptive capacity of shorelines to keep pace with relative SLR.

Nature-based defences are increasingly being used as complements or substitutes to grey infrastructure. These defences mimic or enhance natural features, such as barrier islands, vegetated dunes, coastal wetlands, mangrove forests and reefs (see Box 2.2 for an example). Diverse terminology is used to describe these measures, which include natural infrastructure, green infrastructure, nature-based solutions and ecosystem-based adaptation. There is a distinction between strategies that favour natural defences, which is the protection potential of existing coastal habitats, and those that favour nature-based defences, which is restoration with coastal protection as an objective (Narayan et al., 2016[19]).

Coastal habitats reduce the vulnerability of communities through wave attenuation, sediment capture, vertical accretion, erosion reduction, and the mitigation of storm surge and debris movement (Spalding et al., 2014[14]). A 2016 review found that coastal habitats (which included coral reefs, mangroves, salt marshes, seagrass/kelp beds) reduce wave heights by 35-71% (Narayan et al., 2016[19]). Strategies such as retreat or limiting development in a specific area are often paired with the understanding that leaving a natural landscape in place, or allowing a landscape such as a wetland to regenerate, can then serve as a buffer from coastal hazards.

Box 2.2. The advantages and disadvantages of beach nourishment

Beach nourishment is a nature-based coastal erosion control strategy that involves adding new sand to shorelines in an attempt to stabilise and artificially maintain a minimum beach width. Beach nourishment is a popular measure to combat erosion as it provides a flexible and modifiable approach to adapt to sea-level rise (SLR). It is also reversible, easily modified to the actual rate of SLR, and can complement hard protection measures such as seawalls. The natural appearance of beach nourishment projects also means these schemes are aesthetically pleasing, promoting recreation and tourism. Beach nourishment is gaining in popularity in OECD countries. In the United States, the federal government spends an estimated USD 150 million every year on beach nourishment. In the Netherlands, "the Sand Engine", a EUR 70 million project, was completed in 2011, which is a 21.5 million m^3 pile of sand that juts out into the North Sea, steadily eroding so that beaches down current will be continually replenished.

Beach nourishment can also have disadvantages. First, beach nourishment can threaten coastal biodiversity, both by harming species that relied on the dynamic nature of existing beaches and by disturbing the seabed where offshore dredging happens. This can have downstream impacts on groups such as fishers, who depend on functioning coastal ecosystems for their livelihoods. Nature-based protection can also lock in increased development, similar to the levee effect described above. As beach nourishment is not without costs, getting locked in to a continuous cycle of nourishment could eventually become financially unsustainable. In addition, in some areas, dredged sand is not limitless and it is possible that neighbouring communities end up competing for an increasingly expensive resource.

Sources: McNamara, D.E. et al. (2015[20]), "Climate adaptation and policy-induced inflation of coastal property value", https://doi.org/10.1371/journal.pone.0121278; Gopalakrishnan, S. et al. (2016[21]), "Economics of coastal erosion and adaptation to sea level rise", https://doi.org/10.1146/annurev-resource-100815-095416; Gopalakrishnan, S. et al. (2017[22]), "Decentralized management hinders coastal climate adaptation: The spatial-dynamics of beach nourishment", http://dx.doi.org/10.1007/s10640-016-0004-8.

One of the key differences between nature-based approaches and hard engineering is that ecosystems are highly dynamic in response to physical changes and, in some cases, can recover and regenerate following damage (Spalding et al., 2014[23]). However, regeneration is not immediate, and overall ecosystem resilience can be compromised by poor ecosystem health (Spalding et al., 2014[14]). Another advantage of natural measures is that they can deliver multiple benefits beyond coastal protection through a range of other ecosystem services. These include tourism, recreation, fish nurseries and habitat, transport, and cultural heritage and spiritual benefits (Mehvar et al., 2018[24]; Temmerman et al., 2013[18]; Guerry et al., 2012[25]). Despite the increase in awareness of its benefits in the international policy community (Wong et al., 2014[8]), most examples of implementation in OECD countries remain at a smaller scale (Arkema et al., 2017[26]; Spalding et al., 2014[14]). Additionally, uncertainties about their effectiveness is much higher than engineered defences, which can prevent implementation.

2.2.2. Accommodate

Accommodation strategies aim to reduce vulnerability and are usually implemented via regulatory and planning instruments. They are particularly suitable as a response to occasional, short-term impacts (e.g. impacts from coastal storm events or seasonal flooding) and is an appropriate response when the practicality of protecting coastal assets is outweighed by the costs, and/or the effectiveness would be limited to a relatively short period of time. Examples include changing building codes to emphasise resilient measures (examples in Box 2.3), risk-informed land-use planning that allows space for flood water, and emergency management plans.

Box 2.3. Incorporating sea-level rise resilience in urban building codes for coastal cities

Building codes and design standards have a crucial role in making development resilient to predicted sea-level rise (SLR) impacts through measures such as building elevation, foundation design, moisture entrapment and damage from debris. Examples of cities that have used building codes and design standards to address SLR include:

- Helsinki, Finland, initiated changes to design standards addressing coastal flooding and SLR in the late 1980s, which resulted in the decision to raise floor levels in the inner-city suburb of Ruoholahti from 1 metre to 3 metres above mean sea level (EC, 2009[27]).
- Christchurch, New Zealand, updated its city plan in 2011 to account for climate change-induced SLR and flooding. It now contains provisions that control development in areas vulnerable to flooding, including raised floor levels and set-backs from waterways (Christchurch, 2010[28]).
- Vancouver, Canada, updated minimum flood construction levels to be a metre higher in 2014 to account for SLR projections up to 2100.

Encouraging household-level risk-reduction measures is an accommodation strategy with multiple benefits. Measures such as flood proofing, elevating properties and keeping protective items like sandbags on hand can significantly reduce flood risk (Kreibich et al., 2015[29]), while still being flexible and a low regret risk management strategy, as they do not lock in as high costs as protection or retreat (Wilby and Keenan, 2012[13]). In addition, the use of household measures spreads awareness and responsibility for adaptation beyond the public sector, which is considered a best practice in risk management (elaborated in Box 2.1) (OECD, 2014[4]). Finally, accommodation measures can reduce residual risks of flooding when other measures are in place, and thus are important complements to coastal risk management (Koerth, Vafeidis and Hinkel, 2017[30]).

2.2.3. Avoidance and planned retreat

Retreat reduces exposure through the managed withdrawal of assets and people from hazard-prone areas of the coast. This may involve relocating or abandoning assets in high-risk areas, preventing any new development in coastal areas through risk-informed land-use planning, and/or allowing development to take place on the condition that it will be abandoned if necessary (Nicholls, 2011[31]). Retreat can be planned or reactive, and the latter generally occurs in response to major or repetitive hazard events. The modelling in Chapter 1 suggests that this will be particularly important for managing increasing risks in lower density coastal areas.

While retreat has long been acknowledged as part of the suite of coastal adaptation strategies, it is far less employed than strategies that include elements of protect and/or accommodate (Gibbs, 2016[32]). Retreat policies are highly physically and emotionally disruptive to those directly impacted, and have associated political and legal challenges in implementation (OECD, 2017[5]). In many cases where implementation has been attempted, relocation programmes have suffered from low levels of participation (OECD, 2016[33]). Finally, buying back properties can have high up-front costs – based on early experiences, the financial cost of managed retreat to implementing parties varies from USD 10 000 to well over USD 100 000 per person (Hino, Field and Mach, 2017[7]). Despite these challenges, there are select examples in OECD countries where coastal retreat has been attempted (Table 2.1).

Table 2.2. Examples of coastal retreat in OECD countries

Location	Description	Implementation status
Byron Bay, Australia	Byron Shire Council adopted a policy of retreat in 1988, in which structures would need to be removed once the coastline eroded to within a certain distance of their property. This policy was revised as landowners sued the council on the grounds that the policy devalues their property.	On hold
United States	Since 1989, the Federal Emergency Management Agency has used its Hazard Mitigation Grant Program to purchase properties from willing homeowners after disasters. The land is then restored to open space.	Reactive (after an event)
United Kingdom	The UK government's Coastal Change Pathfinder Programme (see Chapter 7) funded five pilots to test "rollback" schemes between 2009 and 2011. The programme bought out properties at high risk from erosion. Each pilot relocated around ten households in different communities.	Pre-emptive
De Noordwaard, Netherlands	As part of the Room for the River programme, a lengthy community engagement process was conducted to decide how to improve the existing flood risk management system to cope with future climate extremes. This resulted in the decision to lower the dikes surrounding De Noordwaard, and the government supported the resettlement of 75 displaced households between 2009 and 2014.	Pre-emptive
France	The French parliament has adopted a draft bill on coastline retreat that will restrict development within 100 m of the coast. The law will also allow for the retreat of people and assets further inland.	Proposed

Sources: Niven, R.J. and D.K. Bardsley (2013[34]), "Planned retreat as a management response to coastal risk: A case study from the Fleurieu Peninsula, South Australia", https://doi.org/10.1007/s10113-012-0315-4; Verchick, R. et al. (2013[35]), "When retreat is the best option: Flood insurance after Biggert-Waters and other climate change puzzles", http://repository.jmls.edu/lawreview; Defra (2012[36]), *Coastal Change Pathfinder Review Final Report*, https://assets.publishing.service.gov.uk/government/uploads/system/uploads/attachment_data/file/69508/pb13720-coastal-pathfinder-review.pdf; Schut, M., C. Leeuwis and A. van Paassen (2010[37]), "Room for the River: Room for research? The case of depoldering De Noordwaard, the Netherlands", http://dx.doi.org/10.3152/030234210X12767691861173.

Despite the political, legal and social challenges in implementation, retreat is increasingly viewed as a preferable alternative to continued protection in some cases. First, retreat can protect and create new intertidal habitats, which can then themselves serve as flood buffers (Kousky, 2014[38]). Second, it can save on the costs directed towards flood protection measures in the future and has minimal financial costs once implemented, in contrast to recurring costs for the maintenance of protective infrastructure (Verchick et al., 2013[35]; Hino, Field and Mach, 2017[7]). Implementing planned retreat in a way that dedicates sufficient time to the process, ensures community coherence and minimises the costs for affected communities is a better option than the alternative of being forced to move after a disruptive event (OECD, 2017[5]).

2.3. The political economy of coastal adaptation decisions

The potential costs and benefits of adapting to SLR vary significantly between coastal actors (see Table 2.4 for a list of actors). This diversity is due to physical factors, such as the risk of storm surge, expected SLR and the topography of the area (Hinkel et al.,

2015[39]), as well as socio-economic factors, such as the variation in the density and location of development, and the capacity of a community to adapt (Fletcher et al., 2015[40]).

The way the distribution of SLR risk is perceived by coastal stakeholders will drive reactions on how best to manage them and, ultimately, the acceptance of different strategies (e.g. protect, accommodate, retreat) among different stakeholders. The different impacts of strategies (summarised in Table 2.3) will determine politically feasible paths to reform.

Table 2.3. Direct and indirect impacts of coastal adaptation strategies

Strategy	**Direct impact** (i.e. through physical change to coastal risks)	**Indirect impact** (e.g. through tax and investment value)
Protect	• The potential to cause/increase vulnerabilities in other locations, e.g. unwanted impacts to other public or private assets alongside/downstream where the barrier has been constructed[1]	• Deterioration on surrounding natural environment can cause losses in sectors that depend on tourism (e.g. beaches) • Devaluation of property resulting from restrictions on the use of land/view (to create more space for the new/reinforced infrastructure) • Reduction in insurance premiums for those benefiting from increased protection • Depending on public finance scheme, the subsidisation of at-risk properties by the rest of the community
Accommodate		• Increase in property values for the area where development is allowed at the expense of areas where development is forbidden • Costs usually borne by smaller group (those directly at risk) than for protection measures • Development opportunities shift to neighbouring communities
Retreat	• Large financial and physiological impact on households that must relocate	• Depending on public finance scheme, subsidisation of at-risk properties by the rest of the community

1. In contrast to hard protection such as a seawall, beach nourishment at one location can cause the shoreline to erode more slowly at the neighbouring location, depending on the direction of net sediment transport (Gopalakrishnan et al., 2017[22]).

Sources: Gibbs, M.T. (2016[32]), "Why is coastal retreat so hard to implement? Understanding the political risk of coastal adaptation pathways", http://dx.doi.org/10.1016/j.ocecoaman.2016.06.002; Colgan, C.S. (2016[41]), "The economics of adaptation to climate change in coasts and oceans: Literature review, policy implications and research agenda", http://dx.doi.org/10.15351/2373-8456.1067.

Early experiences with coastal adaptation have shown that the adoption of an adaptation strategy often involves social conflict and opposition (Gibbs, 2016[32]). There are numerous examples of conflicts arising over coastal adaptation attempts. For example, on the Italian Adriatic coast, conflicts have arisen between the tourism sector which welcomes beach nourishment as it directly benefits them by maintaining beach-related revenues, and environmental groups who are strongly against introducing foreign materials to the coast (Prati et al., 2016[42]). In Louisiana, small commercial fishing interests have challenged the method of using river diversions to deposit more sediment on the coast, which serve as additional wetland build up and protection (Gotham, 2016[43]). Conflicts can also arise in situations where a small number of properties benefit from a strategy but a community as a whole is expected to fund it, as has been seen in Australia (Fletcher et al., 2015[40]).

In many countries, the impact of adaptation measures, whether real or perceived, on real estate values can create strong support and opposition for different measures. For example, coastal defences can reduce future coastal flood risk, but may also reduce present-day high-value amenities, such as beach width and access. As such, coastal property owners will have a vested interest in influencing coastal decision making and can potentially block measures that reduce the value of their property. This can serve to lock in existing policy choices: for example, a 2015 study in North Carolina (McNamara et al.[20]) estimates that the removal of federal subsidies for nourishment projects would decrease the value of coastal properties by as much as 34%.

In jurisdictions where taxes are calculated based on property values, local governments may also be exposed to a change in value from an adaptation decision. For example, a study undertaken in New York City found that reductions in property value caused by updated flood risk mapping has the potential to reduce property taxes by USD 22 million per year (Dixon et al., 2017[44]).

The way the costs and benefits of protecting, accommodating or retreating from SLR are distributed will, in part, depend on existing policies and institutional arrangements. In the case of residential property, for example, an increase in the risk faced by coastal property will be borne by households in the first instance, through higher insurance premiums, or higher uninsured losses for those unable or unwilling to purchase insurance. At the limit, households may lose the total value of their property due to submergence or coastal erosion. However, policy interventions to subsidise insurance or provide *ex post* disaster relief (such as grants, tax deductions or subsidised loans) shifts some of this cost to taxpayers in lower risk areas.

2.4. The alignment of incentives, capacity and roles in the coastal zone

Coastal adaptation goes beyond the technical issue of building flood defences, elevating houses and risk-based land-use planning: the institutional arrangements behind these strategies matter. Institutional arrangements determine how adaptive capacity is mobilised in the public and private sector through policy frameworks and regulation, incentives, allocation of resources, and co-ordination. These arrangements encompass decisions that involve creating policies or regulations to build adaptive capacity (the enabling environment for adaptation) and action that implements operational adaptation decisions (implementing strategies) (Adger, Arnell and Tomkins, 2005[45]; Wilby and Keenan, 2012[13]).

In 2014, the OECD carried out research on countries' disaster risk-reduction policies, which brought to light how ineffective institutions can undermine the incentives needed for a whole-of-society approach to disaster risk reduction (Box 2.1) (OECD, 2014[2]). Existing institutional arrangements may undermine effective and efficient adaptation, by distorting market signals or providing perverse incentives, and uncoordinated policies can trigger individual economic behaviour that is counter to an overall policy goal of reducing risk (OECD, 2014[2]). Drawing on the findings from the 2014 report, Table 2.4 maps key actors who take decisions related to coastal risk and adaptation, describes drivers of behaviour, and gives examples of areas where misaligned incentives can lead to inefficient outcomes overall.

Table 2.4. An overview of actors, drivers of behaviour and policy misalignments

KEY ACTOR AND ROLE	DRIVERS OF BEHAVIOUR	EXAMPLE OF MISALIGNED INCENTIVES
	PRIVATE ACTORS	
Individuals/property owners • Prospective homeowners take decisions about the location and material of their home. • Existing homeowners can invest in property-level risk-reduction measures, as well as purchase insurance (where available).	• Motivated to reduce the cost of potential damages and preserve the value of their asset. • Face the direct financial costs and intangible consequences (such as mental health impacts) of an extreme event.	If governments assist homeowners in post-disaster recovery and reconstruction, regardless of their insurance take-up prior to the shock, it undermines individual homeowner incentives to invest in *ex ante* risk-reduction or transfer measures.
Property developers • Take decisions about the construction of new housing and investing in maintaining existing housing stock.	• Incentive to preserve property value and reduce additional costs. • Coastal real estate usually has high value due to the proximity to amenities and view of the water.	If property prices/insurance premiums do not reflect risk, and coastal property is highly valued, there will be a strong incentive to continue to invest and build in high-risk coastal areas.
	PUBLIC ACTORS	
Local governments • Often have responsibility and jurisdiction for coastal adaptation through land-use planning, emergency management and educating the community.	• Benefit from development through the generation of local tax revenues. • Can be directly exposed to financial risks from sea-level rise-induced hazards through changes in property values. • Can bear the costs of relief and recovery, reconstruction of public assets, payments as compensation to individuals and businesses (often first in line for providing support).	Local governments may permit construction in risk-prone areas if they gain from increased economic activity and tax revenues, while the costs/portion of costs are borne by other levels of government.
National/state governments • Role in ensuring the relevant actors have adequate incentives and tools to adapt, including the provision of climate risk information, and provision of resources for investments in risk reduction.	• Can bear the costs of relief and recovery, reconstruction of public assets, payments as compensation to individuals, business and/or subnational levels of government, and public insurance/(re)insurance schemes that provide coverage for damages and losses.	Political cycles can discourage long-term investments in sea-level rise adaptation, as their benefits may be less visible in the short run or not visible at all within the period of a government's mandate.

Sources: OECD (2014[2]), *Boosting Resilience through Innovative Risk Governance*, http://dx.doi.org/10.1787/9789264209114-en; OECD (2014[6]), *Water Governance in the Netherlands: Fit for the Future?*, http://dx.doi.org/10.1787/9789264102637-en.

The way coastal incentives, capacity and roles are allocated influence the way each individual actor decides about whether or not to invest in resilience (OECD, 2014[2]). Different approaches to risk allocation imply trade-offs between cost-efficiency, effectiveness and social equity. From an economic perspective, aligning incentives provides a strong mechanism for people to manage their exposure to risk. If an individual is responsible for the costs that are incurred from a hazard event, they will be more likely to invest in preventative measures, or move away from the at-risk area. However, this may run counter to an objective of social solidarity.

Existing institutional arrangements also influence what overall adaptation strategy is implemented. As described above, institutions influence how the risks and costs of adaptation are distributed, which influence which strategies may be politically viable. In a similar vein, the scales at which adaptation decisions are taken and funded can influence the types of adaptation measures being implemented. Building an understanding of these issues is vital to the design of institutions that can improve resilience. Figure 2.1 gives an overview of the key questions needed to understand the institutional arrangements related to coastal risk management.

Figure 2.1. Coastal flood risk management arrangements

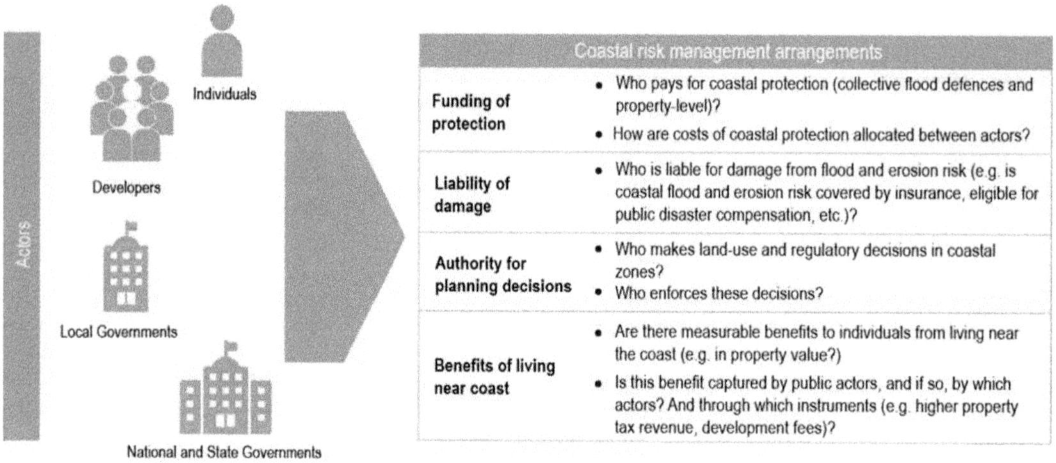

The following section outlines how different institutional arrangements (those covered in Figure 2.1) can influence the choice of adaptation strategies, leading to outcomes that run counter to the goal of cost-efficient and flexible coastal risk reduction.

2.4.1. Funding of protection

Building new and maintaining existing structural coastal defences requires significant resources, which poses challenges for government budgets. A 2011 study found that the additional annual cost of adaptation to SLR through hard defences for Europe alone will be EUR 1.5 billion[1] annually in the 2050s (current prices), excluding annual maintenance costs (Brown et al., 2011[46]).

Funding maintenance is a particular challenge. A 2017 comparative study on disaster risk management (not only coastal) in Austria, France and Switzerland (OECD[5]) found that countries' previous investments have created a significant stock of protective infrastructure; however, the financial allocations for these measures generally do not include a budget for ongoing maintenance expenses. As a result of the lack of financial planning for maintenance of disaster risk prevention infrastructure, the levels of maintenance vary within countries (OECD, 2017[5]). While not focused on coastal protection, it can be extrapolated that funding the ongoing maintenance of coastal protection, especially in the context of SLR, will pose ongoing problems for national budgets. In many European countries, existing protective infrastructure is in need of repair to continue maintaining standards of protection (Alexander, Priest and Mees, 2016[47]). The lack of maintenance of coastal protection infrastructure has led to coastal disasters in the past, with the damage in New Orleans from Hurricane Katrina being a prominent example (Kates et al., 2006[48]).

Given the high costs and public good aspect of coastal defences, they are most often funded by the public sector in OECD countries; however, the funding allocation between levels of government differs across countries. In some countries, such as in Japan and Poland, the national level is directly responsible for providing funding. In others, such as Belgium, Canada and Germany, it is primarily the responsibility of a state or regional government, though there are co-financing arrangements with the national and local (municipal) government. For example, in Germany, as detailed in the case study in Chapter 4, in the *Länd* (state) of Schleswig-Holstein, costs from 2001 to 2013 were 50% covered by the

Länd, 37% by the federal government and 13% by the European Union. Meanwhile, in Sweden, flood (including coastal) defence measures are mainly managed and financed at the local level. This can fall on municipalities, firms, individuals or combinations thereof, depending on land ownership and protection needs (Gralepois et al., 2016[11]). Australia has a model similar to Sweden's, and coastal adaptation funding is predominately the responsibility of local governments, with the exception of some major infrastructure projects that cross jurisdictions and *ad hoc* state funding grants for coastal planning and management works. In some cases, private landholders have responsibility to fund the construction of their own protection (Harman et al., 2013[10]).

In countries where national governments cover the majority of coastal defence costs and solidarity is the guiding principle, the regional nature of the public good provided can cause challenges. For example, a regional or local government on the coast may consider funding an adaptation measure to be socially or economically optimal, while a national government funding the same measure may not, if funding comes from the national tax base (Bisaro and Hinkel, 2018[49]). Conflicts can also emerge from the distribution of public money between a location receiving public support for coastal protection and non-coastal actors paying for this through taxes. For example, in the Netherlands, costs of protection against flood risks are borne by the community at large, including by communities in the east and south of the country which are not part of the main dike system, whereas benefits accrue to a smaller set of stakeholders (OECD, 2014[6]). However, it could be argued that the solidarity principle is justified in this case, as areas not covered by protection measures benefit indirectly from the protection of coastal areas, where the main economic activities of the country are located (OECD, 2014[6]).

In cases where local governments have full responsibility for funding coastal defences, such as areas of the United States and Australia, the ability to raise funds is often cited as a barrier to implementing such coastal risk management measures (Fletcher et al., 2013[50]; National Research Council, 2014[51]). This is partially due to acute political economy factors at the local level (National Research Council, 2014[51]). For all levels of government, coastal adaptation funding needs compete with other priorities. Coastal protection investments are made to avoid longer term damages, and decision makers are rarely rewarded for avoiding crises. Local decision makers face pressure to make investments to address more frequent and immediate issues, as well as operate on short-term political cycles (Brown, Naylor and Quinn, 2017[52]). Conflicting policy and regulation can also cause challenges; for example, in many countries, there are limits on how much local governments can borrow, which makes financing a large-scale project challenging.

There are emerging examples of areas where funding for protection has shifted towards a beneficiary-pays model. In the United Kingdom (Box 2.4), the shift was done in part to encourage community ownership of risk management, and to secure funding over the lifecycle of an investment (Penning-Rowsell and Priest, 2015[53]). Conversely, many towns on the east coast of the United States have used differential property tax rates as an instrument for funding beach nourishment, recognising the political difficulty of raising collective taxes for a project that will disproportionally benefit oceanfront property owners (McNamara et al., 2015[20]).

Box 2.4. Partnership funding: UK model for funding flood defences and coastal protection

The funding system for flood risk management (including coastal flood) in England and Wales underwent a substantial change in 2011. The existing system was funded by block grants from the central government and administered by the Environment Agency. The new system of "partnership" is an arrangement that promotes sharing of costs between the local and national levels. This change shifted part of the burden of investments on those who would benefit from the associated risk reduction.

The cost-sharing agreement is determined by the total value of benefits for households, businesses and environment that result from flood or coastal erosion risks being managed. In addition, the percentage of national funding contributed is on a scale that depends on the income level of a community to favour more high-risk, low-income communities receiving assistance. The policy change included a provision that properties built after January 2012 are ineligible for funding, to avoid encouraging inappropriate development in areas at risk.

One of the primary goals of the policy change was to allow more projects to be funded. In addition, communities with a financial investment in managing risk should have an incentive to manage project costs throughout the project life cycle. Early assessments of this new funding arrangement appear to be favourable and have documented an increase in external funding, although the difficulties of securing contributions at the local scale and from the private sector is still an express concern.

Sources: Defra (2011[54]), *Flood and Coastal Resilience Partnership Funding: An Introductory Guide*, https://www.gov.uk/government/publications/flood-and-coastal-resilience-partnership-funding-an-introductory-guide; Penning-Rowsell, E.C. and S.J. Priest (2015[55]), "Sharing the burden of increasing flood risk: Who pays for flood insurance and flood risk management in the United Kingdom", http://dx.doi.org/10.1007/s11027-014-9622-z.

2.4.2. Financial liability for damage

Many countries have started to take note of the rising costs of publicly funded flood[2] recovery (OECD, 2016[33]). For example, in Canada, payments under the Disaster Financial Assistance Arrangements, the national programme that reimburses provinces and territories for a portion of disaster response and recovery costs, have increased dramatically in the past 20 years. Costs have risen from an average of CAD 291 million per year in the period 1995-2004 to CAD 410 million per year in the period 2005-14, and are projected to increase to more than CAD 650 million annually over the period of 2017 to 2022 (PBO, 2016[56]).

Even without legal or policy frameworks, there is often an expectation that governments will take some responsibility to provide financial support for disaster recovery and reconstruction purposes beyond explicit commitments. These expectations create an implicit contingent financial liability for the government, as well as political risks (Hall et al., 2012[57]). Many countries allocate significantly more funds to disaster response than to risk-reduction measures such as coastal defences (OECD, 2016[33]). While there is limited coastal-specific data, overall disaster spending figures reveal the trend: for example, in Japan, 25% of disaster spending goes to *ex ante* disaster risk-reduction measures, 75% goes to *ex post* spending on recovery and reconstruction; in Mexico, only 3% of disaster spending is allocated to *ex ante* measures, whereas 97% is spent *ex post* on recovery and reconstruction (the reconstruction is required to meet betterment objectives) (OECD/World Bank, forthcoming[58]).

Box 2.5. Monitoring and mitigating the cost of natural disasters risks

Disaster-related costs, including those from coastal risks, can be high, with single shocks causing damages of up to 20% of gross domestic product (GDP), affecting local economies and populations disproportionately.

Governments tend to bear a significant share of the costs of disasters, particularly in countries with modest insurance coverage rate. The nature of these costs ranges from payments made to compensate for business and household losses to public asset recovery. In addition, disaster-related declines in tax and non-tax revenues due to economic disruptions may affect government finances negatively. Government budgets can also be affected by deteriorations in the terms of refinancing or raising new public debt.

In a recent report, the OECD and the World Bank argue that the costs that disasters impose on governments are a type of contingent liability (and contingent revenue loss). Damage to public assets, such as public buildings and infrastructure, are reportedly the largest disaster-related contingent liabilities for central and subnational governments, followed by post-disaster assistance for individual households.

The study shows that many governments have significant information on the sources and potential level of disaster-related contingent liabilities. This information, however, is scattered through different parts of the government and rarely brought together to inform financial planning, including fiscal risk monitoring and mitigation.

The report also shows that disaster costs tend to be higher in countries that have made limited or only very general explicit ex ante commitments to provide disaster recovery assistance. It thus argues that ex ante identification and quantification of disaster-related fiscal risks is key to designing mitigation strategies in the form of clear government commitments for assistance needed to increase countries' financial resilience to natural hazards. Disaster risk-reduction strategies should include clear cost-sharing mechanisms across levels of government that act in a way that encourages stakeholders to carry out disaster risk prevention and mitigation measures. Countries should also consider the formulation of multi-pronged financial strategies that include contingency budgets, risk transfer instruments or catastrophe bonds.

Source: OECD/World Bank (forthcoming[58]), "Boosting financial resilience to disasters: Understanding and strengthening the role of government".

Across the OECD, countries rely on various models to fund response and recovery from a coastal hazard event. Different models of financial liability for damage can be categorised by how direct the link is between experiencing damages and responsibility to pay for those damages. As adapted from Penning-Rowsell and Priest (2015[55]), these categories are:

- loss bearing, where the victim is responsible for all losses
- loss sharing, where losses are spread more widely, for example through flood insurance where individuals contribute premium payments
- compensation, where national, regional or local governments provide financial assistance to those affected by coastal hazards.

Most OECD countries fall somewhere between loss sharing and compensation. The role of national governments varies from very little intervention (e.g. United Kingdom) to a fully state-implemented insurance scheme (e.g. France, the United States) and to recovery mainly covered by public compensation. There are, however, nuances and differences within these distinctions (OECD, 2016[33]).

The design of public assistance mechanisms and insurance programmes has implications for a whole-of-society approach to risk reduction through the possibility of moral hazard. Moral hazard refers to households' lack of inclination to carry out risk-reduction measures or resettle out of flood-prone areas if they can expect to receive insurance pay-outs or public compensation in the event of a disaster (Hanger et al., 2017[59]; OECD/World Bank, forthcoming[58]). Moral hazard can potentially occur between levels of government in countries where subnational governments are responsible for funding protection but national governments are responsible for funding response and recovery (OECD, 2016[33]). In Australia, Canada and New Zealand, post-disaster compensation is provided to subnational governments based on a cost-sharing formula, and reimburses a share of eligible expenses incurred by subnational governments for costs such as emergency response, restoration and reconstruction of public assets. In Mexico, the FONDEN scheme has implemented specific conditions to address moral hazard between levels of government, as subnational governments are only eligible for compensation a second time if they have undertaken certain protection measures as part of initially supported recovery and reconstruction efforts (OECD/World Bank, forthcoming[58]).

Systems based on solidarity can lack an inherent link with risk reduction (with some exceptions), but have the benefit of ensuring widespread and affordable coverage. This can prevent the burden of risk management and recovery from falling solely on households, who may not be well-equipped to respond (Dixon et al., 2017[44]; Hudson et al., 2016[60]; OECD, 2016[33]). For example, research on exposure to flood risks in the United Kingdom suggests that residents of lower social classes were disproportionately exposed to coastal flooding (Walker and Burningham, 2011[61]).

As climate change increases risks, the principle of solidarity may be called into question given the expected rise in the cost of damages and the strong concentration of risks in a few geographical areas. In France, for instance, which is covered by a solidarity-funded national insurance system, municipalities on the Mediterranean coast experienced an average of 6.9 natural disasters between 1982 and 2009, compared with an average of 2.5 in the country as a whole (Clément, Rey-Valette and Rulleau, 2015[62]).

Box 2.6. Coastal risks and rising insurance premiums

Insurance companies can play a key role in coastal adaptation through assessing, pricing and assuming risk. As businesses, they have a strong incentive to understand the risk profile of potential customers so that they can set premiums accordingly. In liberalised markets, the premiums charged will be sufficient to cover those risks and the insurer's costs. While premiums provide a signal to property owners of the current level of risk, they do not provide a signal of how those risks may evolve in future.

Sea-level rise will increase underlying risks due to higher and/or more frequent losses, which increase the challenges of offering affordable coverage. As a result, insurance premiums are likely to rise or coverage will no longer be offered to those owning the riskiest properties (Wolfrom and Yokoi-Arai, 2015[63]). The costs of this will ultimately be borne by property owners, but it could also have negative implications for insurers insofar as it leads to reduced demand or negative public reactions. Unaffordable premiums reduce take-up rates, which then reduces the resilience of households and communities to flood events. Premium increases can additionally reduce property values, increase loan defaults, lower tax revenue and create hardships for current residents in flood-prone areas (Dixon et al., 2017[44]). There may also be transitional impacts for insurers if they fail to reflect changing risk trends in their capital provisions and in the coverage and pricing that they offer.

The benefit of loss-bearing and loss-sharing systems is that they can provide a direct incentive to reduce risk. However, while the ability of risk-based flood insurance coverage to incentivise risk reduction by households has received wide attention in the policy community, in practice this incentive is hindered by low levels of insurance coverage and premium subsidies in many coastal areas (OECD, 2016[33]; Surminski, 2013[64]). For example, there remains mixed evidence of the success of insurance in encouraging risk-reduction behaviour at the household level (discussed more thoroughly in Chapter 3) (Surminski and Thieken, 2017[65]). In addition, coastal communities face significant challenges that limit the deployment of insurance. Risk concentration, which relates to catastrophe events where many insureds are simultaneously impacted, is highly likely in heavily populated coastal areas. This then limits the availability and affordability of coverage (OECD, 2016[33]). Finally, slow-onset, foreseeable climate impacts, such as SLR-induced erosion, are often not insurable (Wolfrom and Yokoi-Arai, 2015[63]).

2.4.3. Authority for planning decisions

Land-use planning can have a significant impact on coastal risk, and inappropriate land-use development can be a substantial driver of increased losses (OECD, 2016[33]). For example, in the United States, high-risk, repetitive loss properties represented 38% of all claims payments between 1978 and 2004 (OECD, 2016[66]). Decision makers should aim to reduce the level of human or fixed assets exposed to flood risk.

Coastal zones are frequently managed by a patchwork of local, regional, national and international authorities looking after specific aspects of land use, such as flooding, transport, development and conservation. For example, in the United States, responsibilities for coastal risk management are shared between a number of federal, state and local agencies, and each agency has its own distinct objectives (National Research Council, 2014[67]). This can lead to a system in which decisions taken by one agency affect other agencies' mandates, and can lead to difficulties in implementing anything other than incremental change (Verschuuren and Mcdonald, 2012[68]; National Research Council, 2014[51]).

In most OECD countries, land-use planning is a local responsibility, but split incentives and capacity constraints may hinder effective implementation (OECD, 2017[69]). In particular, local governments often face pressures to allow development of desirable coastal land, as this leads to increased tax revenue. An underlying challenge in many countries lies with implementation of restrictive land-use regulations at the local level. In Italy, for example, gaps in compliance and number of amnesties provided for properties constructed without regard to flood hazard level have limited the effectiveness of legislative requirements for assessing flood hazard in new construction (OECD, 2016[33]). Some countries have held local decision makers to account for failing to incorporate hazard information into their land-use decisions. In France, responsibility for enforcing hazard zones falls on mayors, who can and have been found liable for ignoring these, such as in the coastal town of La Faute-sur-Mer (OECD, 2017[5]).

The implementation of land-use policies is often a local responsibility, but other levels of government have an important role in providing guidance and incentives (Box 2.7) for risk reduction. In countries where coastal risk management systems is co-ordinated nationally, such as the *plans de prévention des risques (risk prevention plans)* in France or Shoreline Management Plans in the United Kingdom, local implementation gaps have been reported.

Box 2.7. Insurance programmes can encourage better land-use management

In a number of countries, public (re)insurance schemes have been established to provide insurance coverage for flood damages (available for all properties or only residential or high-risk residential properties). In many countries, these schemes specifically include incentives, requirements or exclusions aimed at encouraging flood risk management at the local level.

In the United Kingdom, for example, the reinsurance coverage provided through Flood Re (which is meant to ensure the availability of affordable insurance for high-risk properties) is only available for developments constructed before 2009. This means that developers of more recent properties will need to ensure that the level of flood risk at individual properties is within the risk appetite of private insurers who may otherwise choose not to offer coverage in newly-built high-risk areas, putting at risk the possibility for homeowners to secure mortgage financing (which normally requires comprehensive property insurance coverage).

In the United States, insurance coverage through the public National Flood Insurance Program (NFIP) is only offered in communities that agree to implement a set of minimum NFIP floodplain development standards, including the use of flood maps in development planning, requirements for a base flood elevation and building standards to ensure that new buildings will be protected. In addition, a Community Rating System has been established to provide insurance premium discounts to households in communities that adopt recognised flood risk management practices (land-use planning and other risk-reduction measures) above the NFIP minimum requirements.

Source: OECD (2016[33]), *Financial Management of Flood Risk*, https://doi.org/10.1787/9789264257689-en.

Local governments can also face conflicting advice and capacity constraints in implementing land-use regulations. For example, during post 2013-14 storm recovery in the United Kingdom, central and local funding sources as well as misaligned land-use policies resulted in coastal infrastructure being rebuilt in the same original location, rather than further inland, as was suggested by both local communities and shoreline management plans (Brown, Naylor and Quinn, 2017[70]). In Australia, Canada and New Zealand, concerns around liability are frequently cited as barriers to implementing land-use decisions that account for uncertain future hazards (Verschuuren and Mcdonald, 2012[68]; Lemmen et al., 2016[71]) Box 2.8).

Box 2.8. Liability in planning decisions

In general, a decision by a local government to approve a development in a flood-prone area which is later flooded would not be considered as subject to claims of liability directed towards the relevant decision maker. However, climate change impacts are setting new precedent in countries and protection from liability for local planning decisions may not be assured. For example, in New Zealand, there have multiple cases where a precautionary sea-level rise adaptation measure taken by a territorial authority was challenged by a holder of property rights in the coastal area. In Sweden, local councils have been found liable for flood damage in areas deemed unsuitable for development. In general, liability issues can arise around:

- legal liability associated with the failure of an engineered structure for the owner/operator of the structure (often national governments)
- legal liabilities associated with existing zoning approvals of new development in areas anticipated to be affected by sea-level rise
- legal questions over property rights and with the development of more restrictive zoning regulations aimed at limiting development.

Sources: OECD (2016[33]), *Financial Management of Flood Risk*, https://doi.org/10.1787/9789264257689-en.

2.4.4. Benefits of living near the coast

People choose to occupy or use the coast due to substantial benefits, such as access to the environmental amenities that the coast provides. The benefits of coastal living is reflected in property values: research in the United States found that the prices of houses located within 150 metres of the sea were 100% higher than equivalent properties that are more than 10 km inland (Krause, 2014[72]).

The benefits of coastal living also go beyond homeowners. These benefits accrue to developers, engineers, architects and builders, as well as local and state governments in the form of contracts, profits and tax revenue. Development provides tax revenues, can result in greater local employment and, in some cases, reflects the preservation of historical and cultural community values (National Research Council, 2014[51]). It is therefore often perceived as being in the best interest of the property owner, developer, builder and municipality to undertake new development regardless of future public risk and other externalities.

All things being equal, a property in a risky location should be worth less than an identical one in a safer location; however, in practice the situation is more nuanced. A review of the literature examining the relationship between property value and SLR risk (Beltrán, Maddison and Elliott, 2018[73]; Bernstein, Gustafson and Lewis, 2018[74]; Keenan, Hill and Gumber, 2018[75]; Bakkensen and Barrage, 2017[76]; Warren-Myers et al., 2018[77]) found the following trends:

- In general, future SLR risks alone are not sufficient to reduce coastal property values, especially if the property has yet to be affected by a hazard event (e.g. experienced flooding or erosion). This is mainly due to inaccurate perceptions of risk and inadequate provision of risk information.
- In many cases, the value attached to proximity to coastal amenities outweighs the risk of increased exposure to SLR hazards.
- While information about SLR risk does not always affect value, the experience of actual flooding/erosion of a property is highly likely to adversely affect property values.
- Investments in public risk-reduction measures such as seawalls can raise property values again, as individuals and investors perceive the risks as being lower.
- Once sufficient time has passed without significant hazards occurring, property prices are also likely to increase as the impact of past events fade from memory and individuals discount future risks.

These trends point to a potential "coastal value gap", where the values of coastal properties may not accurately reflect their current or future risk. When a flood or erosion event does occur, the ensuing drop in property value has the potential to be dramatic and cause cascading adverse consequences.

2.5. Impact of institutional arrangements on future adaptation responses

OECD countries vary widely in their approach to coastal risk management, with the level of attention and degree of action often being correlated with the risks they face (Tol, Klein and Nicholls, 2008[9]). In countries that have been exposed only recently to persistent weather events or climate change-related effects, and in cases where there is a lower share of the population at risk, approaches tend to be less developed and more fragmented (Harman et al., 2015[15]). Non-economic factors also play an important role in explaining differences in the approaches to coastal management in different areas. These include different societal views on how to cope with risk, the historic approach to coastal risk management, including past investments in protective infrastructure, experience of floods and the division of institutional responsibilities (e.g. degree of centralisation). While there are large variations among OECD countries' arrangements for coastal risk management, general country typologies, and potential implications for adaptation, are described in Table 2.5.

Table 2.5. Implications of increasing coastal risk for different institutional arrangements

Typology	What will be the impacts of increasing coastal risk?	What adaptation strategies are likely to be prioritised?
1. Centrally funded, centrally co-ordinated (e.g. France, the Netherlands, Poland)	Increasing risk will be distributed throughout the country, and more and more public spending will go towards preparedness and response. This could lead to growing dissatisfaction from those who do not feel the benefits of increased spending on coastal protection, and call existing principals of solidarity into question.	• Heavy reliance on increased protection. • Potential for strong emphasis on large-scale, nature-based infrastructure and innovative responses due to consistent national funding.
2. Centrally supported, locally implemented (e.g. Belgium, Canada, Germany, United Kingdom, United States)	Due to difficulty in raising funds for ongoing maintenance and repair of existing coastal defences, effectiveness will likely drop below current standards. This could lead to a growing burden on emergency management to deal with increasing frequency of flooding events and other ongoing impacts of rising seas, which in turn means increasing costs for the general tax base, especially if risks become uninsurable.	• A mix of hard protection and household-level protection, both hard and nature-based. • Potential for unplanned retreat, especially after a major event, if financial resources cannot be raised for rebuilding and protection. • Low likelihood of transformational change, unless initiated by the community.
3. Local funding, local implementation (e.g. Australia, New Zealand, Sweden)	Increasing risks will be felt by individuals and communities along the coast. In some cases, this direct risk will incentivise individual action, but the lack of co-ordination will likely lead to *ad hoc* responses. It is possible that wealthier communities continue to raise funds for protection, which could have negative downstream effects on communities without the means for similar measures. In the short term, it is likely that local governments continue to pursue policies that are rational from a local perspective, but create inefficiencies overall, such as granting building permits in higher risk areas.	• A mix of *ad hoc* protection (both hard and nature-based) and individual measures, likely correlated to community resources opposed to community risk profile. • Low likelihood of transformational change, unless community initiative.

Notes

[1] The estimated costs of adaptation vary significantly based on the level of future climate change, the level of acceptable risk protection and the framework of analysis (risks protection versus economic efficiency) (Brown et al., 2011[46]).

[2] Comprising riverine and coastal flooding.

References

Adger, N., N. Arnell and E. Tomkins (2005), "Successful adaptation to climate change across scales", *Global Environmental Change*, Vol. 15/2, pp. 77-86, http://dx.doi.org/10.1016/J.GLOENVCHA.2004.12.005. [45]

Alexander, M., S. Priest and H. Mees (2016), "A framework for evaluating flood risk governance", *Environmental Science & Policy*, Vol. 64, pp. 38-47, http://dx.doi.org/10.1016/J.ENVSCI.2016.06.004. [47]

Arkema, K. et al. (2017), "Linking social, ecological, and physical science to advance natural and nature-based protection for coastal communities", *Annals of the New York Academy of Sciences*, Vol. 1399/1, pp. 5-26, http://dx.doi.org/10.1111/nyas.13322. [26]

Bakkensen, L. and L. Barrage (2017), *Flood Risk Belief Heterogeneity and Coastal Home Price Dynamics: Going Under Water?*, https://www.fema.gov/national- (accessed on 30 August 2018). [76]

Beltrán, A., D. Maddison and R. Elliott (2018), "Is flood risk capitalised into property values?", *Ecological Economics*, Vol. 146, pp. 668-685, http://dx.doi.org/10.1016/J.ECOLECON.2017.12.015. [73]

Bernstein, A., M. Gustafson and R. Lewis (2018), *Disaster on the Horizon: The Price Effect of Sea Level Rise*, http://www.zillow.com/ztrax (accessed on 30 August 2018). [74]

Bisaro, A. and J. Hinkel (2018), "Mobilizing private finance for coastal adaptation: A literature review", *Wiley Interdisciplinary Reviews: Climate Change*, Vol. 9/3, p. e514, http://dx.doi.org/10.1002/wcc.514. [49]

Brown, K., L. Naylor and T. Quinn (2017), "Making space for proactive adaptation of rapidly changing coasts: A windows of opportunity approach", *Sustainability*, Vol. 9/8, pp. 1-17, http://dx.doi.org/10.3390/su9081408. [52]

Brown, K., L. Naylor and T. Quinn (2017), "Making space for proactive adaptation of rapidly changing coasts: A windows of opportunity approach", *Sustainability*, Vol. 9/8, pp. 1-17, http://dx.doi.org/10.3390/su9081408 (accessed on 20 July 2018). [70]

Christchurch, C. (2010), "Climate Smart Strategy 2010-2025", https://www.ccc.govt.nz/assets/Documents/The-Council/Plans-Strategies-Policies-Bylaws/Strategies/ClimateSmartStrategy2010-2025.pdf (accessed on 15 June 2018). [28]

Clément, V., H. Rey-Valette and B. Rulleau (2015), "Perceptions on equity and responsibility in coastal zone policies", *Ecological Economics*, Vol. 119, pp. 284-291, http://dx.doi.org/10.1016/J.ECOLECON.2015.09.005. [62]

Colgan, C. (2016), "Journal of Ocean and Coastal Economics The Economics of Adaptation to Climate Change in Coasts and Oceans: Literature Review, Policy Implications and Research Agenda", http://dx.doi.org/10.15351/2373-8456.1067. [41]

DEFRA (2012), *Coastal Change Pathfinder Review: Final Report*, Department for Environment, Food & Rural Affairs, London, https://assets.publishing.service.gov.uk/government/uploads/system/uploads/attachment_data/file/69508/pb13720-coastal-pathfinder-review.pdf (accessed on 6 December 2017). [36]

DEFRA (2011), *Flood and Coastal Resilience Partnership Funding: An Introductory Guide*, Department for Environment, Food & Rural Affairs, London, https://www.gov.uk/government/publications/flood-and-coastal-resilience-partnership-funding-an-introductory-guide (accessed on 7 December 2017). [54]

Dixon, L. et al. (2017), *The Cost and Affordability of Flood Insurance in New York City: Economic Impacts of Rising Premiums and Policy Options for One- to Four-Family Homes*, RAND, https://www.rand.org/content/dam/rand/pubs/research_reports/RR1700/RR1776/RAND_RR1776.pdf (accessed on 10 August 2017). [44]

Driessen, P. et al. (2016), "Toward more resilient flood risk governance", *Ecology and Society*, Vol. 21/4, http://dx.doi.org/10.5751/ES-08921-210453. [16]

EC (2009), *The Economics of Climate Change Adaptation in EU Coastal Areas*, European Union, Luxembourg, https://ec.europa.eu/maritimeaffairs/sites/maritimeaffairs/files/docs/body/executive_summary_en.pdf (accessed on 15 June 2018). [27]

Filatova, T., J. Mulder and A. Van der Veen (2011), "Coastal risk management: How to motivate individual economic decisions to lower flood risk?", *Ocean & Coastal Management*, Vol. 54/2, pp. 164-172, http://dx.doi.org/10.1016/J.OCECOAMAN.2010.10.028. [12]

Fletcher, C. et al. (2015), "Economic, equitable, and affordable adaptations to protect coastal settlements against storm surge inundation", *Regional Environmental Change*, Vol. 16/4, pp. 1023-1034, http://dx.doi.org/10.1007/s10113-015-0814-1. [40]

Fletcher, C. et al. (2013), *Costs and Coasts: An Empirical Assessment of Physical and Institutional Climate Adaptation Pathways*, National Climate Change Adaptation Research Facility, Gold Coast, Australia, https://www.nccarf.edu.au/sites/default/files/attached_files_publications/Fletcher_2013_Costs_and_coasts.pdf (accessed on 18 August 2017). [50]

Gibbs, M. (2016), "Why is coastal retreat so hard to implement? Understanding the political risk of coastal adaptation pathways", *Ocean & Coastal Management*, Vol. 130, pp. 107-114, http://dx.doi.org/10.1016/j.ocecoaman.2016.06.002. [32]

Gopalakrishnan, S. et al. (2016), "Economics of coastal erosion and adaptation to sea level rise", *Annual Review of Resource Economics*, Vol. 8, pp. 119-39, http://dx.doi.org/10.1146/annurev-resource-100815-095416. [21]

Gopalakrishnan, S. et al. (2017), "Decentralized management hinders coastal climate adaptation: The spatial-dynamics of beach nourishment", *Environmental and Resource Economics*, Vol. 67/4, pp. 761-787, http://dx.doi.org/10.1007/s10640-016-0004-8. [22]

Gotham, K. (2016), "Coastal restoration as contested terrain: Climate change and the political economy of risk reduction in Louisiana", *Sociological Forum*, Vol. 31/S1, pp. 787-806, http://dx.doi.org/10.1111/socf.12273. [43]

Gralepois, M. et al. (2016), "Is flood defense changing in nature? Shifts in the flood defense strategy in six European countries", *Ecology and Society*, Vol. 21/4, http://dx.doi.org/10.5751/ES-08907-210437. [11]

Guerry, A. et al. (2012), "Modeling benefits from nature: Using ecosystem services to inform coastal and marine spatial planning", *International Journal of Biodiversity Science, Ecosystem Services & Management*, Vol. 8/1-2, pp. 107-121, http://dx.doi.org/10.1080/21513732.2011.647835. [25]

Hall, J. et al. (2012), "Proportionate adaptation", *Nature Climate Change*, Vol. 2, pp. 833-834, http://dx.doi.org/10.1038/nclimate1749. [57]

Hanger, S. et al. (2017), "Insurance, public assistance and household flood risk reduction: A comparative study of Austria, England and Romania", *Risk Analysis*, Vol. 38/4, pp. 680-693, http://dx.doi.org/10.1111/risa.12881. [59]

Harman, B. et al. (2015), "Global lessons for adapting coastal communities to protect against storm surge inundation", *Journal of Coastal Research*, Vol. 31/4, pp. 790-802, http://dx.doi.org/10.2112/JCOASTRES-D-13-00095.1. [15]

Harman, B. et al. (2013), "Global lessons for adapting coastal communities to protect against storm surge inundation", *Journal of Coastal Research*, Vol. 31/4, pp. 790-802, http://dx.doi.org/10.2112/JCOASTRES-D-13-00095.1. [10]

Hinkel, J. et al. (2015), "Sea-level rise scenarios and coastal risk management", *Nature Climate Change*, Vol. 5/3, pp. 188-190, http://dx.doi.org/10.1038/nclimate2505. [39]

Hino, M., C. Field and K. Mach (2017), "Managed retreat as a response to natural hazard risk", *Nature Climate Change*, Vol. 7, pp. 364-370, http://dx.doi.org/10.1038/NCLIMATE3252. [7]

Hudson, P. et al. (2016), "Incentivising flood risk adaptation through risk based insurance premiums: Trade-offs between affordability and risk reduction", *Ecological Economics*, Vol. 125, pp. 1-13, http://dx.doi.org/10.1016/J.ECOLECON.2016.01.015. [60]

Kates, R. et al. (2006), "Reconstruction of New Orleans after Hurricane Katrina: a research perspective.", *Proceedings of the National Academy of Sciences of the United States of America*, Vol. 103/40, pp. 14653-60, http://dx.doi.org/10.1073/pnas.0605726103. [48]

Keeler, A., D. McNamara and J. Irish (2018), "Responding to sea level rise: Does short-term risk reduction inhibit successful long-term adaptation?", *Earth's Future*, Vol. 6/4, pp. 618-621, http://dx.doi.org/10.1002/2018EF000828. [17]

Keenan, J., T. Hill and A. Gumber (2018), "Climate gentrification: From theory to empiricism in Miami-Dade County, Florida", *Environmental Research Letters*, Vol. 13/5, p. 054001, http://dx.doi.org/10.1088/1748-9326/aabb32. [75]

Koerth, J., A. Vafeidis and J. Hinkel (2017), "Household-level coastal adaptation and its drivers: A systematic case study review", *Risk Analysis*, Vol. 37/4, pp. 629-646, http://dx.doi.org/10.1111/risa.12663. [30]

Kousky, C. (2014), "Managing shoreline retreat: A US perspective", *Climatic Change*, Vol. 124/1-2, pp. 9-20, http://dx.doi.org/10.1007/s10584-014-1106-3. [38]

Krause, A. (2014), *What is Waterfront Worth?*, https://www.zillow.com/research/what-is-waterfront-worth-7540 (accessed on 22 June 2018). [72]

Kreibich, H. et al. (2015), "A review of damage-reducing measures to manage flood risks in a changing climate", *Mitigation and Adaptation Strategies for Global Change*, Vol. 20/6, pp. 967-989, http://dx.doi.org/10.1007/s11027-014-9629-5. [29]

Lemmen, D. et al. (2016), *Canada's Marine Coasts in a Changing Climate*, Government of Canada, Ottawa, http://www.nrcan.gc.ca/sites/www.nrcan.gc.ca/files/earthsciences/files/pdf/NRCAN_fullBook%20%20accessible.pdf (accessed on 23 July 2018). [71]

McNamara, D. et al. (2015), "Climate adaptation and policy-induced inflation of coastal property value", *PlOS ONE*, Vol. 10/3, p. e0121278, http://dx.doi.org/10.1371/journal.pone.0121278. [20]

Mehvar, S. et al. (2018), "Quantifying economic value of coastal ecosystem services: A review", *Journal of Marine Science and Engineering*, Vol. 6/1, p. 5, http://dx.doi.org/10.3390/jmse6010005. [24]

Narayan, S. et al. (2016), "The effectiveness, costs and coastal protection benefits of natural and nature-based defences", *PLOS ONE*, Vol. 11/5, p. e0154735, http://dx.doi.org/10.1371/journal.pone.0154735. [19]

National Research Council (2014), *Reducing Coastal Risk on the East and Gulf Coasts*, National Academies Press, Washington, DC, http://dx.doi.org/10.17226/18811. [67]

National Research Council (2014), *Reducing Coastal Risks on the East and Gulf Coasts*, National Academies Press, Washington, DC, http://dx.doi.org/10.17226/18811 (accessed on 9 January 2018). [51]

Nicholls, R. (2011), "Impacts of sea level rise", *Oceanography*, Vol. 24/2, pp. 144-157, http://dx.doi.org/10.5670/oceanog.2011.34. [31]

Niven, R. and D. Bardsley (2013), "Planned retreat as a management response to coastal risk: A case study from the Fleurieu Peninsula, South Australia", *Regional Environmental Change*, Vol. 13/1, pp. 193-209, http://dx.doi.org/10.1007/s10113-012-0315-4. [34]

OECD (2017), *Land-use Planning Systems in the OECD: Country Fact Sheets*, OECD Publishing, Paris, http://dx.doi.org/10.1787/9789264268579-en. [69]

OECD (2017), *OECD Reviews of Risk Management Policies. Boosting Disaster Prevention through Innovative Risk Governance: Insights from Austria, France and Switzerland*, OECD Publishing, Paris, https://www.oecd-ilibrary.org/docserver/9789264281370-en.pdf?expires=1531472451&id=id&accname=ocid84004878&checksum=FAA505A62C1A385C8165D30455FA2DF2 (accessed on 13 July 2018). [5]

OECD (2016), *Financial Management of Flood Risk*, OECD Publishing, Paris, https://doi.org/10.1787/9789264257689-en (accessed on 5 September 2017). [33]

OECD (2016), *Financial Management of Flood Risk*, OECD Publishing, Paris, http://dx.doi.org/10.1787/9789264257689-en. [66]

OECD (2014), *Boosting Resilience through Innovative Risk Governance*, OECD Reviews of Risk Management Policies, OECD Publishing, Paris, http://dx.doi.org/10.1787/9789264209114-en. [2]

OECD (2014), *Recommendation of the Council on the Governance of Critical Risks*, OECD, Paris, http://www.oecd.org/gov/risk/Critical-Risks-Recommendation.pdf (accessed on 13 July 2018). [4]

OECD (2014), *Water Governance in the Netherlands: Fit for the Future?*, OECD Studies on Water, OECD Publishing, Paris, http://dx.doi.org/10.1787/9789264102637-en. [6]

OECD (2013), *Water and Climate Change Adaptation: Policies to Navigate Uncharted Waters*, OECD Studies on Water, OECD Publishing, Paris, http://dx.doi.org/10.1787/9789264200449-en. [1]

OECD (2013), *Water Security for Better Lives*, OECD Studies on Water, OECD Publishing, Paris, http://dx.doi.org/10.1787/9789264202405-en. [3]

OECD/World Bank (forthcoming), *Boosting Financial Resilience to Disasters: Understanding and Strengthening the Role of Government*, OECD, Paris. [58]

PBO (2016), "Estimate of the average annual cost for disaster financial assistance arrangements due to weather events", http://www.pbo-dpb.gc.ca (accessed on 11 December 2017). [56]

Penning-Rowsell, E. and S. Priest (2015), "Sharing the burden of increasing flood risk: Who pays for flood insurance and flood risk management in the United Kingdom", *Mitigation and Adaptation Strategies for Global Change*, Vol. 20/6, pp. 991-1009, http://dx.doi.org/10.1007/s11027-014-9622-z. [53]

Penning-Rowsell, E. and S. Priest (2015), "Sharing the burden of increasing flood risk: Who pays for flood insurance and flood risk management in the United Kingdom", *Mitigation and Adaptation Strategies for Global Change*, Vol. 20/6, pp. 991-1009, http://dx.doi.org/10.1007/s11027-014-9622-z. [55]

Prati, G. et al. (2016), "Public perceptions of beach nourishment and conflict management strategies: A case study of Portonovo Bay in the Adriatic Italian coast", *Land Use Policy*, Vol. 50, pp. 422-428, http://dx.doi.org/10.1016/J.LANDUSEPOL.2015.06.033. [42]

Schut, M., C. Leeuwis and A. van Paassen (2010), "Room for the River: Room for research? The case of depoldering De Noordwaard, the Netherlands", *Science and Public Policy*, Vol. 37/8, pp. 611-627, http://dx.doi.org/10.3152/030234210X12767691861173. [37]

Spalding, M. et al. (2014), "Coastal ecosystems: A critical element of risk reduction", *Conservation Letters*, Vol. 7/3, pp. 293-301, http://dx.doi.org/10.1111/conl.12074. [23]

Spalding, M. et al. (2014), "The role of ecosystems in coastal protection: Adapting to climate change and coastal hazards", *Ocean & Coastal Management*, Vol. 90, pp. 50-57, http://dx.doi.org/10.1016/J.OCECOAMAN.2013.09.007. [14]

Surminski, S. (2013), "The role of insurance in reducing direct risk: The case of flood insurance", *International Review of Environmental and Resource Economics*, Vol. 7, pp. 241-278, http://eprints.lse.ac.uk/60764/1/Surminski_Role-of-insurance-reducing-direct-risk_2014.pdf (accessed on 19 October 2017). [64]

Surminski, S. and A. Thieken (2017), "Promoting flood risk reduction: The role of insurance in Germany and England", *Earth's Future*, Vol. 5/10, pp. 979-1001, http://dx.doi.org/10.1002/2017EF000587. [65]

Temmerman, S. et al. (2013), "Ecosystem-based coastal defence in the face of global change", *Nature*, Vol. 504/7478, pp. 79-83, http://dx.doi.org/10.1038/nature12859. [18]

Tol, R., R. Klein and R. Nicholls (2008), "Towards successful adaptation to sea-level rise along Europe's coasts", *Journal of Coastal Research*, Vol. 242, pp. 432-442, http://dx.doi.org/10.2112/07A-0016.1. [9]

Verchick, R. et al. (2013), "When retreat is the best option: Flood insurance after Biggert-Waters and other climate change puzzles", *The John Marshall Law Review Annual: Kratovil Symposium on Real Estate Law & Practice*, Vol. 47/8, http://repository.jmls.edu/lawreview (accessed on 6 December 2017). [35]

Verschuuren, J. and J. Mcdonald (2012), "Towards a legal framework for coastal adaptation: Assessing the first steps in Europe and Australia", *Transnational Environmental Law*, Vol. 1/2, pp. 355-379, https://doi.org/10.1017/S204710251200009X (accessed on 9 August 2017). [68]

Walker, G. and K. Burningham (2011), "Flood risk, vulnerability and environmental justice: Evidence and evaluation of inequality in a UK context", *Critical Social Policy*, Vol. 31/2, pp. 216-240, http://dx.doi.org/10.1177/0261018310396149. [61]

Warren-Myers, G. et al. (2018), "Estimating the potential risks of sea level rise for public and private property ownership, occupation and management", *Risks*, Vol. 6/2, p. 37, http://dx.doi.org/10.3390/risks6020037. [77]

Watkiss, P. (ed.) (2011), *The impacts and economic costs of sea-Level rise in Europe and the costs and benefits of adaptation: Summary of results from the EC RTD ClimateCost Project*, Stockholm Environment Institute, https://www.sei-international.org/mediamanager/documents/Publications/sei-climatecost-sea-level-rise.pdf (accessed on 11 October 2017). [46]

Wilby, R. and R. Keenan (2012), "Adapting to flood risk under climate change", *Progress in Physical Geography: Earth and Environment*, Vol. 36/3, pp. 348-378, http://dx.doi.org/10.1177/0309133312438908. [13]

Wolfrom, L. and M. Yokoi-Arai (2015), "Financial instruments for managing disaster risks related to climate change", *OECD Journal: Financial Market Trends*, Vol. 2015/1, https://doi.org/10.1787/fmt-2015-5jrqdkpxk5d5 (accessed on 15 November 2017). [63]

Wong, P. et al. (2014), *Coastal Systems and Low-Lying Areas*, IPCC, https://www.ipcc.ch/pdf/assessment-report/ar5/wg2/WGIIAR5-Chap5_FINAL.pdf (accessed on 17 August 2017). [8]

Chapter 3. Emerging approaches to coastal adaptation

This chapter examines what national governments can do to ensure all relevant stakeholders have the right incentives and tools to adapt to rising coastal risks. It analyses current practices with regard to adaptation to sea-level rise in OECD countries by reviewing national adaptation plans. Finally, it examines what institutional features need to be in place for an efficient, effective and equitable response to coastal risks, drawing on the review of existing practices and the country case study chapters of this report.

This chapter was written by Lisa Danielson and Aurélien Seawert, OECD, and Alexander Bisaro, Global Climate Forum.

3.1. The role of national governments in coastal adaptation

National governments have a crucial role to play in supporting coastal adaptation by ensuring the relevant actors have the correct incentives and tools to adapt, as well as removing potential distortions. Governments should take a proactive approach to create an enabling environment to improve the co-ordination, efficiency and effectiveness of actions implemented at lower levels. Key areas for achieving this include providing access to information, tools and guidance; ensuring that regulations and economic instruments are coherent and avoid perverse incentives; considering climate risks when taking funding decisions; and finally monitoring and evaluating effectiveness of all policy interventions and adjusting accordingly.

The following sections outline the approaches (Table 3.1) being used by national governments to address sea-level rise (SLR)[1]. This overview of national approaches to SLR brings together a content analysis of national adaptation plans, supplemented with other salient literature on SLR adaptation. National adaptation plans have been used because they are available for most OECD countries and the structure of these documents tends to be consistent across countries. A caveat when using this approach is that these documents are not exhaustive and some relevant initiatives may not be included. Nonetheless, they provide a useful overview of relevant activities underway.

The approaches and tools discussed within this section refer to national governments, but many could also be used by local government and communities to adapt to SLR.

Table 3.1. Approach to sea-level rise management mentioned in adaptation plans

Policy lever	Information provision	Regulatory/economic instruments	Dedicated national funding	Monitoring and evaluation
Description	e.g. climate modelling, impact, vulnerability, and/or risk assessments, guidance and tools for other levels of government, business and citizens	e.g. land-use planning, building regulations, coastal protection infrastructure standards, economic incentives for risk reduction	e.g. funding of investment in risk reduction; funding for household-level protection measures	e.g. stakeholder surveys, quantitative and qualitative indicators measuring climate effects, policy process and policy outcome
Australia	●	-	-	●
Belgium	●	-	-	●
Canada	●	●	●	●
Chile	●	-	-	●
Denmark	●	●	-	-
Estonia	●	●	-	●
Finland	●	●	-	●
France	●	●	●	●
Germany	●	●	●	●
Greece	●	-	-	-
Iceland*	-	-	-	-
Ireland	●	●	-	●
Israel	●	-	-	-
Italy	●	-	-	-
Japan	●	●	-	●
Korea	●	●	-	●
Latvia	●	-	-	-
Mexico	●	●	-	●
Netherlands	●	●	●	●
New Zealand**	●	-	-	-
Norway	●	-	-	●
Poland	●	●	-	●
Portugal	●	-	-	●
Slovenia	-	-	-	●
Spain	●	●	-	●
Sweden	●	●	●	●
Turkey	●	-	-	-
United Kingdom	●	●	●	●
United States*	●	-	-	-

Notes:
● Policy instrument referred to in adaptation plans.
- Not available.
* No adaptation plan in place.
** Adaptation plan in development.
Source: For a full list of adaptation plans, please refer to Annex A.

3.2. Information provision

Access to credible and transparent climate projection and risk information is essential for coastal adaptation. Decisions about location, timing and design of coastal adaptation response require trustworthy information about coastal hazards, exposure and vulnerabilities. In addition, scientific information needs to be clearly communicated and understood by affected stakeholders to build a common vision and strategy for greater resilience. Given that better information will become available and new risks will become apparent over time, the analysis of climate risks needs to be an iterative process that monitors the evolution of risks and communicates these to the decision makers and stakeholders who most need this information. The role of national governments is two-fold: the provision of underlying scientific information on sea-level observations, modelling and analysis, and vulnerabilities, as well as information and tools on prevention and responses to coastal impacts (Le Cozannet et al., 2017[1]).

3.2.1. Climate projections and risk information

The International Panel on Climate Change (IPCC) provides authoritative information about future global sea levels, as it gathers evidence from a range of global climate models (Hinkel et al., 2015[2]). The IPCC updated its scenarios of global mean sea-level rise with the release of its Fifth Assessment Report (AR5) in 2013. Most OECD countries have either produced their own national-level sea-level projections or have statistically downscaled projections from IPCC modelling to understand how sea-level rise will affect them (Vallejo and Mullan, 2017[3]). Even with the best possible information, sea-level rise is among the most uncertain of climate change impacts, both in terms of the timing and magnitude of hazards at the regional level (discussed in more depth in Chapter 1). Given these uncertainties, robust adaptation requires sophisticated decision-making processes that proactively plan for different scenarios of sea-level rise impacts (see Box 3.3 for more detail and an example).

Combining sea-level projections with existing coastal flood and erosion hazard assessments, such as flood risk maps, is an emerging practice in OECD countries; however, this is not yet widely established. A 2016 OECD survey found that all surveyed countries[2] had flood maps in place; however, these existing flood maps do not always incorporate future climate change risk (OECD, 2016[4]). For example, in the United States, modelling work incorporating spatially comprehensive flood hazard information finds that national flood maps may underestimate flood exposure by a factor of three[3] (Wing et al., 2018[5]). Some countries are investing in maps that incorporate future SLR hazards. For example, under the Irish Coastal Protection Strategy Study, the Office of Public Works has prepared strategic coastal flood hazard maps for the national coastline representing two future scenarios (mid-range and high-end) up to the year 2100, which take into account both future sea-level rise and glacial isostatic adjustment.

Very few adaptation plans quantify exposure and vulnerability to SLR, with many references to levels of uncertainty surrounding predictions. Although flood and erosion hazard assessments are necessary for effective coastal risk management, they are not sufficient for assessing investment in coastal risk reduction. Information on the exposure and vulnerabilities of communities, including the socio-economic-ecological context, is also needed. This information is essential for informed policy decisions as well as the prioritisation of different actions (OECD, 2017[6]).

Some national governments have assessed nationwide SLR vulnerability. The UK plan specifically details that "about 270 residential and 470 non-residential properties may be lost to coastal erosion by 2030" (DEFRA, 2013[7]). The Australian plan estimates that under a high-end scenario, the equivalent of AUD 226 billion worth of industrial, public and residential properties could be exposed to flood and erosion hazard by 2100 (Department of Climate Change and Energy Efficiency, 2011[8]). France specifies that a one-metre sea-level rise would directly affect the equivalent of around EUR 2 billion worth of national main roads by 2100 (French Government, 2017[9]). In New Zealand, the Parliamentary Commissioner for the Environment commissioned a study of exposed residents and buildings to SLR. The study estimated that SLR of up to 3 metres would affect over 280 000 people and damage buildings with a replacement cost exceeding NZD 50 billion (Bell, Paulik and Wadwha, 2015[10]). In Canada, the qualitative assessment "Canada's marine coasts in a changing climate" assesses climate change sensitivity, risks and adaptation along Canada's coasts.

3.2.2. Communicating climate risk information

Stakeholders' use of climate risk information in decision making depends on the effective communication of sea-level projections combined with the associated risk assessments that incorporates exposure and vulnerability data. In recent years, the production of such climate risk information has improved significantly; however, the use of information by decision makers and policy implementers (e.g. local governments, property developers and households) is largely dependent on the way that this is presented. The challenge is to present climate risk information in a way that is relevant, credible, accessible and easy to understand, with the aim of it being well received by users (EEA, 2015[11]).

Local governments are challenged when faced with multiple conflicting sources of climate information; it is therefore considered a best practice to have a central, authoritative source of information with which to work. One of the main obstacles to effective coastal adaptation is asymmetric access to information on current and future risks. Some of the most detailed and accurate risk information is held by insurance companies, scientific organisations and modelling groups, but is often not sufficiently diffused to cities, businesses, individuals and community groups (Climate-KIC, 2017[12]).

Many OECD countries have created specific organisations or platforms to act as knowledge brokers on adaptation. For example, in Korea, the Adaptation Centre for Climate Change supports central and local governments to develop adaptation measures to climate change and provide guidelines for policy issues associated with climate change adaptation, having assisted Seoul and Incheon in creating adaptation plans that focus on SLR in particular. The government of Canada is in the process of establishing a Canadian Centre for Climate Services which will deliver climate information, data and tools through an online climate information portal. In the United States, the National Oceanic and Atmospheric Administration's SLR viewer web-mapping tool is designed to support community decision making around infrastructure plans and consider performance and reliability for local relative SLR up to the year 2100 (Le Cozannet et al., 2017[1]). The Irish Climate Information Platform (Climate Ireland) includes a section on coastal flooding and managing SLR impacts. The French adaptation platform (Wiklimat), makes explicit links with the national strategy for integrated coastal management as well as with disaster risk-reduction information from the Observatoire National des Risques Naturels. The European Commission has also developed a web-based platform, Climate-ADAPT, that has a specific coastal focus.

Box 3.1. The cognitive barriers to risk perception and the importance for risk communication

One major barrier to coastal adaptation is low risk perception at the individual level, which has cascading effects. If individuals are not aware of risk, they will continue to take risky decisions, such as purchasing property in high-risk areas or not investing in disaster preparedness. In addition, local concerns usually drive local government action. If coastal adaptation is not perceived as a priority, it is unlikely that individual local governments will make significant shifts towards disruptive or unpopular adaptation strategies. Without a good understanding of sea-level rise (SLR) risks, it is also likely that individuals will oppose adaptation strategies that conflict with their private interests. A large body of social science research concludes that individuals can be poor evaluators of risks. Reasons include:

- Individuals often use heuristics, or rules of thumb, to take decisions about risk. For example, individuals may overreact to recent events, be overly optimistic or pare down future probabilities.
- When individuals receive information that is not in line with their underlying values, they generally have trouble updating their beliefs.
- Individuals' trust and ownership of new information is strongly correlated with their evaluation of whether the person communicating that information is trustworthy and knowledgeable.

Given these factors, it can be challenging to communicate SLR risks in a way that effectively convinces individuals to integrate these risks in private decisions and adopt risk-reduction behaviour. SLR risk communication efforts should take into account how people process risk information. For example, individuals may be more likely to accept SLR information when it is presented by someone whose values they share, and when it fits into their existing narratives.

Sources: Colgan, C.S. (2016[13]), "The economics of adaptation to climate change in coasts and oceans: Literature review, policy implications and research agenda", http://dx.doi.org/10.15351/2373-8456.1067; Costas, S., O. Ferreira and G. Martinez (2015[14]), "Why do we decide to live with risk at the coast?", http://dx.doi.org/10.1016/J.OCECOAMAN.2015.05.015; Kousky, C. (2014[15]), "Managing shoreline retreat: A US perspective", http://dx.doi.org/10.1007/s10584-014-1106-3.

A number of countries are providing adaptation guidance to local governments, businesses and the public, which is especially a focus for countries with a decentralised approach to adaptation. For example, Australia has a web-portal "CoastAdapt", which provides tools such as inundation mapping software, local coastline morphological information, coastal climate adaptation decision-making guidance, as well as local and international case studies. The government of New Zealand provides non-statutory guidance to local governments on how to adapt to coastal hazards and climate change. The guidance includes information on adaptive planning, community engagement and how to implement a risk-based approach (Ministry for the Environment, 2017[16]). It is essential that these approaches meet the needs of end users as their actions move through the coastal adaptation policy cycle, from information provision, vulnerability and risk assessments to appraising and selecting adaptation options, and on to monitoring and evaluation actions. In Estonia, guidance material for general planning has a section dedicated to taking climate change into account.

Box 3.2. Early warning systems for risk communication

Early warning systems are an essential component of a policy response to mitigate the loss of life and property from coastal flooding. By providing timely information about hazards (water levels, wave heights) combined with knowledge about the coastal environment and topography, it is possible to facilitate the necessary evacuation of people and the implementation of any emergency flood defences. These systems are vital for risk communication not only before, but also during, an emergency.

Developments in climate modelling have resulted in more sophisticated coastal storm projections, which can accurately predict storm duration and intensity for up to around three days in advance. Nevertheless, the remaining considerable degree of uncertainty surrounding sea-level rise and storm surge trends emphasises the critical need to develop new coastal information systems.

The Estonian adaptation plan includes the objective of improving the country's early warning and public information systems to better communicate information to vulnerable coastal residents. The aim is to increase residents' hazard awareness, their ability to cope during emergencies and to teach them how to help others. Mexico has also set the objective of strengthening risk management through better communication and early warning systems, combined with local evacuation plans to respond to extreme coastal events. The Japan Meteorological Agency has also updated and improved its criteria for storm-surge warnings, especially to homologise the communication of when evacuation is advisory or mandatory.

Source: Adapted from national adaptation plans.

3.3. Incorporating sea-level rise into regulatory and economic instruments

Tackling persistent barriers to coastal adaptation may require reforms of regulation and economic instruments to help achieve a desired and effective outcome (see Chapter 2). Experience from climate change mitigation and disaster risk reduction demonstrates that information campaigns to mobilise action and the provision of information and tools to support risk management can have limited effectiveness on their own. It is essential that the relevant actors also have sufficient incentive to engage in risk reduction.

3.3.1. Mainstreaming sea-level rise risks in land-use decisions

Limiting development in at-risk areas is the first line of defence against coastal hazards, therefore spatial planning policies are key in ensuring climate resilience in coastal areas. Land-use planning can reduce the exposure of new assets to climate hazards, as well as reduce the impact of hazards by dedicating land to natural buffers, such as wetlands and dunes. However, only a few national adaptation plans have aimed to mainstream SLR in existing land-use planning. Generally, land-use planning frameworks are based on historical information or do not integrate future hazard information (OECD, 2017[6]).

Some countries have committed to reviewing existing land-use legislation, regulations and standards, whereas others have already updated standards in order to explicitly address SLR impacts. For example, the Netherlands' National Spatial Plan is a regulatory instrument used to avoid unwanted land-use developments from taking place. It prevents new building activities in specific areas along the coast and identifies emergency water storage areas to be preserved from development along the coastline (Verschuuren and Mcdonald, 2012[17]). Other examples include the *Plan de Prévention des Risques* in France and planning policy statements in England, which both account for SLR margins, as well as Ireland's recently published National Planning Framework, which contains specific policy objectives linked to adapting to SLR.

As described in Chapter 2, the national level tends to set land-use planning frameworks, but local authorities have a critical role in implementing them, and sometimes issue their own regulatory requirements. Consequently, many national governments have binding or non-binding advice for local governments on incorporating SLR into existing regulations. For example, Denmark passed a law allowing municipalities to consider climate change directly in local land-use planning decisions, enabling municipalities to ban construction in certain areas solely due to reasons relating to adaptation (OECD, 2013[18]). In France, local authorities are obliged to take hazard maps into consideration in land-use planning decisions, and mayors can and have been made liable for ignoring hazard zones (OECD, 2017[6]). A draft law is also being considered in France on coastline retreat, which would limit development within 100 metres of the coast and facilitate the planned retreat of people and assets (French Senate, 2018[19]).

Box 3.3. Factoring uncertainty into planning and regulation

A dynamic, forward-looking approach to planning and regulation that explicitly deals with uncertainty is needed to address the changing pace and magnitude of climate impacts. This is especially the case for sea-level rise, where local-level variations reinforce the need to incorporate uncertainty into site-specific adaptation decisions.

The Belgian Sigma Plan was designed in 1977 to protect the coastline of the Scheldt and its tributaries from storm-surge floods. An update was implemented in 2005, as the original plan was insufficient to provide protection for current and likely future sea-level conditions. The revised programme increased the baselines of its protection measures and established controlled flooding areas to allow overflow water to flood during storm surges if needed. A number of potential additional measures have been designed for after 2050 in case they are needed to address sea-level rise that is higher than anticipated.

The Delta Programme in the Netherlands is using "adaptive delta management" to develop flexible strategies that link short-term decisions with long-term needs. This approach identifies multiple potential strategies ("adaptation pathways") that can be alternated between and the first steps make sense under every scenario ("no regret" measures). The circumstances under which it would be logical to move from one approach to another depending on actual sea-level rise developments are studied, along with how options can be kept open to actually enable that transition. The approach has already been applied in several Delta sub-programmes, such as in the Rhine Estuary-Drechtsteden.

Source: Climate-ADAPT (2014[20]), "An integrated plan incorporating flood protection: The Sigma Plan (Scheldt Estuary, Belgium)", https://climate-adapt.eea.europa.eu/metadata/case-studies/an-integrated-plan-incorporating-flood-protection-the-sigma-plan-scheldt-estuary-belgium; OECD (2014[21]), *Water Governance in the Netherlands: Fit for the Future?*, http://dx.doi.org/10.1787/9789264102637-en.

Some countries are promoting the use of ecosystem-based adaptation[4] in their land-use planning; however, few formal mechanisms for this integration exist. Belgium's and the Netherlands' plans both intend to increase the use of natural coastal defences. Mexico's adaptation plan has a prominent focus on ecosystem-based adaptation, and one of the plan's goals is to incorporate ecosystem considerations into land-use planning to increase the country's climate resilience. Many regions and cities in the United States are also focusing on nature-based solutions. For example, around 8 000 hectares of tidal marshes are being restored for coastal protection in the San Francisco Bay (Lubell, 2017[22]). Other US regions, including the state of Florida and other communities along the East Coast, have allocated permits to create "living shorelines". These projects aim to restore natural coastal processes, which can reduce the adverse effects of erosion and storm surge. One regulatory mechanism to enhance this integration is "living shoreline permits". The US Army Corps of Engineers recently streamlined the permitting process for living shorelines in an effort to incentivise these measures and correct the comparative advantage held by hard infrastructure projects in terms of shorter time frames to receive permits.

3.3.2. Integrating sea-level rise margins into infrastructure standards and building codes

An adaptation measure that is being used more widely is applying a climate change safety margin during the design process for hard infrastructure measures, such as dikes, levees and seawalls (Wilby and Keenan, 2012[23]). Coastal defence infrastructure is designed to achieve a level of service (such as protecting a community from a 100-year flood), and in general, this level of service is determined using historical climate information, which does not incorporate changing conditions. Several countries have updated design standards, such as Denmark, Germany, the Netherlands and the United Kingdom. In Germany, dike crests have been widened in order to address uncertainty in future SLR (see Chapter 4). Depending on existing institutional arrangements, these changes differ in their legal status across countries. In some cases they are set out in regulation, whereas in others they take the form of guidance documents. For example, the UK allowances for climate safety margins for sea-level rise are contained in planning regulation and guidance for engineers, while the Canadian Standards Association offers general advice (Wilby and Keenan, 2012[24]).

SLR considerations have been incorporated into building and infrastructure standards beyond coastal protection. For example, in Australia, some regional governments have released technical guidance to ensure infrastructure design is resilient to climate change, with a focus on SLR. The Western Australia government's Standards and Technical Guide on Addressing Climate Change in Road and Traffic Engineering, for example, is helping planners, designers and managers identify climate change risks relevant to the construction of roads and bridges. The state road operator (WA Main Roads) requires that the implications of a 300 mm sea-level rise (450 mm for structures) be considered as part of planning, design and construction for all rehabilitation and expansion projects near coastal areas (Vallejo and Mullan, 2017[3]). Examples of changes in building codes, generally done at the regional or local level, can be found in Box 2.3. When enshrining SLR considerations in infrastructure-related regulation, policy makers should strive to strike a balance between creating consistent, straightforward standards, while taking into account the uncertain and context-specific nature of climate risks (Vallejo and Mullan, 2017[3]).

3.3.3. Integrated coastal zone management

Many countries mainstream SLR considerations into their integrated coastal zone management (ICZM) frameworks, an acknowledged process to deal with current and long-term coastal challenges. ICZM is a long-term, iterative and evolutionary framework that integrates a range of activities and stakeholders across different coastal sectors in order to encourage sustainable development (Wong et al., 2014[25]). The issues found within SLR and coastal adaptation are reasonably similar to those faced within ICZM, which can offer an enabling environment for adaptation measures.

The mainstreaming of SLR into ICZM is particularly common for countries with coastlines on the Mediterranean Sea. The Barcelona Convention, ratified by the EU in 2011, defines a common legal binding framework for ICZM in the Mediterranean. The ICZM Mediterranean Awareness-Raising Strategy considers climate resilience to be one of the key issues for coastal development (Albini et al., 2017[26]). In Spain, local coastal management plans mainstream future SLR projections into ICZM frameworks in order to regulate development along the coastline. Portugal's coastal zone management plans for islands of the Azores archipelago encourages public participation to develop measures that are legally binding and set the potential for land use. They incorporate future climate projections to prevent and manage hazards and to balance economic, social and cultural development while preserving the coastal environment (Albini et al., 2017[26]). Israel's 2004 Protection of the Coastal Environment Law establishes principles and limitations for the sustainable management, development and use of the coastal environment. SLR is mainstreamed into this legislation as the shoreline is officially set at a level that reflects projections to 2100.

There is limited evidence and agreement on the conditions for effective mainstreaming of SLR into ICZM, despite its relatively widespread application. A local-level study at Cork Harbour, the second largest port in Ireland, found that SLR mainstreaming within an ICZM approach led to a faster and more efficient implementation of adaptation measures, as the preparatory steps had already been initiated by the ICZM activities (O'Mahony et al., 2015[27]). A review of this mainstreaming approach in Europe found that the complexity of coastal regulations, as well as an absence of commonly agreed objectives and time frames hinder its implementation and effectiveness (EEA, 2013[28]).

3.3.4. Economic instruments

Economic instruments, such as risk-based flood insurance and property risk disclosure (see Box 3.6), can be well-suited to reducing coastal risks; however, there are few examples where they are effectively used in practice. Using economic instruments to respond to rising coastal risks can yield the following benefits:

- Lower public costs: economic instruments can lower public expenditure as responsibility for risks, and consequently for potential costs, is transferred to the direct beneficiaries of the risk-reduction measures. In addition, part of the decision process of coastal adaptation is transferred to individuals, which then reduces administration costs (Filatova, 2014[29]).
- Flexible and efficient use of space: economic instruments should only remove developments where individual costs do not exceed personal benefits, e.g. those that are economically inefficient (Filatova, 2014[29]).
- Stakeholder involvement: the communication of risks through economic signals, such as the cost of insurance premiums, ensures individuals are aware of their level of risk and builds towards a "whole-of-society" approach to risk reduction (OECD, 2015[30]).

Flood insurance is probably the most studied economic instrument in relation to flood risk (which encompasses coastal flood risk) management. Many countries have acknowledged that the insurance industry has an important role to play in influencing future behaviour in relation to known risks. In theory, the establishment of risk-based insurance premiums can incentivise households to reduce their own risks so that they can access cheaper insurance (Surminski and Thieken, 2017[31]). In practice, there is mixed and limited evidence on the success of insurance in encouraging this behaviour. For example, in Germany and England, areas with high flood insurance penetration rates tend to have lower uptake of household-level protection measures (Surminski and Thieken, 2017[31]). A number of obstacles prevent insurance from acting as an effective economic instrument to reduce coastal flood risk, such as the lack of adequate risk-based pricing, misalignments between the needed prevention investments by policyholders and the premium savings, the short-term nature of insurance contracts, as well as a general uncertainty surrounding the advantages of risk-reduction measures (Crick, Jenkins and Surminski, 2018[32]).

Box 3.4. Government investments in risk reduction to support the insurability of flood risk

Governments have a vital role in supporting the insurability of flood risk through investments in risk reduction at the community and household level. Some OECD countries consider the availability and/or affordability of flood insurance coverage when deciding where to target investments in risk reduction (OECD, 2016[4]). Properties in high-risk areas, commonly developed before the true level of flood risk was established, should be a specific focus for risk reduction given the difficulty of providing a viable insurance offering to households in those areas.

Japan's and Poland's national adaptation plans focus on improving general risk-reduction policies to maintain the viability of insurance coverage. Poland's adaptation plan includes reference to possibly supporting property insurance from public funds and encouraging actions that minimise the consequences of extreme events, including those in the coastal zone (MoE, 2013[33]). Japan's plan also examines the insurability of risks, and commits to upgrading risk management for natural disasters to ensure insurability continues (Japanese Government, 2015[34]).

Few countries have revised financial protection mechanisms as part of their adaptation planning. Two exceptions are Finland and the United Kingdom, where climate change has been one of the factors leading to a change in insurance provision. In Finland, the public insurance scheme has been shifted to a private one in response to rising public costs from flooding. At the beginning of 2014, the state compensation system for flood damages in Finland came to an end and coverage of damages was shifted to private insurance companies (BASE, 2014[35]). In the United Kingdom, a public reinsurance scheme was created with the goal of increasing availability and affordability of private insurance for high-risk properties that were otherwise no longer insurable due to mounting risks. The scheme, called Flood Re, formally cross-subsidises high and low flood-risk households in order to cap flood risk premiums in very high-risk areas (about 2% of households) (Lamond and Penning-Rowsell, 2014[36]). The scheme is reviewed at least every five years and is planned to be in place until 2039, at which point home insurance prices should fully reflect flood risk (elaborated in Box 3.5).

Box 3.5. Transition effects of Flood Re in the United Kingdom

Flood Re was created in 2016 in order to support the private insurance industry and encourage the affordability of flood insurance for policyholders. The scheme works by providing insurance companies with the possibility of reinsuring policies at a highly discounted price. A levy for the subsidised reinsurance is collected from insurers, who can pass on the levy to policyholders. As insurers can pass on their risk for a reduced price, they can charge lower premiums to high-risk policyholders. All homes are eligible for Flood Re, regardless of their flood risk; however, the price of accessing Flood Re reinsurance was set with the aim of making sure that the coverage is only sought for high-risk properties.

In the long term, the main aim of Flood Re is to encourage a transition to a free market that uses risk-reflective pricing. However, to achieve this, a combination of amending premium thresholds and reducing flood risk will be necessary to keep flood insurance affordable. Yet, there are already concerns that the design of the new pool does not sufficiently consider rising flood risks due to climate change nor incentivise flood risk reduction or the improvement of the flood resilience of properties. Indeed, the UK Committee on Climate Change finds that in its current design, Flood Re is likely to be counter-productive to the long-term management of flood risk as it does not provide enough incentives for high-risk households to put measures in place to avoid or reduce flood damage.

The UK government has accepted that risk-reduction efforts are essential for the future affordability of flood insurance, and has pledged to collaborate more closely with other stakeholders. Yet despite the release of a second adaptation plan in 2018, criticisms of the management of Flood Re continue, in particular that not enough action has been taken to manage the transition period ahead of the programme's withdrawal.

Source: Brown, K. (2018[37]), *The New National Adaptation Programme: Hit or Miss?*, https://www.theccc.org.uk/2018/07/19/the-new-national-adaptation-programme-hit-or-miss; Crick, F., K. Jenkins and S. Surminski (2018[32]) "Strengthening insurance partnerships in the face of climate change: Insights from an agent-based model of flood insurance in the UK", http://dx.Doi.org/10.1016/J.SCITOTENV.2018.04.239.

Attempts to change insurance provision have not always proved sustainable. Participation in the US National Flood Insurance Program (NFIP), which helps households to protect themselves financially against inland and coastal flooding, is obligatory for properties with mortgages from federally regulated or insured lenders located in high flood-risk areas (defined as a 1% annual chance of flooding during a 30-year mortgage). Nevertheless, misalignments between NFIP premiums and real flood risks, an inability to reject high-risk applicants, and a significant programme deficit led to the passing of the Biggert-Waters Flood Insurance Reform Act (BW-12), designed to target the fiscal soundness of the programme. The resulting annual premium rate increases of up to 20% for policyholders led to the reform being substantially repealed two years later following sustained political opposition and lobbying on the part of homeowners. Suggestions for further reforms to the programme in the future have focused on phasing in risk-based insurance premiums and ensuring adequate coverage that fully reflects flood risk exposure.

National-level grants or incentives for household-level coastal protection measures remain uncommon. One exception is the United Kingdom, which provided GBP 5.2 million in funding between 2009 and 2011 to support a "property-level protection" pilot scheme, which led to the installation of measures such as flood barriers, non-return valves and airbrick covers in 1 109 properties (Defra, 2014[38]; Surminski and Eldridge, 2017[39]). In the United States, the Federal Emergency Management Agency has three flood risk-mitigation programmes: Pre-Disaster Mitigation, the Hazard Mitigation Grant Program and Flood Mitigation Assistance. Flood Mitigation Assistance includes flood-related grants, which provide grants to local, state and tribal governments and others at the community level to protect individual properties (National Research Council, 2014[40]).

Other than flood insurance and grants for household measures, economic instruments are not mentioned in OECD country adaptation plans as a tool to manage rising coastal risks. Property risk disclosure (described in Box 3.6) shows promise, but there is currently limited evaluation of its scalability, effectiveness or limitations.

Box 3.6. Property risk disclosure

Property risk disclosure is the release of information about a property that is vital to a potential buyer's decision. It offers a potential tool by which buyers can become informed about both a home's history of damage and its exposure to future coastal flood and erosion risk. Sea-level rise (SLR) property risk disclosure can be either voluntary or mandatory. Mandatory disclosure has the benefit of higher compliance rates among sellers and levelling the field; however, it remains uncommon. Only a select few subnational jurisdictions apply mandatory property risk disclosure for coastal risks, particularly certain Australian and US states:

- **California, United States**: since 1998, sellers have been required to complete statements informing buyers if the property is located in a "special flood hazard area". An updated 2017 law obliges sellers to provide greater information to tenants on where they may obtain guidance on coastal flood hazards.
- **Florida, United States**: since 2006, sellers of coastal property seaward of the Coastal Construction Control Line have been required to inform potential buyers that their property "may be subject to coastal erosion and to federal, state or local regulations that govern coastal property".
- **Victoria, Australia**: property sellers must notify buyers on whether the municipality has classified the area at risk of flooding and whether further redevelopment has been prohibited.

The question of whether disclosure of previous coastal flood damage or current SLR risk negatively affects property values has received political attention. For example, the Australian state governments of Queensland and New South Wales rejected proposed mandatory disclosure processes for projected climate risks, including SLR risk, when purchasing a property, citing problems for developers and landowners in obtaining insurance and selling land.

Sources: England, P. (2013[41]), "Too much too soon? On the rise and fall of Australia's coastal climate change law", http://hdl.handle.net/10072/57341http://www.thomsonreuters.com.au/environmental-and-planning-law-journal-online/productdetail/97170; Henstra, D. and J. Thistlethwaite (2018[42]), "Buyer beware: Evaluating property disclosure as a tool to support flood risk management", https://www.cigionline.org/publications/buyer-beware-evaluating-property-disclosure-tool-support-flood-risk-management.

3.4. Dedicated national funding

National-level funding can remove economic barriers that may obstruct efficient adaptation by providing a predictable and sustainable channel for finance, facilitating alignment between adaptation activities and country priorities, and ensuring that financial constraints are not limiting local implementation. National government investments in coastal adaptation additionally have a clear role in promoting joint adaptation, where benefits accrue to various actors, who may be under-provisioned due to the public good attributes of adaptation (OECD, 2013[18]). Securing funding for adaptation is especially important in view of the long-term, complex and uncertain nature of climate change. National-level funding can help to overcome institutional inertia and change long-established approaches to policy development (OECD, 2015[30]).

Very few national adaptation plans have explicit references to dedicated funding for coastal adaptation measures. One exception to this is the Pan-Canadian Climate Change Framework, which includes a commitment to partner with lower levels of governments to invest in traditional and natural infrastructure that reduces risks from climate-related hazards such as coastal flooding (Government of Canada, 2016[43]). Other exceptions are Germany and the United Kingdom, which both include specific funding commitments from the national government. The United Kingdom has established a GBP 2.6 billion six-year capital investment programme (2015-21) to reduce flood and coastal risk, which the 2nd National Adaptation Programme estimates will provide over GBP 30 billion in overall economic benefits (e.g. reduced damages) and benefit 300 000 households by 2021 (Defra, 2018[44]). The UK funding system has also recently been reformed to promote cost-sharing between levels of government (see Box 2.4). In Germany, a special instrument (*Sonderrahmenplan*) to speed up implementation of coastal protection due to climate change risks was established in 2009, which provides an additional combined EUR 25 million for all coastal federal states annually until 2025 (EUR 550 million total) (see Chapter 4). In France, the national government provided EUR 500 million to fund flood prevention measures, particularly in coastal areas, through the National Flood Plan (*plan submersions rapides*) (French Government, 2017[45]).

Other countries have chosen to mainstream coastal adaptation measures into existing financial arrangements or within a broader adaptation strategy. In the Netherlands, coastal adaptation is mainstreamed due to the high priority and cross-sectoral nature of flood risk prevention and water management within the country, with financing for coastal resilience measures falling under the financial responsibility of the Delta Fund (OECD, 2013[18]). Another example is Sweden, where the national government has dedicated funding for local authorities to undertake precautionary measures in built areas with high risk of natural catastrophes.

Box 3.7. Mobilising private investment for coastal adaptation

Public actors are currently the principal funders of coastal adaptation, and the current and future climate challenges related to sea-level rise (SLR) will place increasing pressure on these resources. As such, there is increasing interest in mobilising private investment towards coastal adaptation.

Challenges such as the distribution of liabilities between public and private actors can act as barriers to private investment for coastal projects. Liability risks to private investors related to large-scale coastal adaptation investments can pose significant barriers given the uncertainties associated with climate change and SLR. For example, private actors may be deterred from investing if SLR could lead to extensive property or infrastructure damage for which they would be liable. Conversely, if governments act as insurers of last resort in order to limit the liability of private investors, this could discourage private actors from making the levels of investment required.

Public-private partnerships can align public and private interests by providing incentives to private investors for learning through long-term contracts, while allowing public actors some control over outcomes. Public-private partnerships therefore offer the potential to mobilise private investment in coastal adaptation, especially when operational costs are a large proportion of the overall project costs.

Sources: Bisaro, A. and J. Hinkel (2018[46]), "Mobilizing private finance for coastal adaptation: A literature review", http://dx.doi.org/10.1002/wcc.514; OECD (2016[47]), *Financial Management of Flood Risk*, http://dx.doi.org/10.1787/9789264257689-en; World Bank (2015[48]), *Green Bonds Attract Private Sector Climate Finance*.

A potential misalignment in national funding can occur if funding targets one type of adaptation measure, as this can influence and unnecessarily circumscribe the range of policy options available for local authorities. For instance, if national funding is predominantly directed towards hard defences, local governments may feel inclined to opt for seawalls as opposed to beach nourishment measures, even if this does not represent the best or only option for the coastal community. In Germany, federal and state funding predominantly goes towards the establishment and maintenance of dikes, which can "crowd out" other policy options (Hooijer et al., 2004[49]). In the United States, federal financing for prevention measures through programmes such as coastal resilience grants is directed towards hard infrastructure, meaning that nature-based solutions remain uncommon despite their potential local benefits (Colgan, Beck and Narayan, 2017[50]).

3.5. Establishing monitoring and evaluation frameworks

A comprehensive approach to coastal adaptation should include a process of monitoring and evaluation, in order to understand how to best manage climate risks and improve the effectiveness of actions taken. For coastal adaptation in particular, considerable uncertainty regarding future SLR, storm surge level, and erosion trends and their impact at the local level means that it is essential to continually monitor and regularly evaluate to ensure policy responses are still serving their desired purpose.

Most OECD countries have indicated in their adaptation plans that they plan to design and implement a monitoring and evaluation system at the national level, which includes a focus on coastal areas, but relatively few systems are currently operational (see Table 3.2). To date, adaptation monitoring and evaluation remains far more common at the project and programme level (Vallejo, 2017[51]). Monitoring is also better established than evaluation, often due to an insufficient length of time passed for evaluations to be feasible (Vallejo, 2017[51]).

National monitoring and evaluation systems can broadly serve one of two purposes: 1) promoting a learning process; or 2) focusing on accountability (Dinshaw et al., 2014[52]). France's approach firstly aims to monitor the implementation of coastal adaptation measures, while during evaluation it emphasises a process of continual learning. A mid-term and end-term evaluation of the national adaptation plan (PNACC) allowed the government to take stock of new data regarding SLR and its impact on French coasts. Key recommendations for the elaboration of a second adaptation plan included the endorsement of nature-based solutions and proposals to spatially reshape coastal areas (French Government, 2017[9]). UK monitoring and evaluation, in contrast, is mainly focused on ensuring accountability for actions and determining which measures are most effective. The evaluation approach combines a regular statutory assessment of the overall adaptation plan based on the monitoring of a set of specific, measurable indicators, in addition to non-statutory assessments of shoreline management plans. Evaluations of the effectiveness of these measures have resulted in a change of indicators in certain cases and the adoption of a proactive rather than reactive approach to coastal management (Nicholls et al., 2013[53]).

OECD countries have taken a variety of approaches for their monitoring and evaluation systems for coastal adaptation, with no two systems being identical. Several countries (e.g. France, Germany and the United Kingdom) rely on a mix of mostly quantitative, but also qualitative indicators as a basis for evaluation. These indicators can take the form of effect-based indicators such as sea-level or storm surge levels, process-based, meaning the level of advancement of a particular measure, or outcome-based, meaning the result of a measure in coastal risk reduction. Other countries (e.g. Finland and Norway) prioritise the use of stakeholder surveys and self-assessments over indicators to offer insights on adaptation progress. The Netherlands is currently compiling a list of sea-level rise indicators for the Delta Programme, after having concluded to strike a balance between learning and accountability (Van Minnen et al., 2018[54]).

A number of challenges remain to the full implementation of monitoring and evaluation programmes at the national level. Several of these challenges relate to the nature of climate adaptation itself, which are especially salient in coastal zones. These include long time frames, uncertainty regarding impacts at the local level, difficulties in establishing baselines and targets, and the challenge of discerning causes and effects (OECD, 2015[55]). Further, coastal adaptation does not have common aggregated metrics and is often integrated into other sectoral policies rather than being an independent measure. Therefore, adaptation policy targets at different levels cannot typically be monitored with a single or distinct number of indicators or sources of information like in other policy domains such as climate change mitigation (EEA, 2015[56]). A vital factor of monitoring and evaluating progress of adaptation policies is the establishment of long-term data sets, including the implemented measures, expected effects and eventual outcomes in terms of changes in risks (Vallejo, 2017[51]). The process can also be resource-intensive, particularly regarding data and the human and technical capacities required to collect and interpret it.

Table 3.2. Examples of proposed or operational indicators to monitor coastal adaptation

Country	Type of indicator	Indicator
Australia	◊	Capacity of planning frameworks to support effective management of climate risks in the coastal zone Number of local governments considering climate change risks in land-use planning
Finland	□	Raising of flood banks
	◊	Results of stakeholder surveys on a five-point scale
France	□	Climate change vulnerability maps of coastal zone developed Number of wave recorders installed along coastal areas
Germany	○	Sea level (WW-I-9); intensity of storm surges (WW-I-10)
	□	Investments in coastal protection (WW-R-3)
Spain	□	Process-based indicators on the C3E project[1]
United Kingdom	○	Cost of damage to buildings (disaggregated by coastal erosion, other flooding events)
	□	Capital and revenue spent in flood risk and coastal erosion management against the need
	◊	Urban/built-up areas at risk of flooding (disaggregated by fluvial, coastal and pluvial flooding); uptake of measures to increase resilience and resistance to flood risk in new development

Notes:
○ Effect-based indicator.
□ Process-based indicator.
◊ Outcome-based indicator.
1. The C3E (Climate Change on the Spanish Coast) project identifies the impacts and vulnerabilities linked to climate change along the Spanish coastline. The results of these projections will inform coastal adaptation measures to put in place.
Source: Adapted from national adaptation plans.

3.6. Elements of effective coastal adaptation policy regimes

There is robust evidence and a compelling case for further action to address the consequences of SLR. While not all coastal risks can be avoided, well-prepared coastal communities will be better able to adjust to new conditions, at lower cost, and rapidly bounce back from disasters when they occur. Implementing change takes time, stakeholder engagement and should be guided by the latest scientific evidence and economic analysis. This creates a need for countries to put in place now the elements necessary to effectively respond to SLR.

Physically, SLR differs from existing coastal change due to uncertainty around magnitude and pace of change, as well as the long timescales involved. Both uncertainty and long timescales contribute to low-risk awareness in coastal zones: many inhabitants of flood-prone areas are not aware of new and long-term risks. In addition, the time lag between when costs are incurred to reduce risks and when benefits are realised, as well as the public good nature of adaptation investments, can prevent SLR from being internalised into decisions. As illustrated in Figure 3.1, this can lead to excessive exposure and vulnerability in coastal zones.

Figure 3.1. Challenges for coastal decision making

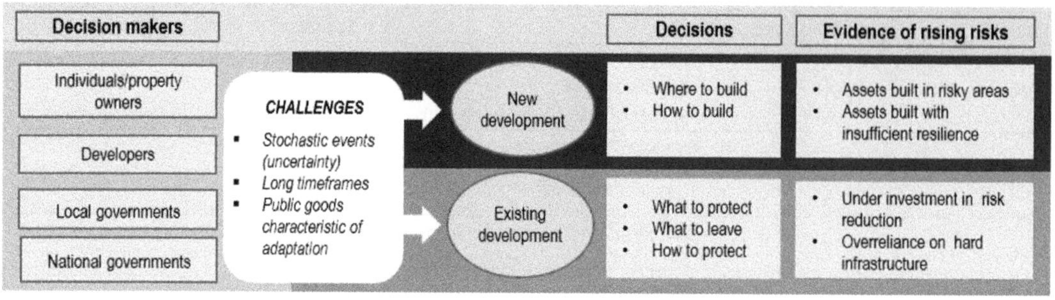

Note: Decisions about what to protect, and to leave, and how to protect encompass decisions between different strategies discussed in Chapter 2 (e.g. protect, accommodate, retreat).

While policy action is apparent, many of the measures currently in place are not commensurate with the challenge. The majority of efforts to date have focused on building the scientific evidence base and disseminating information. However, far fewer countries are using SLR information in regulatory frameworks, and even less have dedicated funding for coastal adaptation. A lack of consideration of SLR in national policies can lead to inefficiencies and sub-optimal outcomes. These include:

- local governments and individuals pursuing policies that are rational from a local or individual perspective but create inefficiencies overall, such as granting building permits in higher risk areas
- moral hazard as property owners and developers who gain the benefits of coastal location, while risks are transferred to others
- increased reliance on hard infrastructure due to political pressure to build coastal defences as the number and value of threatened buildings increases
- increasing costs for the general tax base, especially if risks become uninsurable.

Through the scan of current policies and four in-depth case studies, this study puts forward four principles of a policy framework for coastal adaptation that is equipped to meet the challenges described above. These principles should be taken into consideration by national governments as they further develop and implement their adaptation responses. They are:

1. engage stakeholders early and substantively
2. plan for the future and prevent lock-in to unsustainable pathways
3. align actors' responsibilities, resources and incentives
4. explicitly consider distributional and equity implications of policies.

1. Engage stakeholders early and substantively

Policy makers should engage stakeholders in the early stages of decision making and throughout the entire decision-making process to enhance overall resilience in coastal areas, while supporting community ownership and buy-in.

While engagement is an important component of any policy change, there are specific qualities of coastal adaptation that require extra consideration. These are discussed below.:

SLR risks are complex and difficult to understand. This is in part due to cognitive barriers around understanding risk (see Box 3.1), compounded by the fact that SLR risks are relatively new, have associated uncertainty and very long timescales. In many cases, stakeholders and communities that are not presently concerned with future flood/erosion risks may be more concerned over the perceived negative impacts of proposed adaptation plans and policies themselves.

Coastal adaptation decisions can pose a significant threat to private assets. It is understandable that communities may feel threatened by some adaptation measures – homes are often the most significant material and financial possession people have.

Decisions taken at the individual, household or developer level (e.g. where to build new property) can increase overall exposure and vulnerability, as described in Figure 3.1.

Engaging all affected stakeholders in the policy-making process is needed to ensure the development of a shared vision of risks and shared understanding of an acceptable level of risk. Once this has been achieved, it is possible to discuss and manage trade-offs across stakeholders, who can be differently affected by the economic, social and environmental impacts of SLR, as well as the options to address it. Difficult decisions (e.g. limiting the approval of new properties, relocation of existing properties) should be considered, discussed and planned through a coherent, long-term approach. In addition, engagement must reinforce the roles and responsibilities for risk management and clarify the accountability and liability for damages.

The context-specific nature of SLR reinforces the need to engage stakeholders early on. There is no "one-size-fits-all" coastal adaptation strategy; instead, they need to be tailored to the local context. In view of this, stakeholders can provide decision makers with key information and knowledge of local features, such as where the impacts of SLR are felt most and which objectives should be prioritised. Doing this can improve the quality of decision outcomes and ensure that plans and projects are tailored to be regionally and culturally relevant. Through engagement, stakeholders also develop a sense of ownership over the coastal adaptation process and its outcomes. This increases the trust and confidence of stakeholders towards the approach, who will tend to regard the resulting adaptation measures as more legitimate (OECD, 2015[57]).

In 2015, the OECD undertook an extensive study to determine how engagement processes can contribute to water governance objectives. Box 3.8 lists the principles.

Real-world examples of successful, long-term engagement strategies are needed. Lessons can be drawn from the case of the Marsh Body established in Truro, Nova Scotia (see Chapter 5), as well as adaptation pathways approach used in Hawkes Bay, New Zealand (see Chapter 6).

Box 3.8. OECD 2015 Principles for Stakeholder Engagement

Although engagement processes cannot be easily replicated from one context to another, the following principles are proposed for effective stakeholder engagement:

- **Inclusiveness and equity**: Identify all stakeholders who have a stake in the outcome or that are likely to be affected.
- **Clarity of goals, transparency and accountability**: Define the ultimate line of decision making and the objectives of the engagement.
- **Capacity and information**: Allocate proper financial and human resources to engagement and ensure necessary information is available.
- **Efficiency and effectiveness**: Regularly assess the process and outcomes of stakeholder engagement to learn, adjust and improve accordingly.
- **Institutionalisation, structuring and integration**: Embed engagement processes in clear legal and policy frameworks, organisational structures/principles, and responsible authorities.
- **Adaptiveness**: Customise the type and level of engagement as needed and keep the process flexible to changing circumstances.

Source: OECD (2015[57]), *Stakeholder Engagement for Inclusive Water Governance*, http://dx.doi.org/10.1787/9789264231122-en.

2. Plan for the future and prevent lock-in to unsustainable pathways

Policy makers need to take a long-term approach to coastal planning that actively favours flexibility.

As highlighted in Chapter 1, climate-induced SLR will continue for thousands of years even if greenhouse gas concentrations are stabilised within the 21st century. There remains considerable uncertainty over the rate and magnitude of SLR, particularly at the local level and over long timeframes. This has significant practical consequences, as planning for a 0.5-metre sea-level rise is substantially different from planning for a 2-metre sea-level rise, in terms of the area of land likely to be affected, and the frequency and seriousness of the impacts. Uncertainties about climate impacts additionally represent a cost in themselves, as there is the risk of preparing for a future that is markedly different from the one that materialises. Preparing for the "wrong" future or implementing the "wrong" form of coastal protection has the potential to be more costly than doing nothing. Planning should therefore go well into the future, but also leave room for manoeuvre.

In particular, the uncertainties associated with SLR call for a dynamic, future-oriented approach to planning that explicitly deals with uncertainty. Adaptation planning must consider the impact of time on planning processes, recognising that as conditions and available knowledge change, adaptation options may also need to change (OECD, 2015[30]; 2013[18]). OECD (2015[30]) provides an overview of approaches to plan for uncertainty, and the general principles are to build in flexibility and identify solutions that can perform well against a range of different scenarios. The New Zealand case study provides an example of dynamic adaptive pathways planning. The pathways approach involves testing different responses against a wide range of SLR projections, which informs the development of alternate policy pathways that are robust and flexible. Within each pathway, coastal hazard risk and vulnerability assessments are used to identify vulnerabilities and thresholds of intolerable risk, to develop early signals and decision points for when to switch pathways before reaching the adaptation threshold.

The specific characteristics of SLR increases the value of robustness (the ability to perform across a range of conditions) and flexibility (the capacity to adjust with changing conditions). Policy lock-in occurs when the selection of a coastal adaptation pathway in the short term inadvertently restricts the application of alternative options in the long term. As described in Chapter 2, options such as increased protection can lead to the levee effect – a cycle of increased development in the coastal floodplain based on the perception of increased safety, which can carry the perverse impact of increasing vulnerability in the longer term. Placing value on flexibility and robustness can give preference to innovative measures to address SLR, such as nature-based solutions, which can be easily modified to the actual rate of SLR. Accommodation measures, such as changing building design, also present a more flexible approach that leaves further options available in the future.

A key element of planning is timeframes, as the cost effectiveness of different measures is highly dependent on the time and spatial scales over which it is calculated. For example, replacing a damaged coastal road with the exact same infrastructure is likely to restore business-as-usual in the short term, yet a long-term perspective could bring alternative options, such as an initially more expensive road relocation, into play.

An important aspect of long-term planning is having a vision for the coast. National governments need to communicate the overall objective and vision of coastal resilience to other levels of governments. While local governments may often want to implement measures to reduce coastal risks (such as restrictive land-use planning), in practice this can come up against a variety of governance and political economy challenges. Actions at the national level therefore need to promote a shared approach and long-term explicit commitment to manage the impacts of SLR, with co-ordinated and sustained dialogue between different levels of government.

3. Align actors' responsibilities, resources and incentives

Policy makers need to understand and address the incentives and constraints faced by relevant actors.

As highlighted in Chapter 2, the institutional environment is a determining factor influencing actors' behaviour in coastal risk reduction. If an actor is aware of owning or sharing a risk, but has little reward or incentive attached to managing responsibilities, it can result in increasing risk overall. For example, property developers often do not bear future costs from current development, and as a result lobby for coastal land releases (OECD, 2014[21]). In addition, political economy challenges arise from entrenched policies and institutional arrangements (e.g. property and land rights, existing public infrastructure, stakeholder expectations). Funding arrangements, and related planning and regulatory frameworks, must therefore be well-co-ordinated and designed to minimise moral hazard.

Reforms should ensure that responsibilities, capabilities and resources are also aligned. Multi-level governance challenges, both horizontal (across policy domains) and vertical (across levels of government), can hinder effective implementation. In general, local actors have the necessary local knowledge, as well as jurisdiction, to implement coastal adaptation measures. However, not all adaptation options can be implemented solely at the local level, due to funding constraints or institutional barriers. For example, in Australia, the lack of national funding and co-ordination has led to the disorganised construction of seawalls, which has spread coastal risk (Fletcher et al., 2013[58]). In the United Kingdom, a key barrier noted by local governments is the high upfront cost of adaptive responses such as realigning critical infrastructure, in comparison to stopgap measures that fit with short-term funding cycles (Brown, Naylor and Quinn, 2017[59]). A lack of co-ordinating mechanisms and higher level support can lead to inefficient outcomes overall.

Economic and regulatory instruments can be used to internalise social costs, such as risk-priced flood insurance. However, as described in the section above, there are very few examples of these instruments being implemented to address SLR, and even less empirical evidence about their effectiveness in influencing behaviour. Nevertheless, finding ways to ensure SLR risk is internalised into decisions (e.g. policy, real estate, etc.) will be essential, as this can help to break the potentially damaging feedback loop between real estate values and coastal defence investments. For example, in the United States, property values are significantly higher in areas that use continued beach nourishment (Gopalakrishnan et al., 2017[60]). In the United Kingdom, while new developments are subject to a flood risk assessment and site-specific adaptations are often required, these decisions are taken within the context of the level of protection offered current flood defence infrastructure (Brown, Naylor and Quinn, 2017[59]).

The diagnostic framework in Figure 3.2 outlines a process for identifying where incentives, responsibilities and resources may not be aligned towards risk reduction. Such a framework can help policy makers identify the key actors, understand their interests, and the factors that enable or hinder adaptation. This should be used to ensure that the scale and implications of future coastal change are acknowledged by those with responsibility for the coast and communicated to those who live on the coast.

Figure 3.2. Framework to identify actors/roles, drivers and misalignments

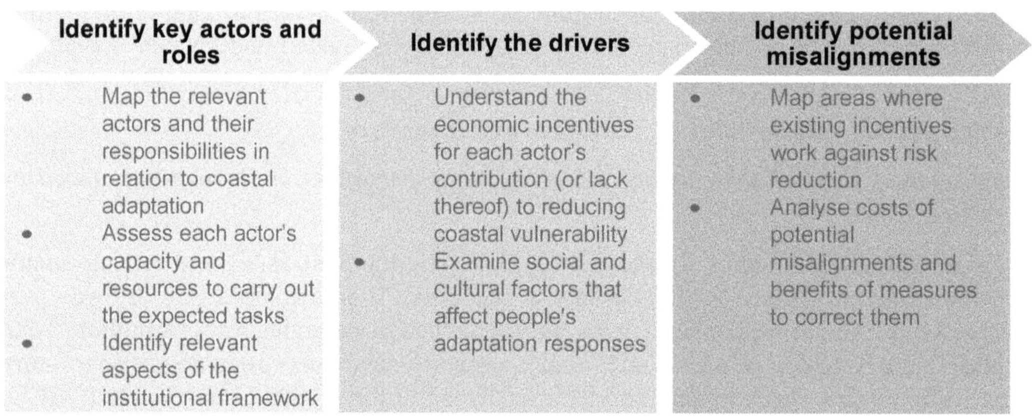

Source: Adapted from OECD (2014[61]), *Boosting Resilience through Innovative Risk Governance*, http://dx.doi.org/10.1787/9789264209114-en.

4. Explicitly consider distributional and equity implications of policies

Policy makers must explicitly address the distributional and equity implications of policies that address coastal risks

Changes to the allocation of risks and responsibilities relating to sea-level rise will have significant distributional impacts. Some adaptation measures may result in significant costs for property owners in areas of risk. These costs can include: the requirement to allow their land to be flooded periodically (for example, the Netherlands), being prohibited to build certain protective structures on their land (various countries) and higher insurance premiums. Given these potential costs, the distributional impacts of policy reforms need to be addressed in the process of implementing reforms.

Understanding the potential socio-economic vulnerability of those exposed to SLR is needed for both public and private SLR adaptation. For government-implemented measures, the prioritisation of options can be based on a measure of economic efficiency (acknowledging that many decisions about coastal adaptation are not taken with strict cost-benefit decision rules – other factors may include local zoning by-laws, future land-use plans, the presence of development-supporting infrastructure, etc.) (Martinich et al., 2013[62]). In a strict cost-benefit analysis, land that is more valuable will be prioritised for coastal protection. This can leave socially vulnerable communities that are located in high-risk areas even more likely to remain exposed and experience disproportionally adverse consequences from SLR. For private adaptation, socially vulnerable groups may not have the resources to implement measures. This is especially salient as many people settled in areas at risk of SLR before information about future hazards was available.

An important first step for policy makers is undertaking detailed risk assessments that account for socio-economic vulnerability and associated adaptive capacity of those in the path of the hazards, as well as the hazards themselves. This can inform future policy design. In some cases, compensation schemes may be required to relieve at least some of the economic burden of being located in a high-risk area.

An example of a policy that explicitly targets potential distributional impacts is the Partnership funding model in the United Kingdom (elaborated Box 2.4), which is a cost-sharing model for flood risk management between national and other levels of government. In this funding scheme, payment rates for households in "deprived areas"[5] are higher than elsewhere.

The question of whether those faced with loss (property, land and/or income) should receive public compensation brings with it legal, political and economic challenges. First, it is often hard to determine whether particular risks could have reasonably been foreseen, and whose responsibility it was to foresee them. Second, the balance between individual responsibility and social solidarity is a political choice, albeit one with implications for the incentives faced by property owners. Decisions about potential compensation should be taken on a consistent, predictable and transparent basis. It will be additionally important that the economic case to support long-term funding should be determined not only by the protection of physical assets, but should also incorporate environmental implications and social justice considerations.

Notes

[1] A similar review of national policies for water-related climate risks, including flooding, was undertaken in 2013 (with country profiles available at: www.oecd.org/env/water-and-climate-change-adaptation-9789264200449-en.htm).

[2] Australia, Austria, Canada, Chile, Costa Rica, the Czech Republic, Estonia, France, Hungary, Iceland, Ireland, Israel, Japan, Latvia, Mexico, Myanmar, New Zealand, Peru, Philippines, Poland, Portugal, the Russian Federation, Spain, Switzerland, Turkey, the United States and Viet Nam

[3] Including inland and coastal flooding

[4] Nature-based coastal defences are a form of ecosystem-based adaptation. Further detail can be found in Chapter 2

[5] Government. Deprivation is assessed using the DCLG's Index of Local Deprivation: https://www.gov.uk/government/publications/english-indices-of-deprivation-2010

References

Albini, A. et al. (2017), *Climate Change Adaptation Practices Across the EU: Mainstreaming Adaptation Policies at Regional and Local Level*, Master Adapt, https://masteradapt.eu/wordpress/wp-content/uploads/2017/07/Master-Adapt-report-A2_v2.pdf (accessed on 21 August 2018). [26]

BASE (2014), *Shifting Responsibilities for Flood Damages in Finland*, https://base-adaptation.eu/shifting-responsibilities-flood-damages-finland (accessed on 20 August 2018). [35]

Bell, R., R. Paulik and S. Wadwha (2015), *National and Regional Risk Exposure in Low-Lying Coastal Areas*, https://www.pce.parliament.nz/media/1384/national-and-regional-risk-exposure-in-low-lying-coastal-areas-niwa-2015.pdf (accessed on 29 August 2018). [10]

Bisaro, A. and J. Hinkel (2018), "Mobilizing private finance for coastal adaptation: A literature review", *Wiley Interdisciplinary Reviews: Climate Change*, Vol. 9/3, p. e514, http://dx.doi.org/10.1002/wcc.514. [46]

Brown, K. (2018), *The New National Adaptation Programme: Hit or Miss?*, Committee on Climate Change, London, https://www.theccc.org.uk/2018/07/19/the-new-national-adaptation-programme-hit-or-miss (accessed on 9 August 2018). [37]

Brown, K., L. Naylor and T. Quinn (2017), "Making space for proactive adaptation of rapidly changing coasts: A windows of opportunity approach", *Sustainability*, Vol. 9/8, pp. 1-17, http://dx.doi.org/10.3390/su9081408. [59]

Climate-ADAPT (2014), *An integrated plan incorporating flood protection: The Sigma Plan (Scheldt Estuary, Belgium)*, https://climate-adapt.eea.europa.eu/metadata/case-studies/an-integrated-plan-incorporating-flood-protection-the-sigma-plan-scheldt-estuary-belgium (accessed on 14 August 2018). [20]

Climate-KIC (2017), "Tackle information asymmetry to accelerate climate change adaptation", Climate-KIC, https://dailyplanet.climate-kic.org/tackle-information-asymmetry-accelerate-climate-change-adaptation (accessed on 1 August 2018). [12]

Colgan, C. (2016), "The economics of adaptation to climate change in coasts and oceans: Literature review, policy implications and research agenda", *Journal of Oceans and Coastal Economics*, Vol. 3/2, http://dx.doi.org/10.15351/2373-8456.1067. [13]

Colgan, C., M. Beck and S. Narayan (2017), *Financing Natural Infrastructure for Coastal Flood Damage Reduction*, Lloyd's Tercentenary Research Foundation, London, https://conservationgateway.org/ConservationPractices/Marine/crr/library/Documents/FinancingNaturalInfrastructureReport.pdf (accessed on 24 July 2018). [50]

Costas, S., O. Ferreira and G. Martinez (2015), "Why do we decide to live with risk at the coast?", *Ocean & Coastal Management*, Vol. 118, pp. 1-11, http://dx.doi.org/10.1016/J.OCECOAMAN.2015.05.015. [14]

Crick, F., K. Jenkins and S. Surminski (2018), "Strengthening insurance partnerships in the face of climate change: Insights from an agent-based model of flood insurance in the UK", *Science of the Total Environment*, Vol. 636, pp. 192-204, http://dx.doi.org/10.1016/J.SCITOTENV.2018.04.239. [32]

DEFRA (2013), *The National Adaptation Programme: Making the Country Resilient to a Changing Climate*, Department for Environment, Food & Rural Affairs, London, http://www.gov.uk/defra (accessed on 28 August 2017). [7]

Defra (2018), *The National Adaptation Programme and the Third Strategy for Climate Adaptation Reporting Making the Country Resilient to a Changing Climate*, Department for Environment, Food & Rural Affairs, London, http://www.nationalarchives.gov.uk/doc/open- (accessed on 31 July 2018). [44]

Defra (2014), *Post-Installation Effectiveness of Property Level Flood Protection Final Report FD2668*, Department for Environment, Food & Rural Affairs, London, http://www.gov.uk/defra (accessed on 24 July 2018). [38]

Department of Climate Change and Energy Efficiency (2011), *Climate Change Risks to Coastal Buildings and Infrastructure*, Australian Government, Canberra, http://www.climatechange.gov.au (accessed on 2 August 2018). [8]

Dinshaw, A. et al. (2014), "Monitoring and evaluation of climate change adaptation: Methodological approaches", *OECD Environment Working Papers*, No. 74, OECD Publishing, Paris, http://dx.doi.org/10.1787/5jxrclr0ntjd-en. [52]

EEA (2015), *National Monitoring, Reporting and Evaluation of Climate Change Adaptation in Europe*, European Environment Agency, https://www.eea.europa.eu/publications/national-monitoring-reporting-and-evaluation (accessed on 9 July 2018). [56]

EEA (2015), *Overview of Climate Change Adaptation Platforms in Europe*, European Environment Agency, Luxembourg, http://dx.doi.org/10.2800/400414. [11]

EEA (2013), "Balancing the future of Europe's coasts; Knowledge base for integrated management", *EEA Report* 12, http://dx.doi.org/10.2800/99116 (accessed on 21 August 2018). [28]

England, P. (2013), "Too much too soon? On the rise and fall of Australia's coastal climate change law", *Environmental and Planning Law Journal*, http://hdl.handle.net/10072/57341http://www.thomsonreuters.com.au/environmental-and-planning-law-journal-online/productdetail/97170 (accessed on 10 August 2018). [41]

Filatova, T. (2014), "Market-based instruments for flood risk management: A review of theory, practice and perspectives for climate adaptation policy", *Environmental Science & Policy*, Vol. 37, pp. 227-242, http://dx.doi.org/10.1016/J.ENVSCI.2013.09.005. [29]

Fletcher, C. et al. (2013), *Costs and Coasts: An Empirical Assessment of Physical and Institutional Climate Adaptation Pathways*, National Climate Change Adaptation Research Facility, Gold Coast, Australia, https://www.nccarf.edu.au/sites/default/files/attached_files_publications/Fletcher_2013_Costs_and_coasts.pdf (accessed on 18 August 2017). [58]

French Government (2017), *Bilan du Plan Submersions rapides 2011-2016*, https://www.ecologique-solidaire.gouv.fr/sites/default/files/170427__livret_Bilan_PSR.pdf (accessed on 24 July 2018). [45]

French Government (2017), *Working towards a 2nd French National Adaptation Plan for Climate Change: Challenges and Recommendations*, French Government, Paris, https://www.ecologique-solidaire.gouv.fr/sites/default/files/ONERC_rapport_2017_EN.pdf (accessed on 13 July 2018). [9]

French Senate (2018), *Développement durable des territoires littoraux*, https://www.senat.fr/dossier-legislatif/ppl16-717.html (accessed on 28 August 2018). [19]

Gopalakrishnan, S. et al. (2017), "Decentralized management hinders coastal climate adaptation: The spatial-dynamics of beach nourishment", *Environmental and Resource Economics*, Vol. 67/4, pp. 761-787, http://dx.doi.org/10.1007/s10640-016-0004-8. [60]

Government of Canada (2016), *Pan Canadian Framework on Clean Growth and Climate Change Canada's Plan to Address Climate Change and Grow the Economy*, Government of Canada, https://www.canada.ca/content/dam/themes/environment/documents/weather1/20161209-1-en.pdf (accessed on 7 December 2017). [43]

Henstra, D. and J. Thistlethwaite (2018), "Buyer beware: Evaluating property disclosure as a tool to support flood risk management", *CIGI Policy Brief* 131, https://www.cigionline.org/publications/buyer-beware-evaluating-property-disclosure-tool-support-flood-risk-management (accessed on 10 August 2018). [42]

Hinkel, J. et al. (2015), "Sea-level rise scenarios and coastal risk management", *Nature Climate Change*, Vol. 5/3, pp. 188-190, http://dx.doi.org/10.1038/nclimate2505. [2]

Hooijer, A. et al. (2004), "Towards sustainable flood risk management in the Rhine and Meuse river basins: Synopsis of the findings of IRMA-SPONGE", *River Research and Applications*, Vol. 20/3, pp. 343-357, http://dx.doi.org/10.1002/rra.781. [49]

Japanese Government (2015), *National Plan for the Adaptation to the Impacts of Climate Change*, http://www.env.go.jp/en/focus/docs/files/20151127-101.pdf (accessed on 28 August 2017). [34]

Kousky, C. (2014), "Managing shoreline retreat: A US perspective", *Climatic Change*, Vol. 124/1-2, pp. 9-20, http://dx.doi.org/10.1007/s10584-014-1106-3. [15]

Lamond, J. and E. Penning-Rowsell (2014), "The robustness of flood insurance regimes given changing risk resulting from climate change", *Climate Risk Management*, Vol. 2, pp. 1-10, http://dx.doi.org/10.1016/j.crm.2014.03.001. [36]

Le Cozannet, G. et al. (2017), *Sea Level Change and Coastal Climate Services: The Way Forward*, Future Earth, http://futureearth.org/projects/news/sea-level-change-and-coastal-climate-services-way-forward (accessed on 13 December 2017). [1]

Lubell, M. (2017), *The Governance Gap: Climate Adaptation an Sea-Level Rise in the San Francisco Bay Area*, http://climatereadinessinstitute.org/wp-content/uploads/2014/03/UC-Davis-Governance-Gap-Sea-Level-Rise-Final-Report.pdf (accessed on 12 September 2017). [22]

Martinich, J. et al. (2013), "Risks of sea level rise to disadvantaged communities in the United States", *Mitigation and Adaptation Strategies for Global Change*, Vol. 18/2, pp. 169-185, http://dx.doi.org/10.1007/s11027-011-9356-0. [62]

Ministry for the Environment (2017), *Coastal Hazards and Climate Change: Guidance for Local Government*, http://www.mfe.govt.nz (accessed on 2 August 2018). [16]

MoE, P. (2013), "Polish National Strategy for Adaptation to Climate Change (NAS 2020)", https://klimada.mos.gov.pl/wp-content/uploads/2014/12/ENG_SPA2020_final.pdf (accessed on 7 December 2017). [33]

National Research Council (2014), *Reducing Coastal Risk on the East and Gulf Coasts*, National Academies Press, Washington, DC, http://dx.doi.org/10.17226/18811. [40]

Nicholls, R. et al. (2013), "Planning for long-term coastal change: Experiences from England and Wales", *Ocean Engineering*, Vol. 71, pp. 3-16, http://dx.doi.org/10.1016/J.OCEANENG.2013.01.025. [53]

OECD (2017), *OECD Reviews of Risk Management Policies. Boosting Disaster Prevention through Innovative Risk Governance: Insights from Austria, France and Switzerland*, OECD Publishing, Paris, https://www.oecd-ilibrary.org/docserver/9789264281370-en.pdf?expires=1531472451&id=id&accname=ocid84004878&checksum=FAA505A62C1A385C8165D30455FA2DF2 (accessed on 13 July 2018). [6]

OECD (2016), *Financial Management of Flood Risk*, OECD Publishing, Paris, https://doi.org/10.1787/9789264257689-en (accessed on 5 September 2017). [4]

OECD (2016), *Financial Management of Flood Risk*, OECD Publishing, Paris, http://dx.doi.org/10.1787/9789264257689-en. [47]

OECD (2015), *Climate Change Risks and Adaptation: Linking Policy and Economics*, OECD Publishing, Paris, http://dx.doi.org/10.1787/9789264234611-en. [30]

OECD (2015), *National Climate Change Adaptation: Emerging Practices in Monitoring and Evaluation*, OECD Publishing, Paris, http://dx.doi.org/10.1787/9789264229679-en. [55]

OECD (2015), *Stakeholder Engagement for Inclusive Water Governance*, OECD Studies on Water, OECD Publishing, Paris, http://dx.doi.org/10.1787/9789264231122-en. [57]

OECD (2014), *Boosting Resilience through Innovative Risk Governance*, OECD Reviews of Risk Management Policies, OECD Publishing, Paris, http://dx.doi.org/10.1787/9789264209114-en. [61]

OECD (2014), *Water Governance in the Netherlands: Fit for the Future?*, OECD Studies on Water, OECD Publishing, Paris, http://dx.doi.org/10.1787/9789264102637-en. [21]

OECD (2013), *Water and Climate Change Adaptation: Policies to Navigate Uncharted Waters*, OECD Publishing, Paris, https://doi.org/10.1787/9789264200449-en (accessed on 2 July 2018). [18]

O'Mahony, C. et al. (2015), "ICZM as a framework for climate change adaptation action: Experience from Cork Harbour, Ireland", *Marine Policy*, http://dx.doi.org/10.1016/J.MARPOL.2015.10.008. [27]

Surminski, S. and J. Eldridge (2017), "Flood insurance in England: An assessment of the current and newly proposed insurance scheme in the context of rising flood risk", *Journal of Flood Risk Management*, Vol. 10/4, pp. 415-435, http://dx.doi.org/10.1111/jfr3.12127. [39]

Surminski, S. and A. Thieken (2017), "Promoting flood risk reduction: The role of insurance in Germany and England", *Earth's Future*, Vol. 5/10, pp. 979-1001, http://dx.doi.org/10.1002/2017EF000587. [31]

Vallejo, L. (2017), "Insights from national adaptation monitoring and evaluation systems", *Climate Change Expert Group Paper No. 2017/3*, https://www.oecd.org/environment/cc/Insights%20from%20national%20adaptation%20monitoring%20and%20evaluation%20systems.pdf (accessed on 9 July 2018). [51]

Vallejo, L. and M. Mullan (2017), "Climate-resilient infrastructure: Getting the policies right", *OECD Environment Working Papers*, No. 121, OECD Publishing, Paris, http://dx.doi.org/10.1787/02f74d61-en. [3]

Van Minnen, J. et al. (2018), "Developments in monitoring climate change adaptation in urban areas: Quick scan of experiences outside the Netherlands", *PBL Note*, https://www.pbl.nl/sites/default/files/cms/publicaties/pbl-2018-developments-in-monitoring-and-evaluating-climate-change-adaptation-in-urban-areas_3018.pdf (accessed on 30 July 2018). [54]

Verschuuren, J. and J. Mcdonald (2012), "Towards a legal framework for coastal adaptation: Assessing the first steps in Europe and Australia", *Transnational Environmental Law*, Vol. 1/2, pp. 355-379, https://doi.org/10.1017/S204710251200009X (accessed on 9 August 2017). [17]

Wilby, R. and R. Keenan (2012), "Adapting to flood risk under climate change", *Progress in Physical Geography: Earth and Environment*, Vol. 36/3, pp. 348-378, http://dx.doi.org/10.1177/0309133312438908. [23]

Wilby, R. and R. Keenan (2012), "Adapting to flood risk under climate change", *Progress in Physical Geography*, Vol. 36/3, pp. 348-378, http://dx.doi.org/10.1177/0309133312438908. [24]

Wing, O. et al. (2018), "Estimates of present and future flood risk in the coterminous United States", *Environmental Research Letters*, Vol. 13, pp. 1-7, http://dx.doi.org/10.1088/1748-9326/aaac65. [5]

Wong, P. et al. (2014), *Coastal Systems and Low-Lying Areas*, IPCC, https://www.ipcc.ch/pdf/assessment-report/ar5/wg2/WGIIAR5-Chap5_FINAL.pdf (accessed on 17 August 2017). [25]

World Bank (2015), *Green Bonds Attract Private Sector Climate Finance*, http://www.worldbank.org/en/topic/climatechange/brief/green-bonds-climate-finance (accessed on 25 July 2018). [48]

Chapter 4. Aligning coastal risk decision making and funding responsibilities on the German Baltic Sea coast

This chapter provides an in-depth look at the German federal state of Schleswig-Holstein, which has differing coastal risk profiles on its North Sea and Baltic Sea coasts. By examining adaptation and coastal protection decisions in several communities on the German Baltic Sea coast, this case study will illustrate the enabling factors and barriers to central government support for local level action to address long-term coastal risks driven by sea-level rise.

This chapter was written by Alexander Bisaro and Jochen Hinkel Global Climate Forum, Berlin and Division of Resource Economics, Humboldt University, Berlin.

4.1. Overview

The German coast, located on both the North Sea and the Baltic Sea, encompasses five federal states (*Länder*): two are densely populated urban areas of Hamburg and Bremen, the other three contain a mix of small to mid-sized towns and sparsely populated rural areas, mostly used for agriculture.

The relevant German laws (state water acts) stipulate that coastal flood and erosion risks are a private responsibility. Only if public interests are concerned, public administration (Federal States, Water and Soil Associations (WSA), municipalities) is responsible. The division of public responsibilities is stipulated in the law. For instance, the state is responsible for the so-called state dikes (i.e. embankments), regional embankments on the islands and coastal erosion protection on the islands, whereas the WSA and (a few) municipalities are responsible for regional embankments along the mainland coast. Further, states also have significant responsibilities regarding adaptation to climate change. The federal government's responsibilities are to support research and knowledge sharing on adaptation, while the states are responsible for developing regional adaptation strategies. The states are also responsible for integrating climate change into planning instruments. Regarding sea-level rise in particular, states are thus responsible for integrating climate change into coastal protection and flood defence (CPCFD) strategies and land-use planning. The extent to which these responsibilities have been formalised varies across states, with some having already enacted laws addressing both climate change mitigation and adaptation (*Klimaschutzgesetz*) and others having only established sectoral plans addressing adaptation (BMUB, 2017[1]).

While there is variation across the different federal states, generally some responsibilities in these areas also remain with local authorities (public obligations as stipulated in the respective laws).

This case study explores how federal state planning and finance for CPCFD, as it is defined in state law and adaptation to sea-level rise (SLR) is addressed in the federal state of Schleswig-Holstein, and how local communities are involved in these processes. The focus is on CPCFD, thus including both hard (e.g. dikes or embankments) and soft (e.g. beach nourishment) measures, and how SLR information is included into decision making and financing of coastal protection. As the case study focuses on current practice, less attention is given to other adaptation measures, such as accommodation or retreat, as these are less prominent in Schleswig-Holstein. Indeed, as we discuss below, the federal state law focuses on "protecting life and limb" with an emphasis on providing CPCFD. While flood insurance has recently become available in Germany, it is not yet widely taken up in coastal areas.

The following section discusses the strengths and weaknesses of governance arrangements addressing coastal risks. In terms of strengths, the federal state master planning process is discussed, and how adaptation has been incorporated into it through building in flexibility to hard protection measures. In terms of weaknesses, sharing of responsibilities presents barriers to local authorities raising funds on their own, due to the lack of transparency of federal state funding decisions, and ambiguity in the law. Further, emerging lessons regarding strengthening existing institutional arrangements to incorporate a consideration of a broader range of adaptation measures and pathways in the federal state planning processes are discussed.

4.1.1. Current flood risk exposure, historical damages and trends

In the German federal state of Schleswig-Holstein, exposure to coastal hazards and risk levels differ at the states' North Sea and Baltic Sea coasts. Extreme high water levels are higher and large storm surge events have occurred more frequently at the North Sea. The most recent significant flood event took place in 1962, with storm surge heights of up to 5.8 m above mean sea level (MSL) (von Storch and Woth, 2008[2]). This event caused widespread damage and hundreds of fatalities. In contrast, at the Baltic Sea, the most recent major flooding event occurred in 1872, with a storm surge height of 2.5-3.3 m above MSL. In these flood risk areas, around 250 000 people live at the North Sea while only 91 000 live at the Baltic Sea. Similarly, assets in the flood risk zone at the North Sea (EUR 31 billion) are about double those at the Baltic Sea (EUR 15 billion). However, gross value added are very similar (EUR 4.3 billion for the North Sea and EUR 4 billion for the Baltic Sea), as are the number of jobs in the flood risk zone (both approximately 85 000) (MELUR, 2012[3]).

Considering future risks, it is projected that sea-level rise will increase storm surge flood hazard in the future, significantly reducing the return periods of major storm surge events. Assessing vulnerability to SLR at national, regional and local levels in Germany, Sterr (2008[4]) notes that it is not possible to ascertain significant trends in extreme storm floods, partly due to the lack of long time-series data. However, applying a sea-level rise scenario of 1 m by 2100 to the current storm flood frequency distribution leads to a significant reduction of return periods for extreme water levels. At Cuxhaven on the North Sea, for example, the current 1-in-100-year flood event is reduced to a 5-year flood event in 2100. While on the Baltic Sea, the reduction in return periods under SLR may be even more significant because of the micro-tidal environment, i.e. the near absence of tides, gives rises to a gentle storm flood frequency curve. Thus, at Travemuende on the Baltic Sea, maximum flood levels, with a return period greater than 1-in-250 years in the past, would be reduced to a 1 in 2-10 year period (Sterr, 2008[4]).

Coastal erosion and cliff retreat is also a salient issue on both the North Sea and the Baltic Sea coasts in Schleswig-Holstein. For instance, the federal state has spent approximately EUR 6 million annually for over 30 years on combatting coastal erosion on the North Sea island of Sylt alone (MELUR, 2012[3]). Future SLR will also exacerbate risks in this regard. A 2005 study found that in the German Wadden Sea area, for SLR rates of up to 5 mm per year, coastal erosion could be addressed with locally available sediment material. For higher SLR rates, locally available sediment would no longer be sufficient to present loss of coastal land areas in the Wadden Sea (MELUR, 2012[3]).

4.1.2. Measures in place in the federal state of Schleswig-Holstein

Historically, coastal flood protection levels have differed widely on each coast. There are 540 km of coast at the Baltic Sea in Schleswig-Holstein, only short sections of which are protected at all. State dikes, the highest level of protection, at an average height of 4.0-4.6 metres above MSL, protect 67 km of coast. An additional 54 km of Baltic Sea coast are protected by regional dikes, which do not have a uniform design standard and generally do not protect to the same level as state dikes (MELUR, 2012[3]). At the North Sea, the situation is quite different, as state dikes protect 364 km of the 553 km long coast, and the state embankments have a general height of about 8-9 m above MSL. These differences reflect varying hydro-morphological settings between the coasts. On the North Sea coast, a mean tidal range of up to 4.0 m has to be considered in the necessary height of embankments, whereas the Baltic Sea coast is a micro-tidal environment. Further, due to the shallow water environment of the Wadden Sea, the surge levels along the North Sea coast are much higher than those along the Baltic Sea coast.

The coastal defence master plan, developed by state governments, is the key coastal risk planning instrument in Germany. It sets out the state dikes' safety standards and areas of general welfare interest. The first Schleswig-Holstein Master Plan was developed in 1963 following the 1962 storm surge, in which the failure of protection led to widespread flooding and several hundred fatalities. The Master Plan is regularly updated (1977, 1986, 2001 and 2012). Flood safety standards have moved towards a more harmonised approach between the North Sea and the Baltic Sea.

The current Master Plan planning process is based on an integrated coastal zone management (ICZM) concept, which was adopted in German federal law in 2006 through the national ICZM strategy (BMU, 2010[5]). The scope of the ICZM strategy is intersectoral planning for the marine environment, as well as coastal land use, and thus entails coastal protection decisions. ICZM stipulates that all relevant stakeholders for a given planning process are able to communicate their interests in the planning process. This includes federal ministries as well as federal states and their ministries, and private sector actors including civil society. The Master Planning process is thus a participatory process and gives the opportunity for public and private stakeholders to comment, and further requires an environmental impact assessment that considers national and EU regulations for nature conservation. A key instrument in this process is the "Advisory Council Integrated Coastal Protection Management", which exists in Schleswig-Holstein since 1999. Under the chairmanship of the minister responsible for coastal protection, coastal protection stakeholders meet twice a year to discuss general aspects of coastal protection, and major individual measures, in an open exchange and in advance of decisions (see Chapter 3). In addition to the coastal and nature conservation administrations, members include the municipal districts, towns and municipalities, water and soil associations, and nature conservation associations. For example, the updates to the General Plan for Coastal Protection, which take place approximately every ten years, are presented and discussed in depth during its creation, in addition to regional citizens' information events. Approval of the plan rests with the Schleswig-Holstein state government. The ministry responsible for CPCFD (Ministerium für Energiewende, Landwirtschaft, Umwelt und ländliche Räume des Landes Schleswig-Holstein, MELUR) establishes the plan, thereby considering all relevant regulations, comments and the environmental impact assessment (BMU, 2010[5]).

The 2012 update of the Schleswig-Holstein Master Plan introduced a uniform flood safety standard of the 1-in-200-year event for the entire Schleswig-Holstein coast, partly to meet the EU Flood Directive. The design water height is thus determined using statistical modeling, incorporating an allowance for SLR, provided the resulting protection level against the 1-in-200-year event is not lower than the observed highest water levels. Further, design water heights SLR allowance used a unified 0.5 m MSLR scenario to 2100 for both the North Sea and the Baltic Sea. The sea-level rise scenarios were updated to reflect increases in the projected level and range of future SLR following the IPCC's Third Assessment Report. SLR of 0.5-1.4 m in this century was thus considered n the 2012 Master Plan.

In order to deal with increased future SLR, and also increased uncertainty, Schleswig-Holstein implemented a flattening of the outer embankment slope and a widening of dike crowns from 2.5-5.0 m during their reinforcement. With this profile, the embankment may be further heightened in a second phase at relatively low cost and little planning efforts. Thus, in two phases, an SLR of about 1.5 m can be accommodated. Dike widening will, as far as possible, occur on the land side of the dike in order not to disturb valuable ecosystems, e.g. salt marshes, on the seaward side.

For areas not under the responsibility of the state, the Master Plan mentions alternative means through which local communities can access federal state funding. For funding purposes, a so-called "*Förderrichtlinie*" (legal conditions for obtaining state funding for CPCFD measures) exists. For instance, the Master Plan mentions that sea-level rise will lead to increasing costs to maintain regional dikes that could overwhelm local authorities. In such cases, the responsibility (and ownership) for these regional dikes can be taken over by the federal state, provided that the dikes in question protect lives and assets comparable to those protected by state dikes. The decision to take over regional dikes is taken on a case-by-case basis and the process must be initiated by the responsible local authority. This is discussed further below (Section 4.2.1).

Finally, a further aspect of the Master Plan concerns measures to protect against coastal erosion. Responsibilities for measures against coastal erosion are stipulated in the State Water Act, i.e. coastal protection measures on islands that are in the public interest (welfare) are a state obligation. For instance, on the island of Sylt, approximately 12 million cubic metres of sand were pumped for beach nourishment at a cost of approximately EUR 61 million between 2001 and 2011. Indeed, annual spending by the federal state at Sylt has been approximately EUR 6 million for combatting coastal erosion since 1983 (MELUR, 2012[3]). Public interest is underpinned by the fact that 22 000 people live on the island and would lose their place of residence if coastal protection were to cease. The State Water Act and its stipulations are the result of a political debate and represents, as such, a societal consensus (decided upon by democratically elected state parliamentarians).

4.2. Coastal protection responsibilities

4.2.1. Centralised federal state decision making

The German Constitution defines coastal protection as a "joint task" for all citizens (§91a), with associated responsibilities, including financial, distributed between three levels of government (federal [*Bund*], state [*Land*] and municipal [*Gemeinde*]) by federal and state laws.

Planning decisions relevant for coastal protection, e.g. on flood safety standards, are taken at the state level and implemented through these planning instruments. The ICZM and Master Plan require stakeholder consultation, as for example, ICZM plans bring together all coastal stakeholders to integrate planning in the coastal zone, including spatial planning, marine uses, biodiversity (e.g. Natura 2000 sites).

At the local level, two types of local authorities are relevant for coastal protection: WSAs and municipalities. WSAs are formalised as public corporations under the 1937 Federal Water Association Act. The law stipulates, first, compulsory membership for all landowners and municipalities within the assigned territory, below an individually defined contour line. The law also empowers WSAs to charge membership fees according to member benefits. The law further stipulates that WSAs can expropriate land for dike construction.

4.2.2. State and regional dikes

The federal state is thus responsible for the construction and maintenance of "state dikes", which "protect life and limb" (State Water Act §64). State dikes protect approximately 90%

of the total flood risk areas in Schleswig-Holstein up to the standard of 1-in-200-year event (MELUR, 2012[3]).

In the remaining flood risk areas, safety standards are lower (MELUR, 2012[3]). In these areas, "regional dikes" may be implemented, and are not required to meet the state flood safety standard of protection against the 1-in-200-year flood event. "Regional dikes" are the responsibility of either the state (on the islands) or local WSAs or local municipalities. These local authorities need to fund a portion of flood risk-reduction measures themselves, but may receive state funding of up to 90% of investment costs, and 30% of maintenance costs (see Section 4.3).

One difficult issue regarding classifying areas for protection by state dikes is that the key legal term underpinning this classification, "general welfare", is difficult to objectively define and measure. As mentioned above, state dikes protect nearly the entire North Sea coast, while several communities on the Baltic Sea coast have people and assets located below the 1-in-200-year flood event level with little or no protection. For example, the Baltic Sea communities of Behrensdorf (40 residents), Strande (90 residents) and Eckernfoerde (600 residents) all have residents living below the 1-in-100-year flood event level (MELUR, 2012[3]).

Communities not protected by measures under the responsibility of the state can receive further federal state support through two principle mechanisms. First, local authorities may apply for the reclassification of regional dikes to state dikes. Reclassification of a regional dike to a state dike can take place if the "purpose or significance" of the dike has changed (State Water Act §67). Second, grant funding from the federal state of up to 90% can be allocated for regional dike investment (strengthening) costs. Grant allocations are decided on a technical basis (as stipulated in the publicly available *Foerderrichtlinie*), in which the responsible federal state agency "decides at its own discretion and within the available budget" (MELUR, 2012[3]).

One reason for these differing approaches to state dike classification is the local interests, which may compete with the public interest in CPCFD. Often measures to improve CPCFD measures, such as state dikes, may interfere with these local interests, as, for example, large dikes may be detrimental to the attractiveness of a beach for tourism. For instance, the Baltic Sea community of Eckernfoerde rejected the offer in the 1970s to establish a state embankment in an attractive area for tourism. Currently, alternative options for flood defence are being explored and negotiated, which would be the responsibility of the city and eligible for 90% co-financing by the state.

4.2.3. State and local responsibilities for coastal erosion

According to state law in Schleswig-Holstein, coastal protection (in the public interest) on the islands is a state responsibility and on the mainland coast a local municipal responsibility. If not in the public interest, coastal protection is the responsibility of the people who benefit. Moreover, the Water Act also stipulates that those whose property is protected can be asked to contribute to the costs of construction and maintenance according to the extent of their benefit (§63(4)).

Thus, where beach nourishment occurs on designated islands, often to ensure island stability and continued existence, the *Land* handles funding and implementation. Extensive beach nourishment has been undertaken by the state at Sylt, as discussed above. In contrast, in areas where beach nourishment addresses other concerns, such as the attractiveness of an area for tourism, local beneficiaries must fund and implement the measures themselves.

For example, in the Baltic Sea community of Strande, erosion of the beach in front of a sea-wall is handled by the municipality.

In practice, determining whether erosion primarily increases flood risk or not has been controversial, and has led to conflicts between state and local levels. In Strande, the municipality has lobbied the state government to assume funding responsibilities for beach nourishment, arguing that despite the presence of a sea-wall, erosion does increase flood risk in the community.

4.3. Coastal risk-reduction financing arrangements

4.3.1. State and regional dike funding

Both the investment and maintenance costs of state dikes as well as regional embankments on islands are 100% funded by the federal state of Schleswig-Holstein (with co-financing from the federal government and the European Union [EU]). For regional dikes along the mainland coast, municipalities or WSAs may receive 90% funding of investment costs from the federal state, and need to cover 10% of these costs themselves. For maintenance of mainland regional dikes, responsible bodies receive a fixed yearly grant from the state. Even this relatively small contribution for investment costs remains a significant barrier in several communities on the Baltic Sea coast (Wolff, 2016[7]). For example, in the community of Strande, the municipality has not provided the approximately EUR 100 000 needed to receive around EUR 900 000 of federal state support for a coastal protection measure.

4.3.2. Federal funding instruments for coastal protection and adaptation

Federal state investment expenditures are funded in part by the federal government and the EU. The EU co-finances 50% of CPCFD measures. At the federal level, the *Bund* pays for coastal planning, as well as 70% of investment costs for CPCFD. The *Land* must pay the remaining 30% of the investment costs for coastal protection measures. Maintenance is financed 100% by the state.

The principle federal instrument for coastal protection funding is the Joint Task for the Improvement of Agricultural Structures and Coastal Protection (GAK). The GAK reimburses 70% of investment costs for coastal protection measures, as mentioned above, paid out as grants to the federal states, and not otherwise covered by EU funding. Within the GAK, a special instrument (*Sonderrahmenplan*) to speed up implementation of coastal protection due to climate change risks was established in 2009. This provides an additional combined EUR 25 million for all coastal federal states annually until 2025 (EUR 550 million total) on the condition that the coastal federal states spent a total of EUR 109 million the previous year (BMEL, 2013). In the years 2015-17, around EUR 8 million were distributed annually to the federal state of Schleswig-Holstein through this instrument for coastal protection (BEL, 2018[6]). EU funding of the GAK itself has varied between 5% and 13% annually (BMEL, 2013).

Since 1962, spending on coastal protection in Schleswig-Holstein amounts to EUR 2.73 billion, with EUR 1.84 billion spent on coastal protection investment and another EUR 862 million of federal state funds on maintenance costs. Since the 2001 Master Plan, total spending is EUR 600 million, with roughly half coming from the federal state, 37% from the federal level (Bund), largely from GAK funds, and another 13% from the EU (MELUR, 2012[3]).

4.3.3. Local funding instruments

At the local level, municipalities are required to fund 10% of coastal flood risk-reduction measures through their general budget. WSAs can raise funds for coastal flood risk reduction through membership fees. However, these are generally not sufficient to cover the 10% of investment costs, e.g. for building new dikes or upgrading existing ones, and are only used for maintenance costs. Further, the state gives a yearly grant for maintenance.

Currently, WSAs face financial challenges in providing adequate coastal flood risk-reduction measures. First, revenue generation is insufficient to finance dike reinforcement and maintenance because the defined areas for fee collection are too small and the fees are too low (Wolff, 2016). Second, even where WSAs are empowered by the law to collect fees, their rights have been challenged. This has been particularly the case in urban areas, where the definition of beneficiaries of protection measures by the WSA has been contested with several lawsuits initiated in urban areas.

Figure 4.1 depicts the coastal decision-making and public finance responsibilities in Schleswig-Holstein. The German federal system distributes responsibilities regarding coastal risk across several levels of governance, and funding responsibilities come from EU, federal, state and local levels, the latter covering both municipal taxes and WSA fees. Some responsibility for funding is put on local entities, i.e. municipalities or WSAs.

Figure 4.1. Coastal governance and financing in the German federal state of Schleswig-Holstein

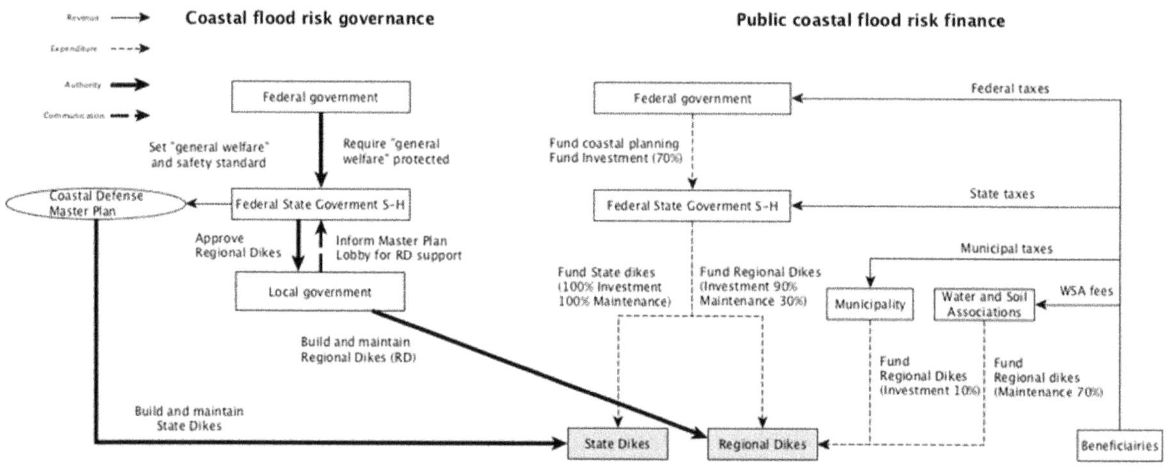

Strengths and weakness of current arrangements

As shown in Figure 4.1, institutional arrangements regarding coastal risk and adaptation distribute responsibilities across different levels of government. Decision-making responsibilities regarding coastal risk are largely centralised with the federal state, though local authorities in some Baltic Sea communities also take on these responsibilities. Funding responsibilities, particularly for coastal protection, also lie largely with the federal state, while it also receives funding from the federal government and the EU. In addition, local-level funding instruments, e.g. the WSA levy, also have a legal basis in state law, and provide a funding source, albeit relatively small.

Coastal protection measures and planning instruments addressing SLR entail a mix of protection measures, both hard and soft, or nature-based, as discussed in Chapter 2. Due to the increasing strain, particularly on local authorities to invest in and maintain protection measures not owned and operated by the federal state, private individual adaptation measures may also become more important in the future (see Chapter 2). Some of the strengths and weaknesses of the mixed institutional arrangements are discussed below, with a large share of responsibility centralised with the federal state, and local authorities taking on responsibility for dike maintenance and combating coastal erosion, particularly in Baltic Sea communities.

4.3.4. Federal state co-ordination and flexibility to address sea-level rise and uncertainty

One strength of the relatively centralised federal state approach is that it has allowed Schleswig-Holstein to address adaptation in a co-ordinated way across most of its coastline. The Master Plan process, as a planning instrument, introduced a co-ordinated approach to SLR incorporating SLR into the safety standards and protection design height determinations. Further, the Master Plan also addressed the uncertainties associated with mid- to long-term sea-level rise in a consistent and coherent manner for the majority of the coastline, as the buffer built into dike upgrades by flattening the outer slope and widening the crest of existing dikes. This will allow future coastal planners to adjust dike upgrades and dike heightening as information on how SLR is progressing becomes available in the future.

A further strength of the centralised aspects of Schleswig-Holstein's approach involves the ability to prioritise dike upgrades across different segments of the coastline and thus take efficiency and equity into consideration in state spending on coastal risk reduction. Public adaptation budgets in particular, and public infrastructure budgets more generally, are strained, thus decisions on coastal risk and adaptation need to carefully consider project prioritisation. The centralised approach of the federal state Master Plan allows for dike upgrading prioritisation based on engineering criteria, e.g. flow rate from overtopping event, as well as socio-economic criteria such as exposed people and assets.

In contrast, one potential weakness of the current arrangements, in the context of increasing SLR risks and associated costs, is that focus remains largely on hard protection measures. The main reason for this is historical. Hard defences have been put in place in reaction to major past flooding events, in particular, at the North Sea. As a result, more than 350 000 people (on both the North Sea and the Baltic Sea coasts) live in flood-prone coastal lowlands behind embankments. Relocation of these people, their assets and the infrastructure is neither feasible nor enforceable (nor is the need to do so inevitable due to available technical options). Further, state legislation and planning instruments shaping public decision making on coastal risk and adaptation to sea-level rise focuses on a "security" approach. The current legislative framework, as well as the historical legacy of major CPCFD works has, thus, committed the federal state to protect large parts of the North Sea coast at ever increasing cost. For the communities where no state responsibilities exist, financing coastal risk reduction is already burdensome, even with federal state support, and financial burden of pursuing hard protection options is likely to become overwhelming with rising seas, even though local communities may receive 90% co-financing for CPCFD investments from the state.

4.3.5. Local barriers to adaptation to sea-level rise

As described above, in those coastal communities where state obligations (i.e. state embankments, regional embankments and beach nourishment on islands) do not prevail, decision making and funding responsibilities regarding coastal risks remain with local authorities, i.e. either municipalities or WSAs, and thus entail some degree of fiscal autonomy for local authorities.

A potential strength of such an arrangement is that it embodies the subsidiary principle, locating decision making with local actors best-placed to understand the interests of the community. In practice, however, local authorities, i.e. municipalities or WSAs, currently struggle to adequately address coastal flood risk, a situation that is likely to worsen under SLR. Municipalities have often been unwilling to finance CPCFD measures out of their general budgets, even when required investments consist of only 10% of project costs with the remainder being covered by the federal state. Local WSAs are empowered under the law to determine fees charged, and control these revenues themselves. That is, they do not pay into more aggregated funds. However, while the level of fees collected by WSAs vary widely, fees collected generally remain too low to fund 10% of investments. Moreover, in some coastal communities, WSAs are not active at all (Wolff, 2016).

An apparent weakness of the current arrangements with respect to local-level adaptation is a lack of transparency in central government funding decisions, e.g. that decisions are taken on a case-by-case basis. This can act as a barrier to mobilising local-level funding. Such a lack of transparency can lead to the perception of unfairness in federal state funding allocation, and inhibit local communities from collectively funding their own adaptation. For example, the key concept of "general welfare" in federal state law determines the respective responsibility of beneficiaries or the federal state to pay for coastal protection, and is somewhat ambiguous. As discussed above, the definition of "general welfare" is not made explicit in state law, and, determining whether a specific project fulfils this criterion is done on a case-by-case basis. Thus, the process of state dike (re)classification has led to the perception among Baltic Sea communities of a lack of fairness in the allocation of state funds for coastal risk reduction. This perception makes the task of local fundraising for CPCFD more difficult because local communities are unwilling to contribute funds when they perceive that other communities are unfairly receiving high levels of state support.

Another weakness of the current arrangements is the lack of co-ordination between associations, which can also act as a barrier to higher fees, and thus greater revenue generation for the WSAs. Higher fees for one WSA can induce households or businesses to leave an area if fees become too high. Moreover, differences in fees between jurisdictions has exposed the WSAs to lawsuits, several of which have successfully challenged the beneficiary definitions used by the WSAs to assess fees (Wolff, 2016).

In order to address these issues, several mechanisms are in place to support co-ordination from the WSAs to higher levels of government in the development of state plans. First, the ICZM concept underpinning Master Planning in Schleswig-Holstein ensures that there is a process in place in which the preferences and interests of local communities are heard. The long-standing WSAs dedicated to coastal risk provide an effective voice for local interests regarding coastal risk, compared to municipalities, who are responsible for a much wider range of issues facing local communities. Second, specific channels for the WSAs or municipalities to apply for federal state support to address coastal risk consist of grant application mechanisms. Strengthening these mechanisms, through knowledge sharing with local authorities, can address the barriers discussed above, and further enable local-level adaptation.

4.4. Conclusions

Summarising, significant historical damages and more frequent large storm surge events have led to institutional arrangements centralising decision-making responsibilities regarding coastal risks and adaptation, particularly on the North Sea coast of Schleswig-Holstein. Such an approach can improve coastal risk reduction and adaptation efficiency, e.g. by prioritising dike upgrades based on hydrodynamic modelling and socio-economic criteria. Further, the centralised approach allowed this state to include flexibility in hard protection measures (i.e. dike crest widening) to account for SLR uncertainties.

Current institutional arrangements, however, focus federal state interventions largely on hard protection measures, and a "security" approach underlies legislation shaping public decision making on coastal risk and adaptation to sea-level rise. As such, hard protection is likely to continue to be implemented where dikes already exist. Coastal protection planning is implemented through an ICZM concept, with an Advisory Council that convenes stakeholders at all levels, and thus provides space for consultation with coastal communities. An important component of these consultations is to increase awareness regarding rising risks due to SLR, and enable communities to avoid increasing exposure by developing in high-risk areas. Yet, local communities where no state CPCFD responsibilities prevail, located mainly but not only at the Baltic Sea, decide on, and partly (10%) fund, their own risk-reduction measures and safety standards. Such communities are unlikely to be able to address increasing coastal risk under SLR because protection is costly, and other collective measures such as retreat are, especially in the affected local communities, highly controversial.

As noted in Chapter 2, transformational change towards a consideration of a broader range of adaptation measures, and coastal adaptation pathways, is difficult due to local considerations, including short-term economic interests, and other public funding obligations that strain the budgets of municipalities, e.g. childcare provision. Nonetheless, mechanisms for local-level participation in federal planning should continue to be supported in concert with the ICZM concept and practice. Indeed, further support for the WSAs dedicated to coastal flood and erosion risk provide a potentially effective voice for local interests regarding coastal risk. A number of existing instruments, e.g. the committee on ICZM, formal environmental impact assessment procedures and a regional conference prior to Master Plan adoption, are available to local communities for participation. Support, and uptake of the mechanisms by which they can participate in, for example, Master Planning processes, in addition to other channels for accessing state support facilitates an integrated approach to coastal risk, particularly at the Baltic Sea. Such instruments may also facilitate a broader approach to adaptation, as local communities require adaptation solutions that can balance a number of interests, e.g. attractiveness for tourism, as well as flood safety and erosion, with investment costs that are often beyond their ability to fund themselves.

Finally, while coastal risk reduction is implemented by federal states in Germany, difficulty in raising sufficient funds for reducing coastal flood risk is likely to lead to an increasing financial burden on the national tax base. As SLR increases coastal risks in Germany, difficulty in raising funds for ongoing maintenance and repair of existing coastal defences could lead to the effectiveness of coastal protection dropping below current standards. This is, in turn, likely to lead to a growing burden on emergency management to deal with increasing frequency of flooding events and other ongoing impacts of rising seas, which in turn means increasing costs for the general tax base, especially if risks become uninsurable. Thus, achieving effective, efficient and equitable adaptation to SLR is in the interest of Germany's coastal populations as well as the country as whole.

References

BEL (2018), *GAK Rahmenplan 2015-2018*, Bundesministerium für Ernährung und Landwirtschaft. [6]

BMU (2010), "Report on the implementation of integrated coastal zone management in Germany: National ICZM report". [5]

BMUB (2017), *Germany's Seventh National Communication on Climate Change*, Federal Ministry for the Environment, Nature Conservation, Building and Nuclear Safety, Berlin, https://unfccc.int/files/national_reports/annex_i_natcom_/application/pdf/26795831_germany-nc7-1-171220_7_natcom_to_unfccc.pdf. [1]

MELUR (2012), "General Plan Kustenschuetz Schleswig-Holstein Fortsetzung 2012. Umwelt und ländliche Räume des Landes Schleswig-Holstein (MELUR), Land Schleswig-Hostein". [3]

Sterr, H. (2008), "Assessment of vulnerability and adaptation to sea-level rise for the coastal zone of Germany", *Journal of Coastal Research*, Vol. 242, pp. 380-393, http://dx.doi.org/10.2112/07A-0011.1. [4]

von Storch, H. and K. Woth (2008), "Storm surges, perspectives and options", *Sustainability Science*, Vol. 3/1, pp. 33-43, http://www.academia.edu/2046785/Storm_surges_perspectives_and_options (accessed on 13 February 2019). [2]

Wolff, C. et al. (2016), "Effects of Scale and Input Data on Assessing the Future Impacts of Coastal Flooding: An Application of DIVA for the Emilia-Romagna Coast", *Frontiers in Marine Science*, Vol. 3, p. 41, http://dx.doi.org/10.3389/fmars.2016.00041. [7]

Chapter 5. Coastal infrastructure realignment and salt marsh restoration in Nova Scotia, Canada

This chapter describes a project to realign a section of the North Onslow dike near Truro, Canada. This project was intended to achieve the multiple goals of reducing dike maintenance costs, enhancing protection of public and private infrastructure, and enhancing resilience to climate change through the restoration of a coastal flood plain.

This chapter was written by Kate Sherren, School for Resource and Environmental Studies, Dalhousie University, Halifax; Tony Bowron, Department of Environmental Science, Saint Mary's University, Halifax and CB Wetlands and Environmental Specialists (CBWES Inc.), Terrance Bay; Jennifer M. Graham, CB Wetlands and Environmental Specialists (CBWES Inc.), Terrance Bay; H.M. Tuihedur Rahman, Department of Geography and Environmental Studies, Saint Mary's University, Halifax and School for Resource and Environmental Studies, Dalhousie University, Halifax; and Danika van Proosdij, Department of Geography and Environmental Studies, Saint Mary's University, Halifax.

5.1. Context

Canada has the world's longest coastline, bordering three oceans, and is thus highly exposed to sea-level rise (SLR) (Lemmen and Warren, 2016). Approximately 38% of Canada's population lives within 20 km of a coast (Manson, 2005). Climate impacts and risks vary across the three coasts in Canada (Lemmen et al., 2016). The Arctic coast makes up 70% of Canada's shoreline, comprising mostly small villages of largely indigenous inhabitants, where sea levels are expected to drop, but where livelihoods and cultures will be affected by declining sea ice, melting permafrost, and coastal erosion and instability. The Pacific coast is dominated by the large population centres of Vancouver and Victoria, both located in the Fraser lowland area that is expected to see the highest relative SLR for the region. Lemmen and Warren (2016) note, however, that the Pacific region faces higher vulnerability to storm surges than SLR.

The Atlantic coast hosts a few small cities but many towns and villages, including unincorporated shoreline developments, all expected to be affected by and vulnerable to SLR and increasingly extreme weather events (Lemmen and Warren, 2016). Examples of climate adaptation planning include especially vulnerable places, such as Les Îles-de-la-Madeleine in the Gulf of St. Lawrence, which has no alternative but to engage in coastal retreat (McClearn, 2018). Nova Scotia is another jurisdiction with significant exposure to SLR, and numerous local innovations. This chapter describes one such project in Nova Scotia, a dike realignment and tidal wetland restoration project that was largely achieved because of its alignment with government policies unrelated to climate, such as wetland compensation and dike divestment.

5.2. Nova Scotia: A coastal jurisdiction

Nova Scotia is a Canadian province perhaps vulnerable to SLR due to its geography and geologic history. The province's 55 000 km^2 are dominated by an isthmus and the large island of Cape Breton (~10 000 km^2), along with thousands of smaller islands. All of the province is located within 67 km of the coast (Chesworth, 2016). There are 13 different coastal ecosystems in Nova Scotia, from the expansive intertidal mudflats and salt marshes of the Bay of Fundy coast to erosive cohesive bluffs on the Northumberland coast (Savard, van Proosdij and O'Carroll, 2016), to complex rocky shores of the Atlantic coast. Its ~7 600 km coast is highly corrugated, with a complex drainage pattern including tens of thousands of lakes and wetlands, its climate is temperate, and it is relatively low-lying, peaking at 536 metres in Cape Breton Highlands National Park.

Geologically, like the rest of the Atlantic provinces, Nova Scotia is undergoing crustal subsidence, or glacial isostatic adjustment, dipping as more northerly and central areas of Canada spring back from released pressure after glaciation (Greenan et al., 2015). Richards and Daigle (2011) project that by 2100 Nova Scotia will become warmer but also wetter and with precipitation coming more frequently via extreme events. Relative sea-level rise projections (incorporating vertical crustal movement) based on the RCP 8.5 scenario of the 5th Assessment Report of the IPCC (2013), modelled by James et al. (2014) predict an upper bound of 1.30 m (median 0.90 m) by 2100. In the upper Bay of Fundy, these projections will most likely be close to an upper bound of 1.20 m due to amplification of tidal range that is also occurring (Greenberg et al., 2012). This area already has the highest tides in the world. In the provincial capital of Halifax, this is projected to result in extreme wave events during storms under all climate scenarios tested (Xu and Perrie, 2012).

Nova Scotia is already seeing the effects of subsidence, independent of climate-driven change; estimates of increases from the Marine Environmental Data Service range from 24 cm to 32 cm per century across four coastal communities in the province (CBCL Limited, 2009). Increases in extreme weather events and storm surges are of primary concern to coastal residents and decision makers in the province (Rapaport, Starkman and Towns, 2017).

Nova Scotia's coasts are sites of long human occupation. Nova Scotia's first people, the Mi'kmaq, relied on coastal settlements for fishing in the spring and summer, moving inland to hunt for food and furs in the fall and winter (Hornborg, 2008). Records of early contact with European explorers and fishers around the busy Atlantic coast date back to the 1500s, but it was in the 1600s that permanent French settlers arrived, later to be called Acadians. Acadians and later settlers converted most of the rich coastal wetlands of the Bay of Fundy coast to farmland by constructing dikes including one-way drains that allow freshwater to flow out at low tide but close at high tide to keep salt water out (called *aboiteau(x)*) (Bleakney, 2004; Butzer, 2002). Diking practices, combined with contemporary development activities (i.e. causeway construction), resulted in the conversion and loss of nearly 85% of tidal wetlands in the Bay of Fundy (Hanson and Calkins, 1996).

Coasts remain a critical part of Nova Scotia's identity and economy. The province has only 920 000 inhabitants, 40% of whom live in the capital area of the Halifax Regional Municipality, and over 60% of whom live within 20 km of the coast (CBCL Limited, 2009). Though most (77%) of the coast is undeveloped, it is also mostly privately owned (87%) and there is significant pressure in and near its many ports, harbours and estuarine settlements like Truro (CBCL Limited, 2009). Nova Scotia grew from the coast inward, and most development flanks coastal roads. While a few industries important to gross dometic product (GDP) rely specifically on coastal resources (e.g. agriculture, fisheries, shipping), most industries rely on coastal infrastructure such as transportation networks and the utilities such as powerlines that tend to follow them (CBCL Limited, 2009). As transportation infrastructure improves, commuting time decreases, expanding development outward from urban centres and putting additional pressure on coastal areas (Millward, 2005).

Nova Scotia's coastal residents are also vulnerable demographically, in part due to aging in rural areas (Gibson, Fitzgibbons and Nunez, 2015), but also due to seasonal population changes: summer amenity in-migration (due to relatively cheap waterfront) and winter out-migration (snowbirds; Northcott and Petruik, 2011). Seniors (those older than 65) are the fastest growing demographic group in Nova Scotia, comprising 15% of the population overall (CBCL Limited, 2009), but more than a quarter and sometimes over 30% of the population in many rural, coastal places, because of lower birth rates, youth out-migration, retiree influxes (including returnees) and lengthening life spans. (Krawchenko et al., 2016; Coulombe, 2006; Newbold, 2008; Foster and Main, 2017). These older residents are often dependent on services that are themselves vulnerable to SLR (Manuel et al., 2015).

Coastal protection in Nova Scotia has to date been dominated by "hard" solutions, such as dikes, berms and shoreline armoring (van Proosdij, Perrott and Carrol, 2013), but these solutions are beginning to fail under SLR and storm surges (Grieve and Turnbull, 2013; CBCL Limited, 2009). In line with growing global attention to ecosystem- and nature-based alternatives to reinforcing hard infrastructure (Narayan et al., 2016; Cheong et al., 2013; Harman et al., 2013), small-scale experiments in living shorelines and salt marsh restoration have been underway locally. Setbacks or "managed retreat" remain uncommon, in part due to local resistance, as described in Box 5.1 (Savard, van Proosdij and O'Carroll, 2016).

Box 5.1. Local resistance to coastal retreat

Local resistance to new forms of adaptation were apparent after the failure in a storm of a natural cobble barrier that has protected a coastal lagoon called Big Lake from the Atlantic Ocean for decades.

Owners of a dozen small homes and cottages around the lake, newly vulnerable to storm surges, have demanded that the natural barrier be rebuilt to protect their homes. The Nova Scotia Department of Natural Resources (NSDNR) had fixed a similar breach in 2010 but refused to do so again, instead recommending that residents "fortify their properties with protective walls, put their homes on stilts and seek coastal-flooding insurance" (CBC, 2018b) and noting the municipality's responsibility for having issued building permits.

While the cobble barrier was natural in origin, after being repaired it became seen by residents as built infrastructure. Over on the Bay of Fundy coast, hundreds of citizens of the small town of Hantsport recently demanded that the province rebuild a privately owned *aboiteau* (type of dike used for land reclamation). The previous one, which had been in a state of disrepair for many years, completely failed in December 2017, restoring the natural hydrology to the system.

Sources: CBC (2018b), "Hantsport residents tell province to fix dam instead of raising road", https://www.cbc.ca/news/canada/nova-scotia/hantsport-residents-tell-province-to-fix-dam-instead-of-raising-road-1.4779312.

The Nova Scotia Department of Agriculture (NSDA) is responsible for the management and maintenance of the province's 260 *aboiteaux* and 241 km of dikes. The resource (human, financial) and engineering requirements to maintain and upgrade this infrastructure stock in order to withstand SLR exceeds the department's current capacity. The NSDA is mandated to protect agricultural landscapes, but a significant portion of the 17 400 ha of land it protects is now used for non-agricultural practices and developments. Along with a number of other government departments, the NSDA is prioritising which dikelands could potentially be decommissioned (breached) and restored to salt marsh (Bowron et al., 2012; van Proosdij, Perrott and Carrol, 2014). In some of these cases, where built assets would still require protection, the construction of new, shorter, dikes built to modern specifications (including SLR projections) is being considered (MacDonald et al., 2010).

Reducing dike infrastructure and restoring provincially significant wetlands has additional benefits beyond ensuring the protection of core agricultural areas and critical infrastructure. These include climate mitigation benefits, in terms of sequestered carbon in salt marsh, often called "blue carbon" (McLeod et al., 2011), as well as climate adaptation benefits (Wollenberg et al., 2018). Nine such restorations have been carried out in Nova Scotia since the first at Cheverie in 2005 (CBC, 2010), including five culvert replacements and four dikes breached, covering a total of 98 ha. A further nine are pending or in construction (five dikes, four roads) representing an additional 338 ha.

The small town of Advocate Harbour provides a useful example of the sensitivities that exist in discussions of dike futures, which so many Nova Scotia towns will have to face in the coming years. The NSDA held a meeting in early 2018 to discuss the future of the agricultural dike that protects numerous homes and businesses in Advocate Harbour (Cole, 2018). Local preferences are strongly for dike reinforcement. One citizen said, "I feel the best option is to fix the dike [sic] … We have to keep our community intact as much as possible and protect our way of life so people can continue to live in Advocate and know that it's going to be a safe place."

Big Lake, Hantsport (Box 5.1) and Advocate Harbour all demonstrate citizen preferences for government intervention with hard options to maintain the *status quo*. This delays difficult decisions to retreat strategically in preparation for what is to come (Sherren, in press). Yet, compared with setback options, investments in hard infrastructure are more expensive and the negative consequences worse if those defences were to fail. Moreover, investment in hard options encourages ongoing development in high-risk areas, as expressed in the quote above, making setback options ever more challenging. Such public sentiments represent – along with limited government budgets – the biggest barrier to coastal adaptation in the region.

5.3. Truro case study: The North Onslow Marsh

Flood risk associated with SLR is a significant driver for action in the case study of the North Onslow Marsh, in Truro, Nova Scotia. Truro is a small regional centre of 12 000 residents located on the floodplain of the Salmon River that flows into Cobequid Bay (Bay of Fundy), and that floodplain is extensively diked: first for agriculture, but now protecting residential, commercial and transportation infrastructure. Even without SLR and storm surges, Truro experiences frequent and severe flooding from the co-occurrence of rainwater accumulation, high tides and ice jams. The region has suffered at least annual floods as far back as records have been kept (CBCL Limited, 2017). None of these events seems to have dampened enthusiasm for floodplain development in the town, meaning repeated exposures for "schools, senior homes and residences ... access roads, commercial areas and industries" (CBCL Limited, 2017). In recent years, research on emergency management has included Truro as a case study (O'Sullivan et al., 2013; Grieve and Turnbull, 2013).

Figure 5.1. Map of North Onslow marsh body

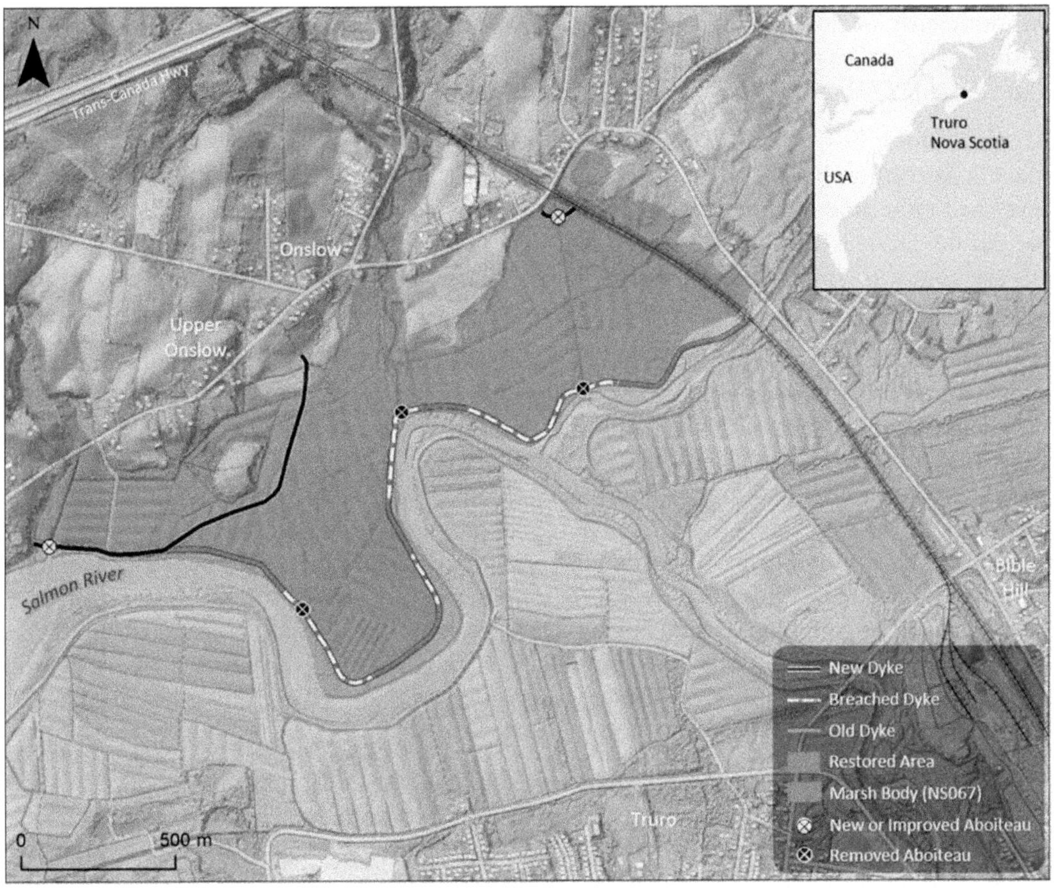

Notes: The North Onslow marsh body being modified (grey), with area to be restored (blue), *aboiteaux* to be removed (black) and new/improved (white), old dike (blue with dotted lines where to be breached), and new dike (black lines).

Source: Jahncke, R. and W. Flanagan (year), Saint Mary's University Department of Geography and Environmental Studies.

While agricultural dikelands dominate the flood plain on which Truro is built, the region is no longer dominated by agricultural employment. In 2016, natural resource industries comprised only 2-4% of employment, dominated instead by retail, healthcare, manufacturing and education sectors (Statistics Canada, 2017). This is reflected in a decline in active farming and the increased abandonment, or "fallowing", of dikelands.

Examinations of Truro's persistent flooding problems and potential solutions were carried out in 1971, 1983, 1988, 1997 and 2006, each inspired by significant flood events. Consistent with the prevailing "command and control" (*sensu* Holling and Meffe, 1996) approach of the time, all of the resulting reports focused on "hard" solutions to the problem. These included raising and strengthening dikes; constructing runoff storage dams, a causeway/tidal dam to "cordon off" Cobequid Bay, or ice control berms; and, approaches to improve drainage and reduce sedimentation such as viaducts, channel straightening and dredging (CBCL Limited, 2017). A significant challenge to addressing this issue has always been the cost involved: Truro and the county of Colchester have relatively healthy balance sheets, but the province's Financial Condition Index suggests they both have inadequate capital reserves relative to the age of their assets, suggesting they may not be able to afford to replace or improve them (NSDMA, 2017). The available technology at the time of those earlier reports, however, made it impossible to distinguish between the various causes of flooding. More recently, efforts to model the river system in combination with the stormwater system has demonstrated the utility of a holistic approach (El-Sharif and Hansen, 2001).

Tropical Storm Leslie in 2012 fuelled a severe September flood in Truro that changed the local conversation (CBC, 2012). Until then, despite the history of flooding, the municipal level had paid little attention to the issue: there existed simply engineering specifications for stormwater such as culvert sizing and new development regulations. The provincial government was considered responsible for the integrity of the dikes on which the region's safety depended.

In that fall 2012 flood, a dike on the North River breached in several places, and politicians and affected citizens alike called for repairs and reinforcement to the dike system (i.e. building it higher) (Hand, 2012). The high school was evacuated and the media shared stories of evacuated residents who live behind dikes, all apparently unaware that the infrastructure was never designed to protect non-agricultural land uses (Tutton, 2012). The breached dike was privately owned and built, but protected numerous businesses, including an important local employer. The province performed repairs for emergency management purposes (Canadian Press, 2012), given that more rain was in the forecast, but the responsibility for ongoing maintenance of this dike was unclear. This flood inspired the creation of a Joint Flood Advisory Committee for the county of Colchester, town of Truro, and Millbrook First Nation, including representation from citizens and provincial government departments.

A comprehensive flood risk study of Truro was commissioned by the Joint Flood Advisory Committee. The consultants developed a set of hydrodynamic computer models to understand the relative influences of rainfall, river hydrology, tides, sedimentation and ice movements using detailed terrain maps derived from Lidar, bathymetric surveys, field measurements and imagery from multiple aerial platforms (Marvin and Wilson, 2016). Climate change projections were explicitly modelled out to 2100. Once these dynamics were understood, which suggested particular sensitivity of the system to rainfall volumes, several dozen flood mitigation options and combinations were modelled. These options were ranked using stakeholder-derived human, land-use and infrastructure priorities (Table 5.1), as well as the protection level that each provided (including in extreme events), its initial and life cycle cost, the value of the land protected, and feasibility given environmental and permitting requirements (CBCL Limited, 2017). Priorities were elicited from targeted stakeholders, as well as at a public meeting with relatively low attendance according to several who were there.

Table 5.1. Stakeholder-derived priorities for the Truro Flood Risk Assessment

Rank	Human health and safety		Land use		Infrastructure services	
1	Life		Hospital		Water supply/treatment	
2	Emergency facilities		Residential properties		Communication	Power supply
3	Necessities of life	Livelihood			Senior homes	Potable water
4	Protection of environment from contamination		Schools		Roads	Wastewater treatment
5	Access to an area		Industrial lane properties		Bridges	
6	Social justice		Agricultural land		Dikes and *aboiteaux*	
7	Regional access routes		Retail properties			
8			Office uses	Recreational facilities		

Source: Adapted from CBCL Limited (2017), *Truro Flood Risk Study*, https://www.truro.ca/living-in-truro/truro-flood-risk-study.html.

It is notable that despite the area's strong farming culture, agricultural lands and dikeland infrastructure ranked low (6) on both land-use and infrastructure categories of priority for flood protection. This is likely because agricultural dikes were designed to allow some flooding; inundation of farmland every few years was expected and considered low risk and perhaps even positive for sediment deposition. By contrast, residential properties ranked high (2). The housing and infrastructure that was allowed to be built in the flood plain has not been due to financial incentives such as increased amenity, real estate value and thus increased taxes: the assessed value per square metre of single residential units is unrelated to either proximity to water or elevation. Rather, this at-risk development was a natural continuation of early development along shorefront and riverfront roads, and the desire by the municipalities to capitalise on the economic development opportunity of passing highway traffic.

The flooding problem in Truro is indeed complex: no single solution was found to be effective through the 2017 analysis. In fact, no measure under CAD 100 million was found to protect more than 20% of the priority areas, and most require costly earthworks (e.g. river straightening, floodway bypass), maintenance (e.g. dredging) and/or the continual spectre of infrastructure failure (dikes and *aboiteau*). Raising dikes was only modelled as effective at its most costly: when constructed as high as locally necessary (6 metres high in some areas, with commensurate design challenges given the footing width of such a dike), and when accompanied by specialised pumping (30% of priority areas protected for CAD 300 million). Additional *aboiteaux* were considered in the 1970s to hasten drainage, but after modelling found ineffective: while they may protect some areas from storm surges, they hold in rainwater that usually accompanies such storms as well as potentially increasing sedimentation. Modelling dike breaches actually reduced flood risk (CBCL Limited, 2017). Raising priority non-residential areas and roadways, and purchasing homes for removal or relocation, protects the most priority areas, but costs around CAD 200 million (as well as likely representing risks of civic conflict).

The analysis above suggests all that planning and regulatory processes should be designed to avoid further floodplain development. In addition, stormwater infiltration systems should be incorporated into new developments or when infrastructure is being replaced (e.g. permeable surfaces, perforating stormwater pipes). This was modelled to reduce flooding in priority areas by 30-40% at low cost.

The consultants also developed an infrastructure-based recommendation, ready to submit for available funding opportunities. The preferred structural scenario was floodplain restoration, including realigning dikes to re-establish the floodplain and thus its water storage capacity. While cost-effective and protecting 29% of priority areas, combining widening dikes with the construction of pumps to pull water out from behind dikes was expected to cost CAD 99 million. Alone, the dike realignment part was only modelled to reduce risk to priority areas by about 1%.

The full report was never publicised, though it can be found on the municipality of Truro's website and media covered its presentation by CBCL (the consultancy that undertook the study) employees at a coastal flooding conference in 2015 (CBC, 2015). A similar flood risk study by CBCL of a neighbouring jurisdiction had inspired the municipal council to seek to rezone a residential area as a high-risk flood zone to halt further development in the face of climate change. Citizens protested because of the possible detriment of real estate values to the 100 homes there (CBC, 2016). No municipality wanted to expose itself to a similar controversy.

5.4. Policy context for management of sea-level rise in Nova Scotia

The transitional space from ocean to land is a crowded jurisdictional space, so this section covers only the context necessary for understanding this case: climate, coasts, dikelands, floods and wetlands.

5.4.1. Climate adaptation

Canada's approach to climate adaptation varies across scales and provincial jurisdictions, and within jurisdictions between government portfolios (e.g. fishing, tourism, energy, infrastructure, transportation), as well as outside to the private sector. An example of inter-jurisdictional collaboration was the Atlantic Climate Adaptation Solutions Project, a 2009-12 partnership between Canada's four Atlantic provinces and the Climate Change Impacts and Adaptation Division of Natural Resources Canada (NRCan) that funded CAD 8.1 million of research on climate adaptation in the region (https://atlanticadaptation.ca). NRCan continues to provide leadership in this space federally, offering funding and instigating science reviews.

Provincially, the Environmental Goals and Sustainable Prosperity Act in 2007 laid the foundation for climate action with incitement to a range of climate mitigation, adaptation and education activities, including ambitious renewable energy targets (e.g. 25% by 2015, achieved; and 40% by 2020). A Climate Action Plan followed in 2009, committing to create a Climate Change Directorate within the NSDE to "work with provincial departments and municipalities, agencies, schools, and hospitals to reduce [greenhouse gas] emissions and ensure that effective adaptation measures are being implemented" (NSDE, 2009). This is a largely enabling and educating role, rather than a regulatory one. Nonetheless, Nova Scotia mandated the creation of municipal climate change action plans by 2014, making it the first province in Canada to require local-level climate action plans.

5.4.2. Coastal protection

All activities in the exclusive economic zone (i.e. 200 nautical miles from mean low tide mark) fall under federal jurisdiction. For example, the Department of Fisheries and Oceans is the central federal agency in charge of managing offshore activities, while Environment and Climate Change Canada protects water resources from pollution. Above that mean low tide mark, the province dominates. The NSDNR is an important provincial agency for coastal protection decision making with a jurisdiction that includes: beaches, crown lands and provincial parks, trails on lands and over watercourses. The NSDNR also holds responsibility for protecting and conserving endangered species and conserving wildlife and their habitats, except for fish species that are controlled by the Department of Fisheries and Oceans (DFO, 2009). The NSDA controls dikelands (see the next section).

"Nova Scotia has at least 45 pieces of international, federal, provincial, and municipal legislation that deal with its coastal resources" (CBCL Limited, 2009). Yet critical pieces of legislation are missing, such as to guide coastal protection in the province. A long delayed Coastal Strategy is currently in development by the NSDE (Grady, 2018). Decisions in some contexts to abandon or retreat some of this hard infrastructure at the coast in the face of SLR have been hindered by the perceived political costs. Private landowners control most coastlines and have certain roles and responsibilities in risk management decision making and implementation, but as has already been seen, the weak regulatory context creates ambiguity.

Dikelands

The NSDA is responsible for developing and managing dikes and dikelands under the Agricultural Marshland Conservation Act 2000 (Robinson, van Proosdij and Kolstee, 2004). The Minister of Agriculture can decide on developing, maintaining, improving and protecting dikes, dikelands and agricultural marshlands, subject to the approval of the Governor in Council. The Governor in Council can appoint an Agricultural Marshland Conservation Commission to advise the Minister of Agriculture about dike, dikeland and marshland protection and maintenance. This commission also hears appeals related to this act and approves by-laws made by the Marsh Body. The Minister of Agriculture can also appoint a marshland administrator who is responsible for performing administrative duties imposed by the act. Proposed changes to dikelands must also be cleared with the Mi'kmaq First Nations and the Nova Scotia Department of Communities, Culture and Heritage, which is responsible for archaeological resources – including Acadian dikelands themselves as well as other resources found in areas protected by dikes – via the Special Places Protection Act (1989) (NSDE, 2005).

Individual landowners play a significant role in the governance of dikelands. A marsh body is a collective of marshland owners who petition the Marshland Conservation Commission to be incorporated (almost like a small municipality) for a marshland section (an area of marshland that may be effectively dealt with as a unit in the construction and maintenance of works – the Agricultural Marshland Conservation Act, 2000). This body can acquire, sell and lease personal property, and can decide on constructing and repairing dikes at its own expense or in an agreement with the Minister of Agriculture. This body also makes by-laws, which are subjected to the approval of the commission.

A marsh body needs to have an executive committee to perform the administrative activities of the body, and assess and value marsh and dikelands. Notably, the chair and secretary of the committee are endowed with the authority equal to the mayor and treasurer of a town to decide on any activity (e.g. dike restoration, drainage maintenance). The executive committee is supervised by the Governor in Council, who can suspend the authority of the committee should the committee cause any permanent injury to the marsh and dikelands. The Governor in Council can, therefore, revert the activities and authority of the committee to the Marshland Conservation Commission. Moreover, the Agricultural Marshland Conservation Commission performs the marsh body's roles and responsibilities in the absence of an active marsh body (Office of the Legislative Counsel, 2000).

Wetlands

The NSDE has jurisdiction over identifying and protecting salt marshes as wetlands of special significance (Environment Act), and reversing historic wetland loss in the province with restoration (Wetland Conservation Policy). Part of the no-net-loss provincial Wetland Conservation Policy (2011) is the requirement that construction work that destroys wetland must be compensated, usually like with like (Austen and Hanson, 2007). A typical offset depends on the type and quality of wetland lost and gained. For instance, freshwater to freshwater compensation requires a 2:1 ratio, two hectares created or restored for every one lost, but it would likely be 4:1 for salt marsh replaced by fresh, or 1:1 for fresh replaced by salt. The most desirable compensation projects are salt marshes, as well as wetlands in parks or drinking water catchments, and restoration is more desirable than creation (as the latter often fails). These differences are due to the extent of coastal wetland or salt marsh losses in Nova Scotia, estimated at 85% on the Bay of Fundy (Hanson and Calkins, 1996).

The NSTIR has many such "compensation" transactions because of its road construction and infrastructure maintenance. Much such maintenance in the face of SLR involves raising infrastructure, which means going not only up, but also "out", to ensure stability, resulting in bigger project footprints. This only exacerbates the "coastal squeeze" underway on foreshore habitats because of coastal infrastructure (Pontee, 2013). The NSDNR is also interested in wetlands for the habitat functions it provides for waterfowl, for instance via the Eastern Habitat Joint Venture of the North American Waterfowl Management Plan.

Flood risk management

Although the federal government no longer holds direct dike and dikeland management responsibilities, it has played an important role in flood risk management. In 1975, the federal government initiated the Flood Damage Reduction Program (FDRP) in collaboration with all provincial and territorial governments (ECCC, 2013). The central objective of this programme was to identify and designate flood risk areas and to encourage the provincial governments not to build, approve or finance any new development in the designated zones. These agreements also aimed to discourage the provincial governments from intervening via "cost-ineffective" structural measures (e.g. dikes, dams) if preventive and non-structural options were available, like mapping or zoning, or if these structural measures were found to be cost-effective and supportive for non-structural measures. In addition, flood damage compensation has been strongly discouraged for any new development in the designated zones (ECCC, 2013).

Truro was one of the high-risk areas identified by the FDRP, but the town was informed after a 1988 study that it would only get one more damage payment after which those would cease. The FDRP was wound down in 1999 (de Loë and Wojtanowski, 2001). Other funds have filled the gap. Today, Public Safety Canada funds a CAD 200 million National Disaster Mitigation Program (2015-20), including disaster financial assistance arrangements, under a co-funding agreement between the federal and the provincial governments. This fund is administrated in Nova Scotia by the Emergency Management Office of the Department of Municipal Affairs (NSDMA), covering up to 50% of eligible provincial projects: flood risk assessment, flood mapping, flood mitigation planning and investment in non-structural and small-scale structural flood risk mitigation projects. The NSDMA also administers the federally funded New Building Canada Fund (also known as the Small Communities Fund), for municipalities and villages with a population of less than 100 000 to develop disaster risk-reduction infrastructures and utility infrastructures.

The federal government has an alternative funding scheme for promoting climate adaptation through influencing infrastructural development at the municipal level. The federal government launched the Gas Tax Fund in the 2005 federal budget as an *ad hoc* funding mechanism for municipal infrastructural development, which was made permanent in 2011 as a stable fund with an endowment of CAD 2 billion per year along with a yearly increment of 2%. This fund is distributed on a per capita basis with a minimum level of funding for least populated regions (0.75% of total fund), regulated under joint agreements between the federal and the provincial governments (Dupuis, 2016). Disaster mitigation is one of the 11 eligibility categories for federal infrastructural expenditure under this fund, including storm water and other utility infrastructures (NSDMA, 2015a). In order to access these funds, the federal government mandated that integrated community sustainability plans be developed by each municipality to guide the effective use of the funding (NSDMA, 2007), and Nova Scotia additionally requires a municipal climate change action plan. Not all municipalities have the in-house capacity to carry out such planning, so many of these plans were developed or facilitated by outsiders, such as consultants or academic teams (Warburton and MacKenzie-Carey, 2013).

Beyond the federal funds mentioned above, the NSDMA operates two other funding schemes for municipal infrastructure (NSDMA, 2015b):

1. The Flood Risk Infrastructure Investment Program (mentioned earlier) is a provincial government initiative to fund inland flood water management infrastructure studies and development programmes (e.g. river training, floodway improvement, flood intensity mitigation, floodwater contamination).
2. The Provincial Capital Assistance Program co-funds high-priority municipal infrastructure programmes to reduce the cost burden for municipal governments, including storm sewer systems.

In general, however, the government of Nova Scotia is concerned with freshwater flooding rather than coastal; there are no legislation, policies or processes yet in place to guide decisions around planning or retreat options (NSTIR Environmental Analyst).

Municipalities along the coastline in Nova Scotia hold important roles, responsibilities, power and authority in flood risk management given under the Municipal Government Act 1998. As directed in this act, every municipal government can develop municipal planning strategies, a document that contains a detailed layout of existing infrastructure and admissible future development along with other land-use practices (e.g. agriculture, recreation). Municipal governments can also enact land-use by-laws for the execution of the municipal planning strategy. However, municipalities are not required to put these strategies in place: because of very different resourcing and in-house skills, 40 out of 51 municipalities have developed comprehensive strategies, including Truro; the other 11 municipalities have only single-issue coverage (GNS, 2018). The plans are guided by a statement of provincial interest (NSDMA, 2016), which is a provincial government guideline managed by the Department of Municipal Affairs for developing the municipal planning strategies and land-use by-laws, covering five broad areas: 1) drinking water; 2) flood risk areas; 3) agricultural land; 4) infrastructure; and 5) housing.

The guidelines for flood risk areas are based on the erstwhile Nova Scotia-Canada FDRP, which identified high flood areas (NSDMA, 2016). Infrastructural development is highly discouraged in these high-risk areas under this guideline, although the enforcement of the guideline falls under the jurisdiction of the municipal governments (NSDMA, 1998). Since most of the coastal protection infrastructure (e.g. dikes, dams) and coastal public land (e.g. beaches, wetlands, crown lands) managements are vested in the provincial agencies, and agricultural marshland management is vested in the NSDA and the marsh bodies, none of the guidelines directly address coastal flooding. That said, a number of the municipal climate change action plans in the Bay of Fundy do include coastal protection infrastructure such as dikes, and even go so far as to reference foreshore and fringe marsh size requirements, so municipalities can wield considerable authority in coastal areas if they so choose.

At present, coastal flooding is not an insurable hazard covered by the majority of insurance companies, but in May 2018, The Co-operators became the first insurance company to cover coastal flooding and storm surge damages through its Comprehensive Water Policy. Such products require good risk mapping, which is only now becoming available, but an additional complication is that "flood-related losses are often directly attributable to under-investment in public infrastructure, poor asset management, obsolete building codes and ineffective land-use planning" as well as a lack of functioning wetlands. As the Truro case study demonstrates, however, the line between coastal and overland flooding is sometimes fuzzy.

Even with flood mitigation by homeowners and communities, insurance experts suggest the increasing expense of insurance products, and dwindling support or capacity for taxpayers to subsidise rebuilding when large-scale events occur, will require serious consideration of retreat options and other nature-based options (Moudrak et al., 2018). In fall 2017, the Insurance Board of Canada was asked to chair a working group by Canada's Minister of Public Safety, "charged with creating a roadmap for ensuring that flood risk is transferred from taxpayers to those who hold the risk". A potential move to increasing homeowner responsibility runs contrary to perceptions held by residents, as heard in towns like Big Lake, Hantsport and Advocate Harbour.

5.5. Dike realignment and salt marsh restoration at North Onslow

The Onslow-North River Dike Realignment and Tidal Wetland Restoration project was a collaboration between government, community, academic and industry partners. Initiated by the NSTIR in co-operation with the NSDA and the NSE, the primary purpose of the project was to create a "bank" of salt marsh "habitat credits" for offsetting the loss or damage to wetlands arising from future NSTIR infrastructure projects. Being part of the Bay of Fundy's Minas Basin, tidal influence within the Salmon River that runs past Truro extends upriver beyond the North Onslow (NS067) project site. The position of the site at the confluence of the Salmon River and North River creates complex patterns of water, sediment and ice movement, which result in high maintenance costs for dike and *aboiteau* infrastructure, the build-up of ice in winter, and an increased risk of flooding. As such, the project was also intended to:

- reduce ongoing dike maintenance costs for the NSDA by reducing the total length of dike and number of *aboiteaux*
- enhance the protection of both public and private infrastructure, as well as viable farmland
- reduce flood risk and enhance resiliency for climate change through the restoration of floodplain, one of several actions recommended by the 2017 Flood Risk Study (CBCL, 2017).

No residential buildings would need to be relocated under this strategy, but some small berms would need to be added to one property to ensure its protection. Access to some electrical transmission infrastructure will need to be maintained as the former dikeland is converted to foreshore marsh, as it would be too costly to move.

5.5.1. Governance

CB Wetlands and Environmental Specialists (CBWES), in partnership with Saint Mary's University and Queens University, was commissioned in December 2016 to develop a dike realignment and restoration design plan for the "northern parcel" of the Onslow-North River dikeland. The scope of work included working with the NSDA and the marsh body to determine the optimal location for new dikes and construction materials (e.g. "borrow pits"), identifying the location and size of breaches in the old dike, creating a restoration design for the tidal wetland, and anticipating habitat response to restoration. This component was financed by the NSTIR as part of the wetland compensation process.

In Nova Scotia, any proposed activity that has the potential to alter the boundaries of a marshland section for which the marsh body is incorporated requires consultation with and agreement by two-thirds majority vote of the marsh body, in accordance with the Agricultural Marshland Conservation Act (2000, c.22, s.13b). The marsh body engagement process expanded upon the consultation process as outlined in the Marshland Act, engaging with the members of the marsh body and bordering landowners and inviting them into the project design process. Consultation with Canadian National (CN) Rail and Nova Scotia Power was also necessary due to the presence of rail and power transmission infrastructure on the project site. Finally, an archaeological resource assessment was required.

At project initiation, the site was a mix of forage (hay, grazed) and fallow agricultural land. The NSDA could not afford to maintain the dike, and there was an *aboiteau* in need of replacing to remain functional. The majority of the dikeland property needed for the project was purchased by the NSTIR in 2016 in anticipation of the project. However, several parcels adjoining the floodplain had not been purchased. For these parcels, flood vulnerability was assessed and mitigation actions would be recommended as part of the design. Despite its agricultural origins, the site is complex for this kind of realignment: the CN Rail line defines its eastern border, the 1763 Onslow Island Cemetery is within its western boundary and a power transmission line dissects the site. Consultation with CN Rail and NS Power was necessary to address any potential risks to their respective infrastructure either through the inclusion of flood protection measures or their relocation, but were notified along with other landowners they were late to join the planning table.

Following consultation with NSDA staff and additional analysis of the marshland, which included site history, habitat conditions and hydrology, several preliminary dike alignments were drafted as a proof of concept to guide early planning and consultation. Various dike realignment and tidal wetland restoration design options were tested using Delft 3D hydrodynamic modelling software (including tidal, overland and river flows) and validated with the same field measurements of water levels and sediment transport as available to CBCL for its flood risk study. All such validation work is hampered by inadequate records; for instance, a lack of long-term tide gauges near the site. The closest permanent gauge operated by the Canadian Hydrographic Service is 200 km across the Bay of Fundy, in Saint John, New Brunswick; all other available tide gauge records come from short-term consulting or research projects.

5.5.2. Consultation

The intent was to collaboratively arrive at a realignment and restoration design that was not just accepted, but supported, by the marsh body. This was to be achieved through a series of community hall style meetings, a special topic meeting and "kitchen table" conversations with individual stakeholders. Prior to the initiation of this project, however, the Onslow Marsh Body was not active and so the first step in the process was to reactivate the group and provide it with the structure, information and tools needed to effectively participate. At the first meeting, the idea and rationale for the project was presented. The questions arising from the marsh body at this stage were about alternative solutions to the flooding problems, which were difficult to debunk given that the CBCL report was not yet publicly available. A second challenge was difficulty interpreting the flood modelling maps: when residents saw the modelled flood boundary under preliminary scenarios, they struggled to understand how rarely the water would reach that level given the hypertidal conditions of that site (Archer, 2013[1]).

Over the period of meetings, the most contentious issue proved to be the issue of mosquitoes. Concern was raised that the restoration to tidal wetland habitat would lead to an increase in mosquito populations like what was experienced in Moncton following the opening of the Petitcodiac tide gates (Gerwing et al., 2017). This was of particular concern to a landowner who ran a nearby tourist attraction. To address this issue, experts from the region were invited to discuss the process of monitoring for mosquito larva in their stormwater impoundments in fallow dikelands, and applying larvicide as necessary to limit mosquito levels. In addition, once predator populations became established in the salt marsh, they would eventually control mosquito populations, and effective drainage would ensure balance was maintained.

The marsh body's final meeting presented the proposed realignment design, answered any remaining questions and conducted a vote in accordance with the Marshland Act to vary the boundaries of the dike and by doing so allow the project to proceed. While adjacent landowners could attend, only marshland owners could vote. Each landowner gets a single vote, regardless of how much land they might own, and a two-thirds majority is needed. The Marsh Body Chair reported that the landowners appreciated that they were "sure giving us a lot of time to think about this." The vote passed unanimously, with two caveats: 1) that a pest-management protocol be developed as part of the project, including monitoring; and 2) that ongoing communication with the marsh body be maintained.

5.5.3. Design

With the successful marsh body vote and a final alignment selected, the technical specifications of the design could be finalised (Figure 5.1), which would mitigate concerns of the creation of additional mosquito breeding habitat, create healthy salt marsh ecosystems and hopefully reduce flood risk for Truro. The fundamental control on the structure and function of tidal wetland habitat is flooding with salt water (Mitsch and Gosselink, 1986; Neckles and Dionne., 2000). It is the hydroperiod (frequency and duration of tidal flooding) of a wetland that determines the area of marsh directly available as habitat, and thus useful as compensation credits. The first step of such design is modelling the outright removal of the barrier, in this case the dike, to see how the site would naturally flood. This also allows for the identification of features, areas or infrastructure that are likely to be at risk or negatively affected. Modifications to the design and the incorporation of mitigation measures (i.e. new dikes, ditching, amending land elevation) to alleviate these effects can then be explored and modelled.

For this project, it was determined that two new dikes would need to be constructed landward of the existing structure: 1) the primary dike (1 km) along the western end of the site to protect active marshland and the historic cemetery; and 2) a small dike in the eastern corner of the site to protect infrastructure owned by CN Rail. In addition, for effective flooding to occur, and to reduce standing water, which could serve as mosquito breeding habitat, a channel network would need to be created and the old dike breached in several places. Dike breach and channel widths were calculated using hydraulic geometry (Graham, 2012; Williams and Orr, 2002), and channel locations selected based on the channel network delineation and relict historic tidal channels identified in historic aerials. Three of the four existing *aboiteaux* would be eliminated, including the large three-barrel structure on McCurdy Brook, and a new *aboiteau* constructed within the eastern dike to ensure protection and drainage of low-lying lands above the rail line. LiDAR DEM, topographic surveys and several tide gauges deployed by CBCL in 2014 and CBWES in 2017 helped the design of the hydraulic network for the new marsh.

5.5.4. Implementation

The implementation of the above design is still underway. The archaeological phase one assessment, conducted in accordance with the Nova Scotia Special Places Protection Act under a Heritage Permit by a consulting firm, noted an artefact scatter at the northern end of the proposed inner dike footprint of a kind already recorded within the Maritime Archaeological Resource Inventory. No additional significant archaeological resources were identified in the area; however, as mentioned earlier, the inner dike was moved slightly to the east to avoid any potential damage to the 250-year-old cemetery situated on an upland portion of the marshland.

Monitoring will be extensive, as this realignment represents an important precedent. Although not yet provincially mandated, over the last 15 years, the NSTIR has funded baseline (pre) and 5-year post-restoration monitoring at all of its tidal wetland restoration sites. CBWES is responsible for data collection and analysis of changes in hydrological condition, vegetation, water quality, soils and sediments, marsh morphology, nekton biology, and marsh surface elevation change. Saint Mary's University will also track its geomorphological change, for instance monitoring sediment accretion using drones, as well as working to quantify the carbon sequestration potential represented by the restored salt marsh. It is also estimated that within 8-10 years post-breach, the restored North Onslow tidal wetland will be operating as a near optimum salt marsh habitat and regulating (e.g. acting as a storm buffer) ecosystem services.

While a comprehensive cost-benefit analysis (including in-direct ecosystem and flood mitigation benefits) was not performed for this project, the direct costs accounting currently available supports the North Onslow realignment as a cost-effective option. It is estimated that the dike realignment will result in approximately CAD 520 000 of savings (Table 5.2). Additional benefits such as carbon sequestration and flood mitigation will be empirically quantified as the project proceeds, and be used to inform future decisions. The current land value of the land protected is CAD 400 000, excluding utility (NS Power) and federal infrastructure (e.g. CN Rail).

Table 5.2. Direct costs of maintaining dike in place (including "topping" to predicted 2055 high-water levels) versus realignment of dike infrastructure and tidal wetland restoration

2018 CAD

Maintain status quo and top dike in place		Realignment of dike infrastructure	
Upgrade McCurdy's brook *aboiteau*	1 500 000	Land purchase (18 parcels, 92.5 ha)	798 000
Top 3.5 km of dike in place	500 000	Archaeology	71 559
Estimated ten-year standard maintenance	180 000	Earthworks and breach	625 000
		Feasibility, design and baseline	161 000
Total	2 180 000	Total	1 655 559

5.6. Outcomes and lessons learnt

This project remains under construction, so its effectiveness in reducing flood risks in Truro has yet to be tested. There are many uncertainties: the lag time involved in the re-establishment of the tidal wetland and its ability to play an effective buffer role; the impact of dike realignment on sedimentation patterns and ice movement; and how such changes will affect the dynamic hydraulic system in place. As with previous tidal wetland restoration projects undertaken by CBWES (Bowron et al., 2012), a comprehensive five-year post-restoration monitoring programme will help fill this gap in understanding. Despite the inability to reflect directly on the physical outcomes, it is possible to identify several other outcomes and lessons for governance of this kind of social and landscape change.

First, thanks to effective collaboration across scales of government, a lack of climate change or coastal protection policy did not hamper action toward climate adaptation in this case study. A number of pieces fell into place at the same time that allowed this project to be put forward as a potential solution to many problems, and allow multiple jurisdictions to work together. Marginal dikeland came up for sale at the same time as the NSTIR needed wetland credits to offset its construction work. The size of the projected salt marsh habitat restoration that would be involved (~93 ha) was particularly attractive to the NSDE, with its responsibility over the no-net-loss Wetland Policy. This allowed the NSDE to offer half the normal offset ratio to the NSTIR as is usually required. This agreement with the NSDE meant that the NSTIR could make the case for purchasing the dikeland at a price attractive to the landowner. The capital costs of the dike infrastructure protecting that marginal land were already problematic for the NSDA, and the department was already engaged in a prioritisation process for informing dikeland decisions such as maintenance, realignment or abandonment. In this case, realignment would reduce the length of dike to be maintained from 3 000 m to 1 250 m. The non-NSTIR half of the cost of the project could be provided by National Disaster Mitigation Program funds via the municipality, thanks to reasonable modelling evidence from the CBCL flood risk analysis that widening the dikes would contribute to the reduction of flood risk in Truro.

The above represents a positive outcome for wetland coverage, construction offsets, dike maintenance and landholder compensation. It is worth noting that this collaboration came about in part because of constrained budgets.

Climate adaptation is notably absent from that list of clear wins. This is because despite strong evidence of the utility of such approaches for flood and erosion protection, as well as potentially climate mitigation through sequestration, it is not yet known whether the restored marsh will prove adaptive to SLR in this complex setting. In the absence of strong policy, it is difficult to credit any of the above positive outcomes to government commitment around climate action. Yet, the NSDE was a critical guide to this process in more ways than the wetland offset agreement discussed above. The NSDE Climate Change Directorate has been working to change the culture in government around climate issues for many years, including running courses for government managers.

Even if the flood protection outcomes are uncertain, the value of the replicable process is not. As such, climate goals underlie the whole undertaking, and if successful, the project will serve as an important precedent. It is an important start on this long-term project of adaptation, and a relatively low-risk one, given that the project is already meeting so many other goals.

This project is not, of course, a no-risk option. Changing any one thing in a hydrologic system as dynamic as Truro's can lead to unexpected outcomes. The dike realignment design being used in this project has not been systematically modelled for its impacts on flood or public safety upstream of the predicted extent of penetration of tidal waters for 2100. For instance, it is possible that the change in hydrology resulting from this project could exacerbate sedimentation issues in the main river channel, alter local flood and drainage patterns, or adversely affect the behaviour of ice. Similarly, while an option may have performed well in terms of the per cent of overall priority areas where flood risk was mitigated, people may still be at risk in specific places. There is some indication from modelling of similar options by CBCL that a dike realignment project such as this one could shift some flood risk to other specific areas, such as low-income housing sites upstream. This remains to be seen, but is an important consideration.

Given the tendency to prefer *status quo* landscapes, this project represents an important opportunity to show Nova Scotia citizens what adaptation may look like, on the land and in public process. The social achievements of this project could lead to greater cultural change. This project created a marsh body organisation where none was previously active. It engaged that group in difficult conversations with a range of government representatives and researchers. The proponents listened meaningfully and made adaptations to their plan, including dike placement and adding monitoring for mosquitoes. The NSDE Adaptation Specialist noted that one thing that is lost by the fact that climate adaptation was not the explicit project goal, was the fact that this is the first time affected residents in Nova Scotia have voted for a managed retreat: basically sacrificing private land for ecosystem purposes.

It is possible that this project set an important precedent: it was quickly followed by a similar verdict about a managed realignment proposal on the Cornwallis River to the west. Such outcomes with informed, engaged citizens are a significant departure from recent headlines presented above about similar situations in Advocate Harbour, Hantsport and Big Lake. Effecting "public good" landscape changes of this type is a non-trivial social challenge. However, the marsh body came together, reviewed the options, asked questions and voted in favour of change. As the NSDE carries out public consultation for the long-awaited Coastal Strategy, projects like this one provide important leverage as well as a place for Nova Scotians to observe salt marsh restoration and the potential role it can play in adaptation. The comprehensive monitoring framework established will contribute to a growing database of pre- and post-empirical field data and visual representations of the changing landscape.

It is argued by many involved in this process that the Bay of Fundy and its erstwhile salt marsh ecosystem itself must be considered a stakeholder of such decisions. The salt marsh ecosystem that is restored may represent a range of ecosystem services, including fish nursery habitat, storm buffer and carbon sequestration through so-called "blue carbon".

The multifunctionality of wetlands that allowed other policies to be used to achieve this project. Ecosystem services may well be a useful way of exploring the costs and benefits of other such nature-based adaptation options (ICF, 2018).

There is a desire by the NSDA and other proponents of this project to carry out similar projects elsewhere in Nova Scotia, including on the south side of the Salmon River from the North Onslow project. That southern lobe of dikeland is closer to the town centre, as well as being more actively farmed. Additional creative approaches may be necessary where farmers are unwilling to sell land, such as the NSDA negotiating trades of dikeland parcels rather than simply buying out active producers, as one of its goals is to maintain agriculture where viable. The expansion of the dike realignment strategy may struggle in the absence of a strong provincial strategy and leadership on coasts and climate. Nonetheless, this project represents an important learning experience as well as precedent: an exemplar of the value of a genuine and patient consultation process.

References

Archer, A.W. (2013), World's highest tides: Hypertidal coastal systems in North America, South America and Europe", *Sedimentary Geology*, Vol. 284-285, pp. 1-25, https://doi.org/10.1016/j.sedgeo.2012.12.007.

Austen, E. and A. Hanson (2007), "An analysis of wetland policy in Atlantic Canada", *Canadian Water Resources Journal*, Vo. 32/3, pp. 163-178, https://www.tandfonline.com/doi/pdf/10.4296/cwrj3203163.

Bowron, T.M. et al. (2012), "Salt marsh tidal restoration in Canada's maritime provinces", In: Roman, C. and D. Burdick (eds.), *Tidal Marsh Restoration*, Island Press/Center for Resource Economics.

Canadian Press (2012), "Province to fix Truro-area dike, after all", *The Chronicle Herald*.

CBC (2010), "Acadian dikes breached near N.S., N.B. border", *CBC News*, https://www.cbc.ca/news/canada/new-brunswick/acadian-dikes-breached-near-n-s-n-b-border-1.939841.

CBC (2012), "Flooding widespread near Truro after rain pounds N.S.", *CBC News*, https://www.cbc.ca/news/canada/nova-scotia/flooding-widespread-near-truro-after-rain-pounds-n-s-1.1135675.

CBC (2015), "Truro flooding leads to ambitious study on coastal threats", *CBC News*, https://www.cbc.ca/news/canada/nova-scotia/truro-flooding-leads-to-ambitious-study-on-coastal-threats-1.2984728.

CBC (2016), "East Hants council votes to designate area as high-risk floodplain", *CBC News*, https://www.cbc.ca/news/canada/nova-scotia/shubenacadie-resident-flood-risk-1.3698616.

CBC (2018a), "Frustrations and finger pointing mount over damaged berm", *CBC News*, https://www.cbc.ca/news/canada/nova-scotia/frustrations-mounting-over-to-plan-to-repair-damaged-berm-1.4725945.

CBC (2018b), "Hantsport residents tell province to fix dam instead of raising road", *CBC News*, https://www.cbc.ca/news/canada/nova-scotia/hantsport-residents-tell-province-to-fix-dam-instead-of-raising-road-1.4779312.

CBCL Limited (2009), *The 2009 State of Nova Scotia's Coast - Technical Report,* Halifax, Nova Scotia.

CBCL Limited (2017), *Truro Flood Risk Study,* Town of Truro, https://www.truro.ca/living-in-truro/truro-flood-risk-study.html.

Cheong, S.-M. et al. (2013), "Coastal adaptation with ecological engineering", *Nature Climate Change,* Vol. 3, pp. 787-791, https://doi.org/10.1038/nclimate1854.

Chesworth, N. (2016), "Economic impacts of tourism in rural Nova Scotia", In: Matias, Á., P. Nijkamp and J. Romão (eds.), *Impact Assessment in Tourism Economics*, Springer International Publishing, Cham, Switzerland.

Cole, D. (2018), "Advocate Harbour residents concerned about future of dike protecting community", *Amherst News*, https://www.cumberlandnewsnow.com/news/local/advocate-harbour-residents-concerned-about-future-of-dike-protecting-community-183450.

Coulombe, S. (2006), "Internal migration, asymmetric shocks, and interprovincial economic adjustments in Canada", *International Regional Science Review,* Vol. 29, pp. 199-223, https://doi.org/10.1177/0160017606286357.

de Loë, R. and D. Wojtanowski (2001), "Associated benefits and costs of the Canadian Flood Damage Reduction Program", *Applied Geography,* Vol. 21/1, pp. 1-21, . https://doi.org/10.1016/S0143-6228(00)00013-8

DFO (2009), *The Role of the Provincial and Territorial Governments in the Oceans Sector,* Fisheries and Oceans Canada, Ottawa, Ontario, http://waves-vagues.dfo-mpo.gc.ca/Library/337906.pdf.

Dupuis, J. (2016), "The Gas Tax Fund: Chronology, funding and agreements", Library of Parliament, Ottowa, Ontario, https://lop.parl.ca/staticfiles/PublicWebsite/Home/ResearchPublications/InBriefs/PDF/2016-99-e.pdf.

ECCC (2013), "Flood Damage Reduction Program", Government of Canada, Ottawa, Ontario, http://ec.gc.ca/eau-water/default.asp?lang=En&n=0365F5C2-1.

El-Sharif, A. and D. Hansen (2001), "Application of SWMM to the flooding problem in Truro, Nova Scotia", *Canadian Water Resources Journal,* Vol. 26, pp. 439-459.

Foster, K.R. and H. Main (2017), *Finding a Place: Understanding Youth Outmigration from Shrinking Rural Communities,* Social Sciences and Humanities Research Council of Canada, https://dalspace.library.dal.ca/bitstream/handle/10222/73932/Finding%20a%20Place%20v1.pdf?sequence=1.

Gerwing, T.G. et al. (2017), "Short-term response of a downstream marine system to the partial opening of a tidal-river causeway", *Estuaries and Coasts,* Vol. 40/3, pp. 717-725, https://doi.org/10.1007/s12237-016-0173-2.

Gibson, R., J. Fitzgibbons and N.R. Nunez (2015), "Nova Scotia", In: Markey, S. et al. (eds.) *State of Rural Canada*, Canadian Rural Revitalization Foundation, http://sorc.crrf.ca/ns.

GNS (2018), *Municipal Land Use Planning Comprehensiveness*, Government of Nova Scotia, Halifax https://data.novascotia.ca/Municipalities/Municipal-Land-Use-Planning-Comprehensiveness/m3zv-87rm (accessed on 12 July 2018).

Grady, C. (2018), *Coastal Protection Act: A Future Scenario Analysis of Coastal Policy in Nova Scotia, College of Sustainability Undergraduate Honours Theses*, Dalhousie University, http://hdl.handle.net/10222/73873.

Graham, J. (2012), *Considerations for Salt Marsh Restoration Design in a Hypertidal Estuary.* Master's Theses, Saint Mary's University, http://library2.smu.ca/handle/01/24807#.XGVsslxKjcs.

Greenan, B. et al. (2015), "Estimating sea-level allowances for Atlantic Canada under conditions of uncertain sea-level rise", *Proceedings of the International Association of Hydrological Sciences,* Vol. 365, pp. 16-21, http://dx.doi.org/10.5194/piahs-365-16-2015.

Greenberg, D.A. et al. (2012), "Climate change, mean sea level and high tides in the Bay of Fundy", *Atmosphere-Ocean,* Vol. 50/3, pp. 261-276, https://doi.org/10.1080/07055900.2012.668670.

Grieve, M. and L. Turnbull (2013), "Emergency management in Nova Scotia", In: Henstra, D. (ed.), *Multilevel Governance and Emergency Management in Canadian Municipalities*, McGill-Queen's Press-MQUP.

Hand, A. (2012), "Truro residents call for better infrastructure to prevent flooding", *CTV News Atlantic,* https://atlantic.ctvnews.ca/truro-residents-call-for-better-infrastructure-to-prevent-flooding-1.969708.

Hanson, A. and L. Calkins (1996), *Wetlands of the Maritime Provinces: Revised Documentation for the Wetlands Inventory*, Environment Canada, Canadian Wildlife Service, Atlantic Region.

Harman, B.P. et al. (2013), "Global lessons for adapting coastal communities to protect against storm surge inundation", *Journal of Coastal Research*, Vol. 31/4, pp. 790-801, https://doi.org/10.2112/JCOASTRES-D-13-00095.1.

Holling, C.S. and G.K. Meffe (1996), "Command and control and the pathology of natural resource management", *Conservation Biology,* Vol. 10/2, pp. 328-337, . https://doi.org/10.1046/j.1523-1739.1996.10020328.x

Hornborg, A.-C. (2008), *Mi'kmaq Landscapes: From Animism to Sacred Ecology,* Ashgate, Aldershot, England.

ICF (2018), *Best Practices and Resources on Climate Resilient Natural Infrastructure*, Canadian Council of Ministers of the Environment, https://www.ccme.ca/files/Resources/climate_change/Natural_Infrastructure_Report_EN.pdf.

IPCC (2013), *Climate Change 2013: Climate Change 2013: The Physical Science Basis. Contribution of Working Group I to the Fifth Assessment Report of the Intergovernmental Panel on Climate Change*, Stocker, T.F. (eds.), Cambridge University Press, New York, NY, https://www.ipcc.ch/site/assets/uploads/2017/09/WG1AR5_Frontmatter_FINAL.pdf.

James, T.S. et al. (2014), "Relative sea level projections in Canada and adjacent mainland United States", *Geological Survey of Canada*, http://dx.doi.org/10.4095/295574.

Krawchenko, T. et al. (2016), "Coastal climate change, vulnerability and age friendly communities: Linking planning for climate change to the age friendly communities agenda", *Journal of Rural Studies,* Vol. 44, pp. 55-62, https://doi.org/10.1016/j.jrurstud.2015.12.013.

Lemmen, D.S. and F.J. Warren (2016), "Synthesis", In: Lemmen, D.S. et al. (eds.), *Canada's Marine Coasts in a Changing Climate*, Government of Canada, Ottawa, Ontario, www.nrcan.gc.ca/sites/www.nrcan.gc.ca/files/earthsciences/pdf/assess/2016/Coastal_Assessment_Synthesis_en.pdf.

Lemmen, D.S. et al. (eds.) (2016), *Canada's Marine Coasts in a Changing Climate*, Government of Canada, Ottawa, Ontario, www.nrcan.gc.ca/environment/resources/publications/impacts-adaptation/reports/assessments/2016/18388.

MacDonald, G. et al. (2010), "The legacy of agricultural reclamation on channel and pool networks of Bay of Fundy salt marshes", *Estuaries and Coasts,* Vol. 33/1, pp. 151-160, https://doi.org/10.1007/s12237-009-9222-4.

Manson, G.K. (2005), "On the coastal populations of Canada and the world", *12th Canadian Coastal Conference*, Dartmouth, Nova Scotia.

Manuel, P. et al. (2015), "Coastal climate change and aging communities in Atlantic Canada: A methodological overview of community asset and social vulnerability mapping", *The Canadian Geographer,* Vol. 59/4, pp. 433-446, https://doi.org/10.1111/cag.12203.

Marvin, J. and A.T. Wilson (2016), "One dimensional, two dimensional and three dimensional hydrodynamic modeling of a dyked coastal river in the Bay of Fundy", *Journal of Water Management Modeling,* Vol. 25, pp. 404, http://dx.doi.org/10.14796/JWMM.C404.

McClearn, M. (2018), "Sea change: Short on options, Îles de la Madeleine residents make a strategic retreat from rising seas", *The Globe and Mail*, https://www.theglobeandmail.com/canada/article-sea-change-iles-de-la-madeleine.

McLeod, E. et al. (2011), "A blueprint for blue carbon: Toward an improved understanding of the role of vegetated coastal habitats in sequestering CO_2", *Frontiers in Ecology and the Environment,* Vol. 9/10, pp. 552-560, https://doi.org/10.1890/110004.

Millward, H. (2005), "Rural population change in Nova Scotia, 1991-2001: Bivariate and multivariate analysis of key drivers", *The Canadian Geographer,* Vol. 49/2, pp. 180-197, http://dx.doi.org/10.1111/j.0008-3658.2005.00088.x.

Mitsch, W.J. and J.G. Gosselink (1986), *Wetlands,* Van Nostrand Reinhold Co, New York, NY.

Moudrak, N. et al. (2018), Combating *Canada's Rising Flood Costs: Natural Infrastructure is an Underutilized Option*, prepared for the Insurance Bureau of Canada, www.ibc.ca/ab/resources/studies/natural-infrastructure-is-an-underutilized-option.

Narayan, S. et al. (2016), "The effectiveness, costs and coastal protection benefits of natural and nature-based defences", *PLOS ONE,* Vol. 11/5, e0154735, https://doi.org/10.1371/journal.pone.0154735.

Neckles, H. and M. Dionne (eds.) (2000), *Regional Standards to Identify and Evaluate Tidal Wetland Restoration in the Gulf of Maine,* Wells National Estuarine Research Reserve, Wells, Maine.

Newbold, K.B. (2008), "Interprovincial migration and retirement income transfers among Canada's older population: 1996-2001", *Environment and Planning A: Economy and Space,* Vol. 40, pp. 1501-1516, https://doi.org/10.1068/a39188.

Northcott, H.C. and C.R. Petruik (2011), "The geographic mobility of elderly Canadians", *Canadian Journal on Aging*, Vol. 30/3, pp. 311-322, http://dx.doi.org/10.1017/S0714980811000262.

NSDE (2005), *Adapting to a Changing Climate in Nova Scotia: Vulnerability Assessment and Adaptation Options, Final Report,* Government of Nova Scotia, Halifax, Nova Scotia, https://climatechange.novascotia.ca/sites/default/files/uploads/Adapting_to_a_Changing_Climate_in_NS.pdf.

NSDE (2009), *Toward A Greener Future: Nova Scotia's Climate Change Action Plan,* Government of Nova Scotia, Halifax, Nova Scotia.

NSDMA (1998), *Municipal Government Act,* Nova Scotia Department of Municipal Affairs, Halifax, Nova Scotia, https://nslegislature.ca/sites/default/files/legc/statutes/municipal%20government.pdf.

NSDMA (2007), *Integrated Community Sustainability Plans: Municipal Funding Agreement for Nova Scotia,* Canada-Nova Scotia Infrastructure Secretariat, Halifax, Nova Scotia, https://novascotia.ca/dma/pdf/mun-icsp-guide.pdf.

NSDMA (2015a), *Federal Gas Tax Fund*, Nova Scotia Department of Municipal Affairs, Halifax, Nova Scotia, https://novascotia.ca/dma/funding/infrastructure/gas-tax-fund.asp (accessed on 12 July 2018).

NSDMA (2015b), "Municipal infrastructure programs", Nova Scotia Department of Municipal Affairs, Halifax, Nova Scotia, https://novascotia.ca/dma/funding/infrastructure.asp (accessed on 12 July 2018).

NSDMA (2016), "Statements of provincial interests", In: Nova Scotia Department of Municipal Affairs (ed.); *S.N.S. 1998, c. 18*, Nova Scotia Department of Municipal Affairs, Halifax, Nova Scotia.

NSDMA (2017), "Financial condition indicators", Nova Scotia Department of Municipal Affairs, Halifax, Nova Scotia, https://novascotia.ca/dma/finance/indicator/fci.asp.

O'Sullivan, T.L. et al. (2013), "Unraveling the complexities of disaster management: A framework for critical social infrastructure to promote population health and resilience", *Social Science & Medicine,* Vol. 93, pp. 238-246.

Office of the Legislative Counsel (2000), *An Act for the Conservation of Agricultural Marshland,* Nova Scotia House of Assembly, Halifax, Nova Scotia, https://nslegislature.ca/sites/default/files/legc/statutes/agricmar.htm.

Pontee, N. (2013), "Defining coastal squeeze: A discussion", *Ocean & Coastal Management,* Vol. 84, pp. 204-207, https://doi.org/10.1016/j.ocecoaman.2013.07.010.

Rapaport, E., S. Starkman and W. Towns (2017), "Atlantic Canada", In: Palko, K. & D.S. Lemmen (eds.), *Climate Risks and Adaptation Practices for the Canadian Transportation Sector 2016,* Government of Canada, Ottawa, Ontario, https://www.nrcan.gc.ca/sites/www.nrcan.gc.ca/files/earthsciences/pdf/assess/2016/Chapter-8e.pdf.

Richards, W. and R. Daigle (2011), *Scenarios and Guidance for Adaptation to Climate Change and Sea-Level Rise - NS and PEI Municipalities,* Atlantic Climate Adaptation Solutions Association, www.gov.pe.ca/photos/original/ccscenarios.pdf.

Robinson, S., D. van Proosdij and H. Kolstee (2005), "Change in dykeland practices in agricultural salt marshes in Cobequid Bay, Bay of Fundy", *BoFEP Conference Proceedings*.

Savard, J.-P., D. van Proosdij and S. O'Carroll (2016), "Perspectives on Canada's east coast region", In: Lemmen, D.S. (eds.), *Canada's Marine Coasts in a Changing Climate*, Government of Canada, Ottawa, Ontario, https://www.nrcan.gc.ca/sites/www.nrcan.gc.ca/files/earthsciences/pdf/assess/2016/Coastal_Assessment_Chapter4_EastCoastRegion.pdf.

Sherren, K. (in press), "From climax thinking toward a non-equilibrium approach to public good landscape change", In: Jacquet, J., J. Haggerty and G. Theodori (eds.), *Coordinating Research on the Social Impacts of Energy Development: Synthesis Across the Social Sciences*. Social Ecology Press.

Statistics Canada (2017), *Census Profile (Truro Population Centre and Truro Census Metropolitan Area) 2016 Census. Catalogue no. 98-316-X2016001,* Government of Canada www12.statcan.gc.ca/census-recensement/2016/dp-pd/prof/index.cfm?Lang=E.

Sullivan, H. (2016), "Saltwater marsh to be created as part of flood mitigation efforts", *Truro Daily News*, https://www.trurodaily.com/news/local/saltwater-marsh-to-be-created-as-part-of-flood-mitigation-efforts-148671/.

Tutton, M. (2012), "Flooding drenches Nova Scotia as east coast readies for Leslie", *The Globe and Mail*, https://www.theglobeandmail.com/news/national/flooding-drenches-nova-scotia-as-east-coast-readies-for-leslie/article4534524/.

van Proosdij, D., T. Bowron and N. Neatt (2014), "Development and application of guidelines for managed realignment to maximize adaptive capacity and ecosystem services", Saint Mary's University, Maritime Provinces Spatial Analysis Research Centre, Halifax, Nova Scotia.

van Proosdij, D., B. Perrott and K. Carrol (2013), "Development and application of a geo-temporal atlas for climate change adaptation in Bay of Fundy dykelands", *Journal of Coastal Research*, Special Issue 65/1, pp. 1069-1074, https://doi.org/10.2112/SI65-181.1.

Warburton, A. and H. MacKenzie-Carey (2013), *Using an EMO-Based Hazard Risk Vulnerability Assessment Process for Municipal Climate Change Action Plan Development,* Nova Scotia Environment Climate Change Directorate, Halifax, Nova Scotia, https://climatechange.novascotia.ca/sites/default/files/uploads/2012-2013_Truro.pdf.

Williams, P.B. and M.K. Orr (2002), "Physical evolution of restored levee salt marshes in the San Francisco Bay Estuary", *Restoration Ecology,* 10/3, pp. 527-542, https://doi.org/10.1046/j.1526-100X.2002.02031.x.

Wollenberg, J.T., J. Ollerhead and G.L. Chmura (2018), "Rapid carbon accumulation following managed realignment on the Bay of Fundy", *PLOS ONE,* Vol. 13, e0193930, https://doi.org/10.1371/journal.pone.0193930.

Xu, F. and W. Perrie (2012), "Extreme waves and wave run-up in Halifax Harbour under climate change scenarios", *Atmosphere-Ocean,* Vol. 50/4, pp. 407-420, https://doi.org/10.1080/07055900.2012.707610.

Chapter 6. Clifton to Tangoio Coastal Hazards Strategy 2120, Hawke's Bay, New Zealand

This chapter describes the process behind the Clifton to Tangoio Coastal Hazards Strategy 2120, a process led by a partnership of local communities. The case study illustrates how various stakeholders can work collaboratively to take long-term decisions on complex and uncertain challenges, how the dynamic adaptive planning pathways method can work in practice, and the importance of open conversations about accountability and responsibility.

This chapter was written by Emma Corbett, Ministry for the Environment and Simon Bendall, Mitchell Daysh Limited.

Acknowledgments: Thanks to the Hawke's Bay Regional Council, Hastings District Council and Napier City Council for their support in the development of this case study.

Technical support to the Council's and community were provided by Aramanu Ropiha, Infometrics, Maven Consulting Ltd, Mitchell Daysh Ltd and Tonkin & Taylor Ltd. Details of these assessments can be found at https://hbcoast.co.nz/resources/ . Living at the Edge, a research collaboration funded by the NZ National Science Challenge acted as a "critical friend" to the process and provided independent advice and assistance.

6.1. Overview

New Zealand has one of the longest coastlines in the OCED and one of the smallest populations. This, along with its varied landscape, makes developing adaptation responses challenging, particularly when considering how the costs of those responses will be met. As an island nation, New Zealand has strong social and cultural connection with its coastline, and it provides unique habitats for indigenous fauna and flora. It is also the focus of much economic activity. Today around 65% of the population and major infrastructure are located within 5 km of the coast.

Climate change poses an increasing risk to these important coastal areas, in particular because sea-level rise (SLR) increases exposure to coastal hazards. This exposure is exacerbated by ongoing coastal development and rising property values. Over the last 100 years, the sea level around New Zealand has risen at an average rate of 1.8 mm per year. As New Zealand is geologically active, rising sea levels are also exacerbated by tectonic effects of uplift and subsidence. Global projections estimate further rises by 0.2-0.4 m by 2060 and 0.3-1.0 m by 2100.

The levels of risk exposure in different regions in New Zealand are illustrated in Figure 6.2. Using a combination of population and infrastructure measures, the highest coastal risk exposure is in the Hawke's Bay and Canterbury regions.

Sea-level rise is, however, only part of the picture. Climate change is also expected to affect New Zealand's coastal areas through increased coastal erosion; more frequent and extensive coastal flooding; higher storm surges; saltwater intrusion into coastal aquifers and further inland in estuaries; and changes in surface water quality, groundwater characteristics and sedimentation. Risks to the coastline from a range of these impacts and the responses that are needed will be specific to each local area.

Figure 6.1. Levels of coastal risk exposure in New Zealand determined by resident population, buildings, roads, railway, airport and jetties/wharves for land elevations less than 1.5 m

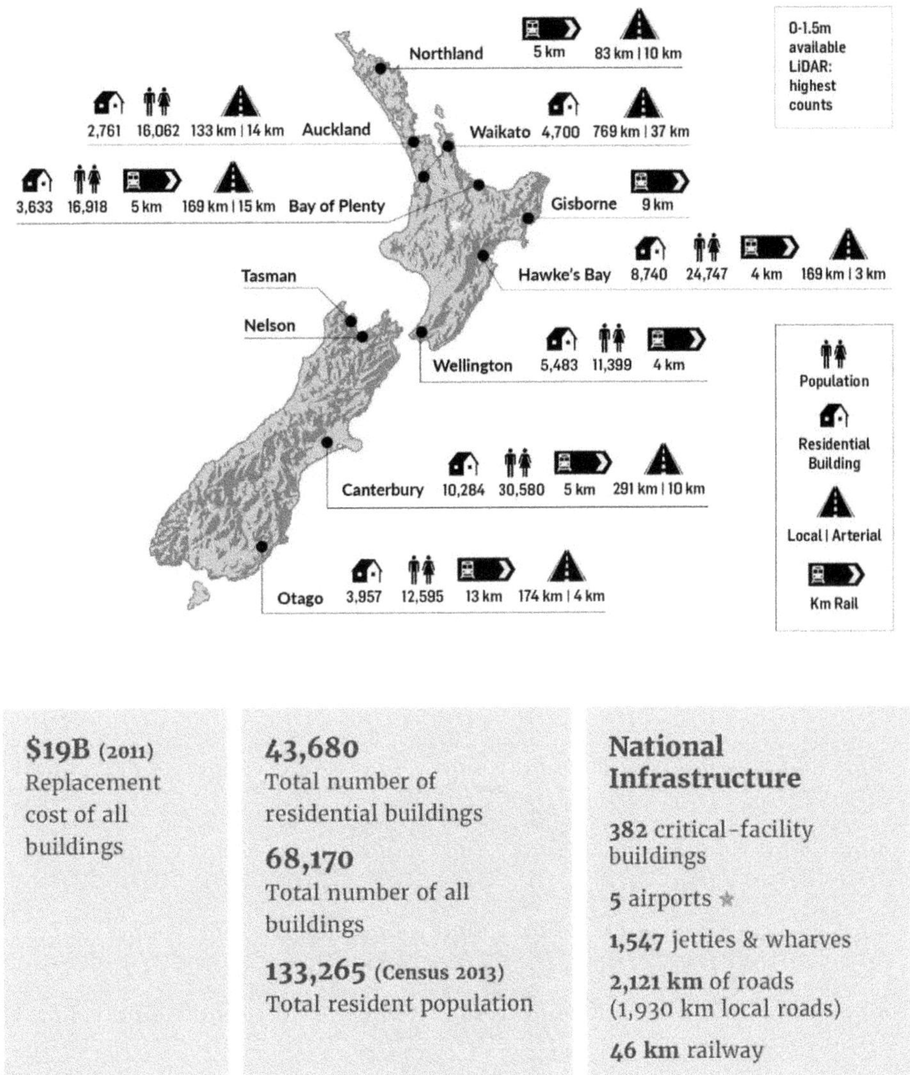

Note: The boxes above show aggregated results from regional totals where LiDAR4 data were available. All dollars in NZD.

Source: Bell, R., R. Paulik and S. Wadwha (2015), National and regional risk exposure in low-lying coastal areas, Prepared for the Parliamentary Commissioner for the Environment, https://www.pce.parliament.nz/media/1384/national-and-regional-risk-exposure-in-low-lying-coastal-areas-niwa-2015.pdf

In New Zealand, the central government works at a national scale to improve resilience to the impacts of climate change. It does this by: providing the national-level legislative and policy framework; issuing information and guidance to support local government and businesses to take effective adaptation decisions; funding research and publishing information on climate change impacts; and preparing for and responding to major natural hazard events.

Local government has responsibilities to prepare communities for and manage the risks of climate change and are considered best-placed to understand what is appropriate for their region based on the local changes they can expect to experience. Local government is also required to consider the effects of a changing climate on communities and incorporate climate change into existing policy and regulatory frameworks, plans, projects and decision-making procedures, for example, when making choices about the use of land.

Māori are the indigenous people of New Zealand and *tangata whenua* rights and interests are represented in the Treaty of Waitangi, which is one of the founding documents of the country.

6.1.1. Current central government initiatives

In early 2018, a group of government-appointed technical experts provided recommendations on actions New Zealand needs to take to adapt to climate change. The group concluded that New Zealand is in the early stages of planning to adapt to the impacts of climate change and more needs to be done to reduce the risks and build resilience to the changing climate. The group's recommendations are summarised in Figure 6.2 and include core mechanisms needed (dark blue) and supporting functions (light blue).

Figure 6.2. Climate Change Adaptation Technical Working Group's recommendations for effective adaptation in New Zealand

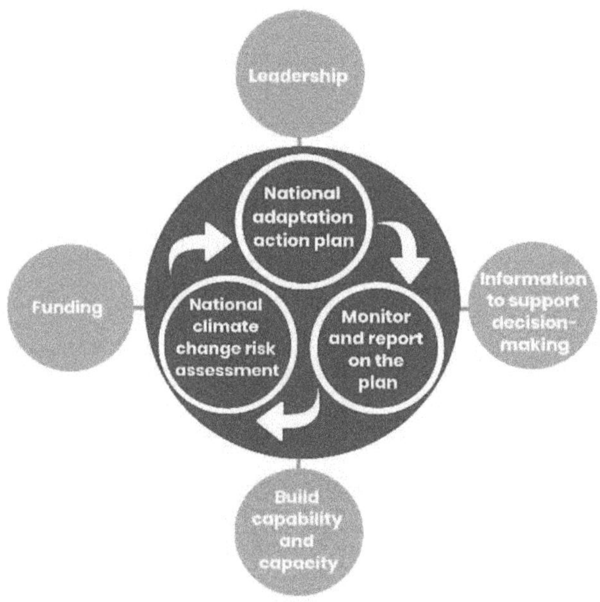

At the time of writing, the government is progressing work to consider how the group's recommended actions can be implemented, including how to fund adaptation responses and how to support local communities to effectively respond to climate change in their local areas.

Proposals for a National Climate Change Risk Assessment and a National Adaptation Plan (the government's response to the National Climate Change Risk Assessment) are currently being considered as part of the its Zero Carbon Bill. This would include the establishment of a Climate Change Commission to provide advice on climate change adaptation and monitor the implementation of the National Adaptation Plan. These proposals are expected to be legislated in 2019.

While central government continues to develop national-scale responses, New Zealand is taking action at a local level. At the coast this is informed by the Ministry for the Environment's publication "Coastal hazards and climate change: Guidance for local government" released in 2017 as an update to earlier guidance material. This guidance aims to support local government[1] to manage and adapt to the increased coastal hazard risks posed by climate change and sea-level rise. It:

- provides information on the potential effects of climate change on coastal hazards, incorporating the latest science and feedback from stakeholders
- recommends a new "adaptive pathways" approach to coastal hazards planning that is dynamic and flexible and that responds to the long-term uncertainty of climate chance effects
- outlines collaborative approaches to engaging with communities and local government roles and responsibilities
- recommends a ten-step decision-making process that councils and communities can follow when planning for the effects of climate change on coastal hazards.

Figure 6.3. Ten-step decision cycle: Coastal hazards and climate change: Guidance for local government

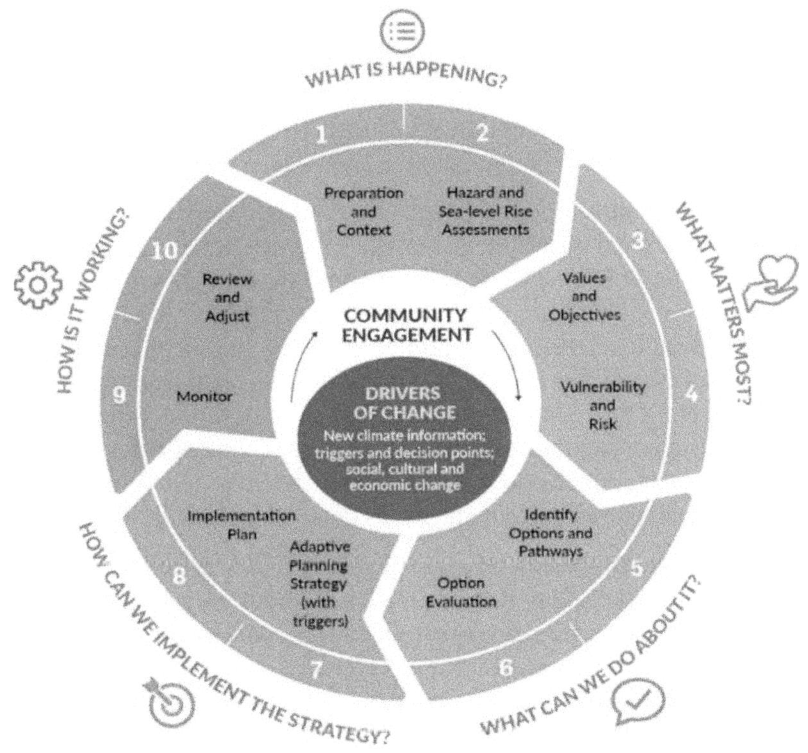

6.2. Clifton to Tangoio Coastal Hazards Strategy 2120, Hawke's Bay, New Zealand

The Hawke's Bay region is located on the eastern coast of the North Island of New Zealand. The region's 353 km coastline supports a diverse range of habitats underpinned by the unique geological history of the area. The region is dominated by Hawke's Bay itself, which is 94 km across its widest point and includes the region's largest population centres of Napier and Hastings. The region has a population of 164 000 (June 2017) and is renowned for its horticulture, with large orchards and vineyards on the plains. In the hilly parts of the region, sheep and cattle farming are dominant along with forestry blocks.

Natural disasters, storms, coastal erosion and inundation along Hawke's Bay's coastline have, and continue to damage, property and threaten people's safety and well-being. In 1931, the region was devastated by a magnitude 7.8 earthquake, New Zealand's deadliest natural disaster. The earthquake resulted in significant loss of life, damage to property and infrastructure, and coastal areas around Napier were uplifted by around 2 metres by the quake, and around 40 km^2 of seabed became dry land. From a coastal processes perspective, the effects of this dramatic change are still being felt today, with coastal margins continuing to adjust to these altered physical conditions.

To plan and respond to the ongoing challenges and community concerns associated with coastal hazards, local government and *tangata whenua* in Hawke's Bay are developing a long-term strategy. The Clifton to Tangoio Coastal Hazards Strategy 2120 ("the strategy") takes a co-ordinated approach to identifying and responding to coastal hazards and the influence of SLR over the next 100 years. It is designed to create a platform for long-term planning and decision making in the Hawke's Bay region.

The first iteration of the strategy focuses on the most populated stretch of the coastline in Hawke's Bay; from Clifton in the south to Tangoio in the north. This area includes the city of Napier; coastal communities including Whirinaki, Te Awanga and Haumoana; and key infrastructure such as the Port of Napier and the Hastings Wastewater Treatment Plant.

The strategy is being developed through a Joint Committee formed by elected representatives from the local government: Hawke's Bay Regional Council, the Napier City Council and the Hastings District Council, and groups brought together for Treaty of Waitangi settlement processes including: He Toa Takitini, Mana Ahuriri Incorporated and the Maungaharuru-Tangitū Trust. The Joint Committee has been formally established under the Local Government Act (2002)[2] and therefore has legal standing and is subject to standed Council meeting procedure and protocol, including the requirement for meetings to be held publicly. Supporting the Joint Committee is a Technical Advisory Group formed by senior staff from each council and led by an independently appointed project manager. The strategy is being developed in four stages, as detailed in the following sections.

The strategy was originally developed to respond to issues raised in a technical report commissioned by the Hawke's Bay Regional Council and to ongoing community concern about the effects of coastal hazards. It also provided an opportunity for the councils to work together on a complex cross-boundary issue.

6.2.1. Stage 1: Defining the issue

The Hawke's Bay coastline has long history of coastal hazards impacts. To assess future risks, the focus area between Clifton and Tangoio was divided into 16 coastal "units". The units were based on a combination of communities of interest, coastal processes, land area units and topography (Figure 6.4).

Within each unit, the possible extent of coastal erosion and coastal inundation over the next 100 years was modelled and mapped, and risks associated with those hazard extents assessed. The process was broadly consistent with that defined in "Coastal hazards and climate change: Guidance for local government". For coastal erosion, a range of potential SLR scenarios was modelled to develop probabilistic erosion lines (i.e. erosion lines mapped with probabilities of occurrence at different time periods). SLR scenarios of between 0.6 and 1.5 metres (with a mode of 1.0 metre) were used over the 100-year planning horizon. For coastal inundation, a building block approach was used where the inundation hazard extents were mapped based on a 1% AEP (or 1 in 100-year) storm surge event + wave set-up at the coast + 0.5 metre (at 2065) or 1.0 metre (at 2120) of SLR. It was acknowledged that these values may be reached sooner or later than the prescribed years; however, it provides a good indication of vulnerability based on current information. Tsunami risks were also identified at this early stage; however, due to the nature of tsunami risks, they have been considered a civil defence and planning issue rather than one that requires a long-term adaptive response.

The 100-year hazards assessment confirmed that in some units, immediate risks are high and in the longer term these become significant. The Joint Committee acknowledged that the issues faced were challenging, emotive and complex and any strategy to resolve them would require community involvement in a broadly agreed and technically sound response. For example, this coastline has a long history of coastal hazards effects and a wide range of strongly held opinions on what should be done, and who should be responsible for implementing such responses. In addition, there are historical, cultural, social, ecosystem and economic values attributable to this coastline that are under threat from the effects of climate change. Further, any response(s) made (e.g. defending with hard structures, retreating from the coast, etc.) to address risks from climate change could be as damaging or deleterious to these values as not responding at all.

Figure 6.4. Assessment cell evaluation panel areas and coastal units

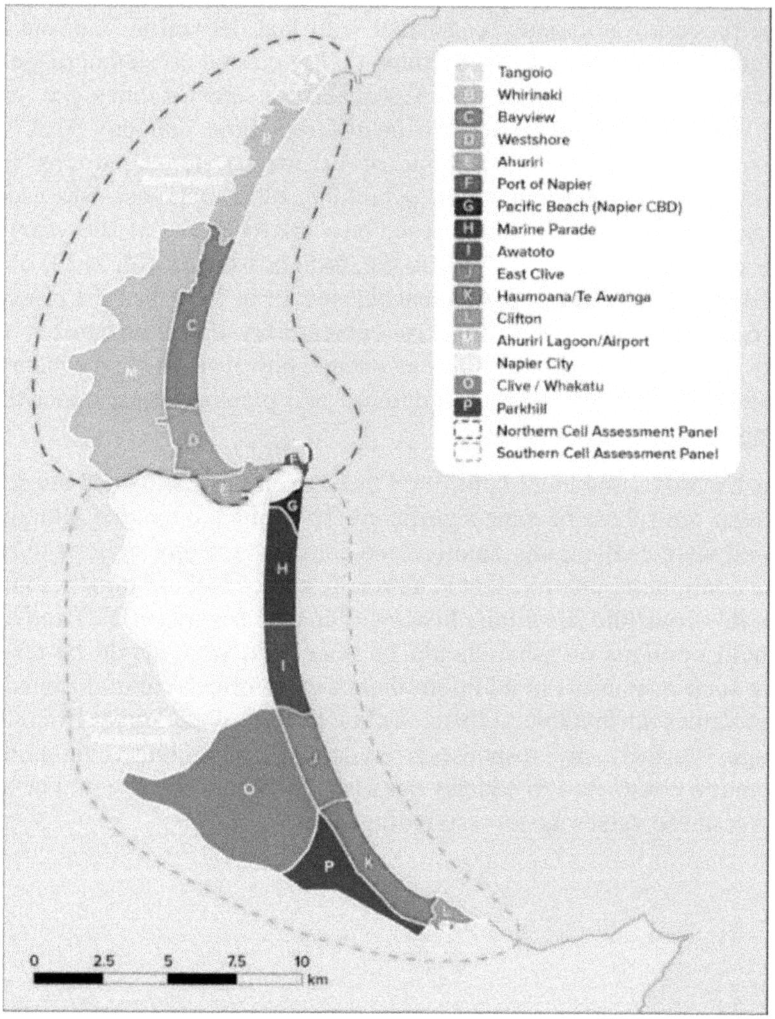

Note: The landward units (M to P) incorporate areas that may be affected by coastal inundation.

6.2.2. Stage 2: Framework for decisions

The aim of this stage was to work with the community to design a decision-making framework that would result in well-considered and broadly supported long-term plans for responding to the risks and hazards identified in Stage 1. The resulting, agreed framework comprised of:

- two assessment panels to represent the interests of *tangata whenua*, communities and agencies exposed to coastal hazards risks
- facilitated workshops to work through a structured decision-making process to develop and evaluate potential options/pathways for responding to identified risks over time in priority coastal units
- the application of multi-criteria decision analysis (MCDA), dynamic adaptive planning pathways (DAPP) and real options analysis methodologies

- the development and delivery of assessment panel recommendations for preferred options/pathways back to each council for final decision making.

6.2.3. Stage 3: Develop responses

Stage 3 involved the formation of the assessment panels and the implementation of the decision-making framework developed in Stage 2. The panels completed their work through a series of 11 facilitated workshops and other supplementary work including site visits and public meetings that took just over 12 months to complete. The following sections outline this process in more detail.

Panel structure

The assessment panels were formed to consider the strategy in two distinct "cells": 1) a Northern Panel to focus on the area from the Port of Napier north to Tangoio; and 2) a Southern Panel to focus on the area from the Port of Napier south to Clifton. The reasons for adopting this cell structure were that it:

- grouped the 16 units with interrelated coastal processes into two manageable "cells"
- deliberately crossed jurisdictional boundaries to ensure that each Partner Council was functionally involved in both panel areas
- struck a good balance between administrative and process cost efficiency and community representation; too many panels would be difficult to operate, but with fewer panels the number of panel members required for appropriate representation purposes increases.

With a two-panel design, panel seats were pre-defined to provide a good cross-section of interested and affected parties. A series of public meetings was held within each coastal community and more broadly to call for volunteers for each of the available community positions. For organisation/agency members, nominations were sought from their respective agency.

Panel process

The assessment panels worked through a structured decision-making assessment process completed through a series of 11 workshops during 2017 (Figure 6.5).

Figure 6.5. Assessment panels and decision-making assessment process

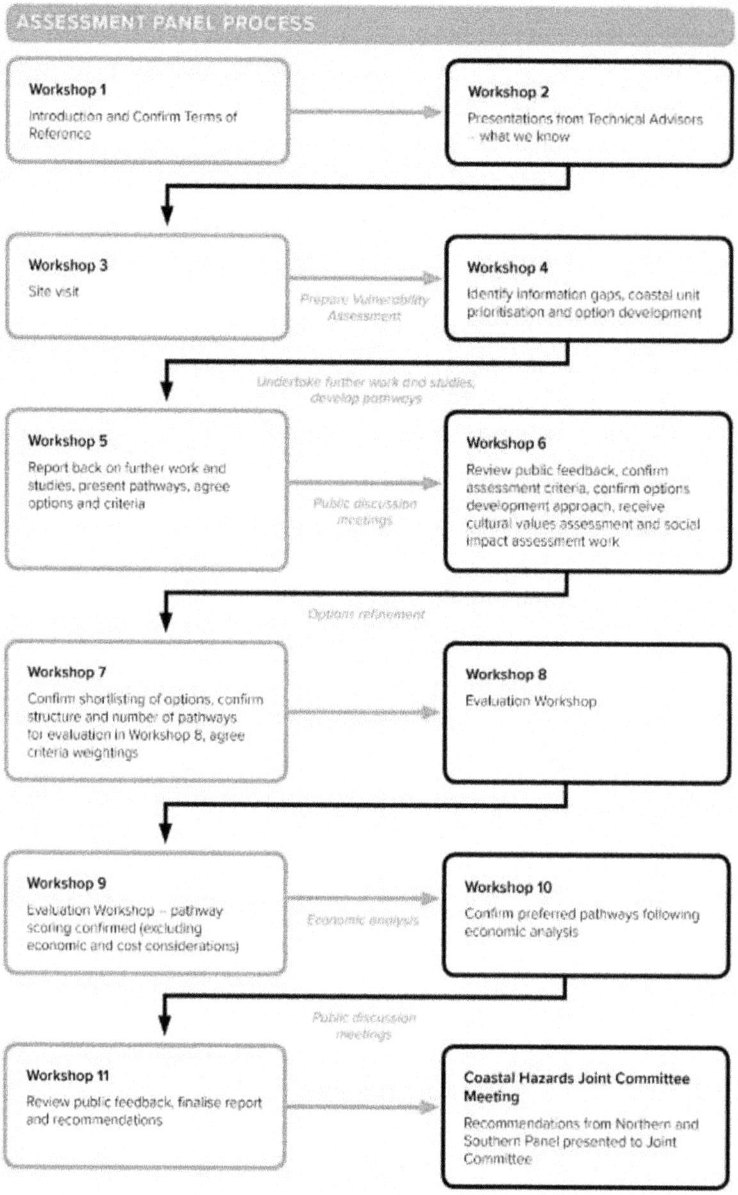

Decision-making tools

The assessment panels employed the decision-making framework that was developed in Stage 2 to arrive at their recommendations. The framework was designed to respond to complex technical information, long time frames, high levels of uncertainty, and multiple (and sometimes competing) values and interests. The framework included MCDA and DAPP. These were supported by:

- a coastal hazard assessment
- a coastal risk assessment

- a cultural values assessment
- a social impact assessment and valuation
- a real options analysis.

Multi-criteria decision analysis

MCDA is an established technique for assessing multiple and sometimes complex options. Generally the process involves the "scoring" of multiple options against defined criteria (e.g. social, cultural, environmental, economic) to determine an overall preferred option that balances sometimes competing values. The criteria developed and adopted by the panels are outlined in Table 6.1.

The assessment panels determined that economic considerations were critical to whether a given pathway could be implemented. As economic considerations were a critical failure issue, rather than a measure of performance, separate economic analysis was undertaken and cost considerations were undertaken separately to the MCDA process.

Table 6.1. The criteria developed and adopted by the panels

	Criteria	Description
Technical assessment criteria	Manages the risks of storm surge inundation	• Reduced exposure to risks from storm surge inundation • Meets objectives over long time frames • Proportionate to the scale and nature of risk
	Manages the risks of coastal erosion	• Reduced exposure to risks from coastal erosion • Meets objectives over long time frames • Proportionate to the scale and nature of risk
	Ability to adapt to increasing risks	• Readily responds to uncertain climate outcomes • Includes measures to support future adjustments
	Risk transfer	• Exacerbation of hazard risk in other areas • Transfer of risk to others, including future generations

Impact assessment criteria	Socio-economic impacts	• Social effects, for example:
		  o effects on community safety
		  o loss of amenity value
		• Decline in recreational values, community facilities
		• Indirect economic/industry impacts (e.g. tourism, fishing)

	Relationship of Māori and their culture and traditions with their ancestral lands, water, sites, *waahi tapu* and other *taonga*	• Impacts on any cultural sites of significance • Maintains access to, and enables the carrying out of, customary activities
	Natural environments impacts	• Impacts on natural coastal ecosystems • Impacts on the natural character of the coastal environment

Dynamic adaptive planning pathways

DAPP has particular utility for taking decisions in the coastal context where ever-changing risk profiles are present, and there is increasing (with time) uncertainty around rates and magnitude of changes. Importantly, DAPP does not prescribe a single, final solution. Flexibility is retained, and future options are left open for future decision points.

This general approach was employed by the assessment panels in the development of "pathways" for each unit. In this strategy, the DAPP process was adapted, whereby pathways were formed for each unit as a combination of short-term (0-20 years), medium-term (20-50 years) and long-term (50-100 years) hazard response actions. An example pathway is shown in Figure 6.6.

Figure 6.6. Example pathway

Short term 0-20 years	→	Medium term 20-50 years	→	Long term 50-100 years
Beach renourishment	→	Renourishment + groynes	→	Managed retreat

Six potential pathways were developed for each priority unit. The pathways were designed to represent the spectrum of possible responses, from low intervention to softer engineering (e.g. beach renourishment), hard engineering (e.g. sea walls) and retreat. The pathways were then assessed using MCDA to determine an order of preference in terms of each pathway's performance against the defined criteria.

Cultural values assessment and hīkoi *(tour of the area)*

A cultural values assessment provided an overview of the cultural values in the coastal area from Clifton to Tangoio to guide the decision making, and included:

- a brief history of the pre-settlement patterns of occupation
- *whakapapa* (genealogy) of the original occupants and how they are manifest in present *hapū* (sub-tribes)
- a compilation of *wāhi tapu* (places sacred to Māori) and sites of significance that are registered by public sector agencies
- *hapū* management plans with cultural values that are registered with local government
- agreements between *hapū* and the Crown related to the Treaty claimant process
- identification of gaps in the information reviewed with proposed remedies.

The report was supplemented with a cultural values *wānanga* (educational seminar) and *hīkoi* (site visit) for panel members, hosted by Matahiwi Marae (*marae* being a traditional meeting ground). Following a *powhiri* (formal welcome ceremony) at Matahiwi Marae, the *hīkoi* took members from both assessment panels on a bus tour of the entire strategy area, highlighting historical use and occupation, and places and sites of significance. This provided important contextual information for panel members as they embarked on the decision-making process.

Social impact assessment and valuation

The social impact of coastal hazards (inundation and erosion) on the communities in each unit was assessed by external consultants engaged by the councils to cover the northern and southern priority units. The purpose of the studies was to provide a clearer understanding of social issues and impacts from coastal hazards through meaningful engagement with community stakeholders. In addition, this assessment provided an analysis of social outcomes that would occur if there were no human intervention to address coastal hazards (beyond current interventions); and a valuation (estimated monetary value) of those outcomes using social impact measurement methodologies (social return on investment).

The studies were developed from interviews with residents and stakeholders and supported by other background information and reports.

The assessments assumed a *status quo* scenario, i.e. no change in interventions compared to those carried out at the present time. In effect, this provided a "baseline" social impact associated with doing nothing in response to coastal hazards. The projected social outcomes were valued using financial proxies and value mapping to estimate a social cost (in monetary terms) to each community. When asked to consider the effects of a do nothing response to coastal hazards, a common theme from those that were interviewed was the large proportion of social outcomes attributable to negative well-being among those residents whose properties are most at risk to the threat of coastal hazards. This negative well-being is a function of anxiety and concern caused by:

- their ability to take necessary action to protect their property from erosion and storm surges (what are the solutions, what will the government do?)
- current and future insurability of homes (excesses, exclusions, and eventual refusal to provide cover)
- ability to raise mortgage finance (which is directly related to insurability)
- future saleability of property as hazards increase
- physical damage caused by erosion or storm events
- perceived "oppression" by territorial authorities using regulatory powers to force retreat as the only option.

The studies provided useful insights and references for panel members to inform their decision making. Further application of this work has been in the development of a funding model in parallel to the work of the assessment panels, where the assessed social impact of coastal hazards has assisted a preliminary consideration of potential public-private apportionment of costs for implementing hazard-mitigation responses. This work is ongoing.

Real options analysis

Real options analysis (ROA) was used as the primary means of applying economic analysis to the pathways. ROA is an expanded version of cost-benefit analysis that assesses whether there is value in waiting for more information before an expensive and possibly irreversible investment is undertaken, and whether an alternative investment might suffice in the meantime. The ROA provides a costing assessment that enables decision making that can be flexibly implemented over time as the climate changes and as impacts increase. This ensures that decisions taken today do not create further risks which are costly to reverse in the future, and that a range of options have been assessed for their ability to meet community objectives over time. Broadly, the results of the ROA demonstrated that a flexible investment strategy, enabling a change of course in the future, is more likely to deliver a lower cost outcome overall than pursuing a single option.

Community feedback sessions

Two community feedback sessions were held for each panel (four sessions in total) as part of the decision-making process. Meetings were structured as "drop in" sessions, allowing members of the public to attend at any time during a two-hour window to meet panel members and council staff, receive information, and provide feedback. The feedback sessions were held at important junctures in the process; the first sessions assisted panel members to confirm their approach and initial thinking; the second allowed panel members to test their preliminary outcomes before finalising their recommendations.

6.3. Outcomes achieved to date

The key outcomes achieved in the strategy to date include:

- Stage 1: production of a comprehensive hazard and risk assessment using probabilistic and other methodologies for 16 defined coastal units within the strategy area.
- Stage 2: development of a decision-making process to apply MCDA, DAPP and ROA methodologies through a community-led assessment process to develop responses to the hazard risks identified in Stage 1.
- Stage 3: establishment of two community-based assessment panels to apply the decision-making process developed in Stage 2. The panels produced a series of recommendations for the Joint Committee that were presented in a joint report. These included:
  - which of the 16 defined coastal units the partner councils should prioritise for response
  - a recommended 100-year adaptive pathway for each of the 9 priority units
  - a range of supplementary recommendations for the partner councils to consider in support of the recommended pathways.

The full package of recommended pathways represents a relatively high degree of intervention, where most locations are proposed for some form of coastal defence structures for the short and medium term. Managed retreat has only been recommended as a long-term response at this stage. While the adaptive nature of the pathways allows this to change over time if necessary to respond to changing hazard risks, overall this is perhaps an unsurprising result, and reflects a commonly expressed desire to protect and preserve coastal communities for as long as can be practicably achieved.

The panel's report and recommendations were adopted by the Joint Committee and recommended back to each partner council. Decisions have now been endorsed by each council for the commencement of Stage 4 to develop and test the panel's recommendations for implementation.

6.4. Lessons learnt

The process taken to develop the strategy is a first of its kind in New Zealand. Key lessons learnt include:

- **Take your time and plan carefully:** Coastal processes and climate change are complex subject areas. However, we do have time to develop considered and collaborative responses. Careful planning and investing time upfront to work openly with communities pays dividends later.
- **Collaboration with the community:** Bringing community members to the table to work alongside partner council officers on a challenging problem can change relationship dynamics by removing the people from the problem, and focusing on

the problem itself – but this does take time. Experience in this project showed that it took 4 or 5 workshops (out of an 11-workshop programme) to build trust and establish strong working relationships.

- **Facilitating knowledge exchange:** A process like this facilitates a significant amount of information exchange. Partner council officers learn far more about local issues and perspectives from this type of engagement than a more formal public meeting could ever provide. For community members, regular and ongoing interactions with subject area experts through an intensive programme of workshops increases knowledge, but also enables that knowledge to filter out into communities through incidental engagements and conversations with neighbours and friends. This assists to dispel misinformation; a common challenge in this area.
- **Blending political, technical and academic:** Success in this project can in large part be attributed to the effective blending of key inputs and working hard to keep those with interests in its outcomes strongly connected to the process and activity engaged throughout. Allowing either political debate, technical information or academic theory to dominate proceedings would likely have led to an unbalanced process; blending these inputs proved to be a successful approach.
- **Community led process, rather than a council-down process:** In a traditional council-led project, a concept is developed, perhaps with options, and then presented for community and stakeholder feedback. This process flipped the traditional approach on its head, with community members developing the concept and presenting it back to the partner council for consideration. This required a leap of faith from partner councils, but ultimately has produced a more robust outcome that has been developed by, rather than for, communities.
- **Pinch point – who pays:** Defending, retreating, accommodating or doing nothing at all; all carry significant financial burden, the question is how the costs should be shared, and by whom. The answers have not yet been developed in Hawke's Bay, and ultimately remain unresolved at a national scale. The government's response to the Climate Change Adaptation Technical Working Group's (refer to Section 6.1.2) recommendations also aims to address funding as a key issue.

6.5. Challenges ahead

The strategy is now moving into Stage 4, which will develop and test the detail of the pathways recommended by the assessment panels for implementation. Recognising that Stage 3 sought to develop multiple options for comparison purposes, and to recommend preferred options, Stage 4 is concerned with concept development and testing and securing broader community approval before moving into actual implementation. This last point is important; inevitably, partner councils will have to decide how to fund responses. Those living inland will likely be asked to contribute something, if not as much as those living on the coast. Securing broader buy-in will be important and critical to overall successful implementation.

This work has been scoped and planned to occur through three phases:

- Phase 1: Pathway Concept Development, Testing and Planning
- Phase 2: Wider Community Consultation and Approvals
- Phase 3: Pathway Implementation Projects.

This work presents a range of key challenges that must be resolved before any physical works can start under the guise of the strategy. Some of the key implementation challenges ahead include:

- Where the benefits of physical works programmes will be realised (i.e. the apportionment of public and private benefit) and where costs should fall as a result.
- Whether the pathways can be affordably implemented as a whole-of-coast package.
- Which partner council(s) should assume responsibility for implementing the physical works programmes and owning the new assets.
- Confirming priority and order of works, noting that some priority units will require more urgent action than others.
- Assessing the environmental effects of the physical works programme, including a consideration of cumulative effects, and any mitigation needed for permitting.
- Collaboratively developing signals and triggers to support each pathway. Signals and triggers will be used as forewarning and ultimate decision points for when to switch to the next action in a given pathway.

At the time of writing, with funding support from each of the partner councils, the Joint Committee is commencing work to develop responses to these challenges. The working relationship established between the councils in the development of this strategy is a notable example of cross-council collaboration, and the degree of co-operation has been highly successful at both the political and staff level. The process has also brought councils and communities closer together and has developed a more collaborative approach to problem solving. While it is essential that processes such as these are tailored to particular local circumstances, the approach developed in Hawke's Bay has many aspects that can be readily adapted for use by other jurisdictions.

Notes

1. Local government in New Zealand consists of regional councils (regional focus on environment resource management and other regional functions) and territorial authorities (responsible for local service provision including roads, water, town planning and other functions). These are collectively referred to as "councils" within this case study

2. The Joint Committee has been formed under Clause 30(1)(b) of Schedule 7 of the Local Government Act 2002 and is deemed to be both a committee of the appointing local authority and a committee of each other local authority or public body that has appointed members to the committee.

Reference

Bell, R., R. Paulik and S. Wadwha (2015), *National and regional risk exposure in low-lying coastal areas*, Prepared for the Parliamentary Commissioner for the Environment, https://www.pce.parliament.nz/media/1384/national-and-regional-risk-exposure-in-low-lying-coastal-areas-niwa-2015.pdf (accessed on 29 August 2018). [1]

Chapter 7. "Rollback" in North Norfolk, United Kingdom

This chapter focuses on an area of North Norfolk, England, where an innovative "rollback" approach to adapting the local area to increased coastal erosion risk was trialled. The approach did not involve traditional coastal defence, which was considered uneconomic, but instead harnessed land-use planning policies with some "pump priming" funding to pursue a number of local projects.

This chapter was written Nick Haigh, Lead Analyst, Floods & Water, Department for Environment, Food & Rural Affairs, United Kingdom, with contributions from Rob Goodliffe, North Norfolk District Council, Cromer, United Kingdom and Kellie Fisher, Environment Agency, United Kingdom.

7.1. Institutional arrangements for coastal flooding and erosion risk

In the United Kingdom, policies for managing the risks associated with coastal flooding and erosion are devolved to the national administrations. For England, the Flood and Water Management Act 2010 has set out the requirement for a national framework for managing risk to be issued by the national environmental regulator, the Environment Agency. The current version of this framework has been set out in "Understanding the risks, empowering communities, building resilience: The national flood and coastal erosion risk management strategy for England" (Environment Agency, 2011). This sets out a high-level framework (Figure 7.1) which empowers various actors to plan for and manage risk, including future pressures such as sea-level rise (SLR).

The key vehicle for strategic planning of coastal erosion risks in England has been the shoreline management plan (SMP). This is overseen by a coastal erosion risk management authority, a local authority whose functions include planning shoreline management activities with input from the Environment Agency and the delivery of coastal erosion risk management activities (using powers under a range of legislation). The SMP is a local strategic plan put together by groups of key stakeholders in defined coastal areas. First-generation plans were issued in 1996, and the current second-generation plans were generally completed in 2009. The SMPs take account of future projections of SLR driven by climate change.

An important aspect of the risk management framework is that it is largely permissive. This means powers are granted to authorities to act to manage risk, but there is generally no legal obligation to provide a particular level of risk management. As such, citizens do not have legal rights to protection levels or other outcomes. However, central and local governments make significant public resources available to manage risk, through political decisions supported by assessment of costs and benefits. Such resources have been deployed over many years to provide locally appropriate protection through coastal defence construction, as well as information provision such as mapping and warning. Land use and other local planning takes account of risk.

At the local level, environmental, economic and technical assessments do not always conclude, however, that tangible defence against risks is deliverable, even in the presence of factors such as expected sea-level rise, which is key to the case study described in this chapter.

Capital costs for protection for those where it is viable are mostly met by the national Exchequer, albeit with increasing contributions from local partners (see Partnership Funding, (Box 2.4). Revenue costs such as maintenance of defences are often met by coastal local authorities, although such sources have undergone significant reductions in recent years. Conversely, flood defence maintenance is more often funded by the National Exchequer. Within local areas, some taxation may be used to support coastal protection, although local funding and financing is in practice heavily constrained. Occasionally, major business beneficiaries in areas (e.g. tourism facilities, energy infrastructure providers) may contribute funding.

Figure 7.1. Overview of flood and coastal erosion risk management in the United Kingdom

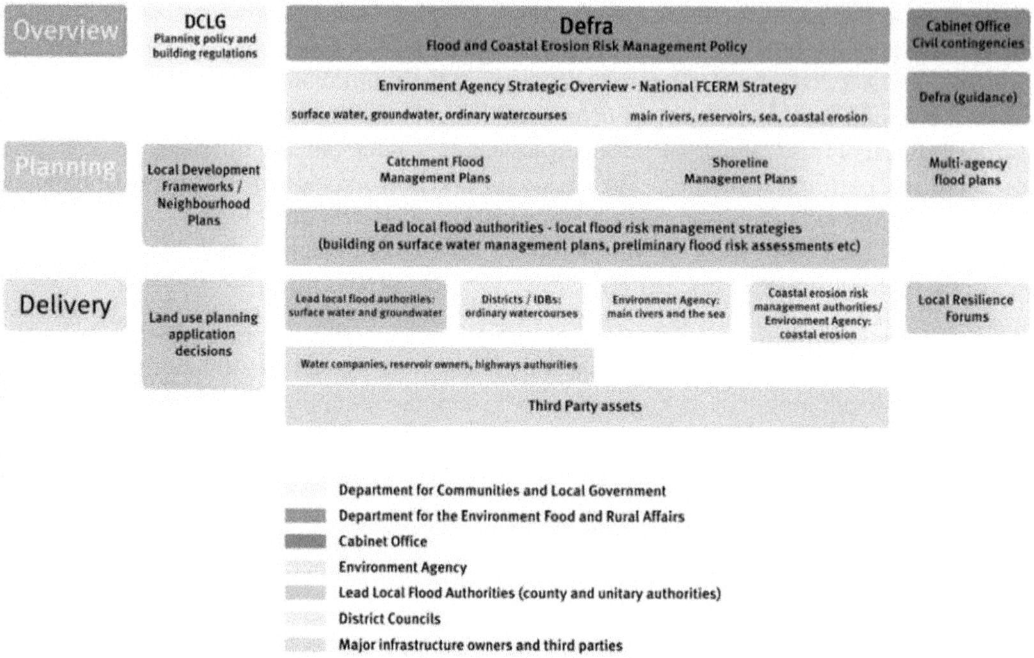

In terms of liability for damage, flood risk is generally covered by private insurance (currently supported by a publically subsidised pool, Flood Re), though coastal erosion is not. Private property owners are liable for erosion damage and loss. Disaster compensation has generally not been offered by public authorities as there is no funding or policy basis, though in the case of flooding, public grants for property resilience have occasionally been offered (though more for inland events). In the United Kingdom, as elsewhere, there are general benefits to living on the coast, though this can be offset by some coastal areas being economically peripheral (e.g. distant from employment centres). In areas where coastal defence investment becomes unjustified, perhaps departing from past policy, property value can quickly disappear, which can cause transitional difficulties.

7.2. North Norfolk and Happisburgh

7.2.1. The area and the Shoreline Management Plan

The area of focus is Happisburgh, a village on the northeast Norfolk coast. The coastline in this area is under inherent and active erosion pressure because of its geology and morphological conditions. This is in contrast with some neighbouring areas of coast which are more stable and indeed rely on the study area for sediment supply.

Happisburgh is a small, historic rural coastal settlement with a population of around 900 at the 2011 Census. The area is relatively deprived, with a position at around 25% in the English Index of Multiple Deprivation (where the lower the percentage, the more deprived).[1] Wider population density in the area is relatively low; the nearest significant town is around 10 kilometres away (North Walsham). The economy of the wider locality is largely driven by tourism and agriculture, though with some out-commuting to economic centres further afield such as Norwich, Great Yarmouth, and the more local tourism centres of Cromer and Sheringham.

The vulnerability of the area to coastal erosion has been assessed in the SMP for this part of Norfolk (East Anglian Coastal Group, 2012[1]). SMPs cover the whole coastline of England and Wales, and are non-statutory documents for coastal defence planning. Alongside catchment flood management plans, the SMPs are a form of high-level plan in the Flood and Coastal Erosion Risk Management National Strategy published by the Environment Agency (see above). The SMPs are put together collaboratively by groups representing coastal interests (flood management authorities, local authorities and others). They present plans taking account of the prevailing UK Climate Projections science report on future SLR, with supporting modelling estimating the interaction between this, sea flooding and rates of coastal erosion.

The latest (second) edition of the SMP covering the area from Kelling, on the north coast of Norfolk, to Lowestoft Ness, about 90° clockwise around the coast to the east, was finalised in August 2012 by the East Anglian Coastal Group. Happisburgh is broadly in the centre of this stretch of coast. Along with others, the overall plan area was defined at national level with regard to broad-scale coastal processes (morphology). There is little observed transfer of sediment between this plan area and others, which makes it an independent cell in which interdependencies are "internalised" and hence suitable as a planning "unit". Within the plan area, however, there is significant transfer of sediment between areas. By nature or design, areas of economic importance such as Sheringham, Cromer and Great Yarmouth are either morphologically stable, protected or receivers of sediment. Other localities in the plan area are inherent suppliers of sediment, even if this is or has been moderated by coastal management.

Figure 7.2. Norfolk Shoreline Management Plan area in the wider context

Number 6 in legend, includes related catchement flood management plans

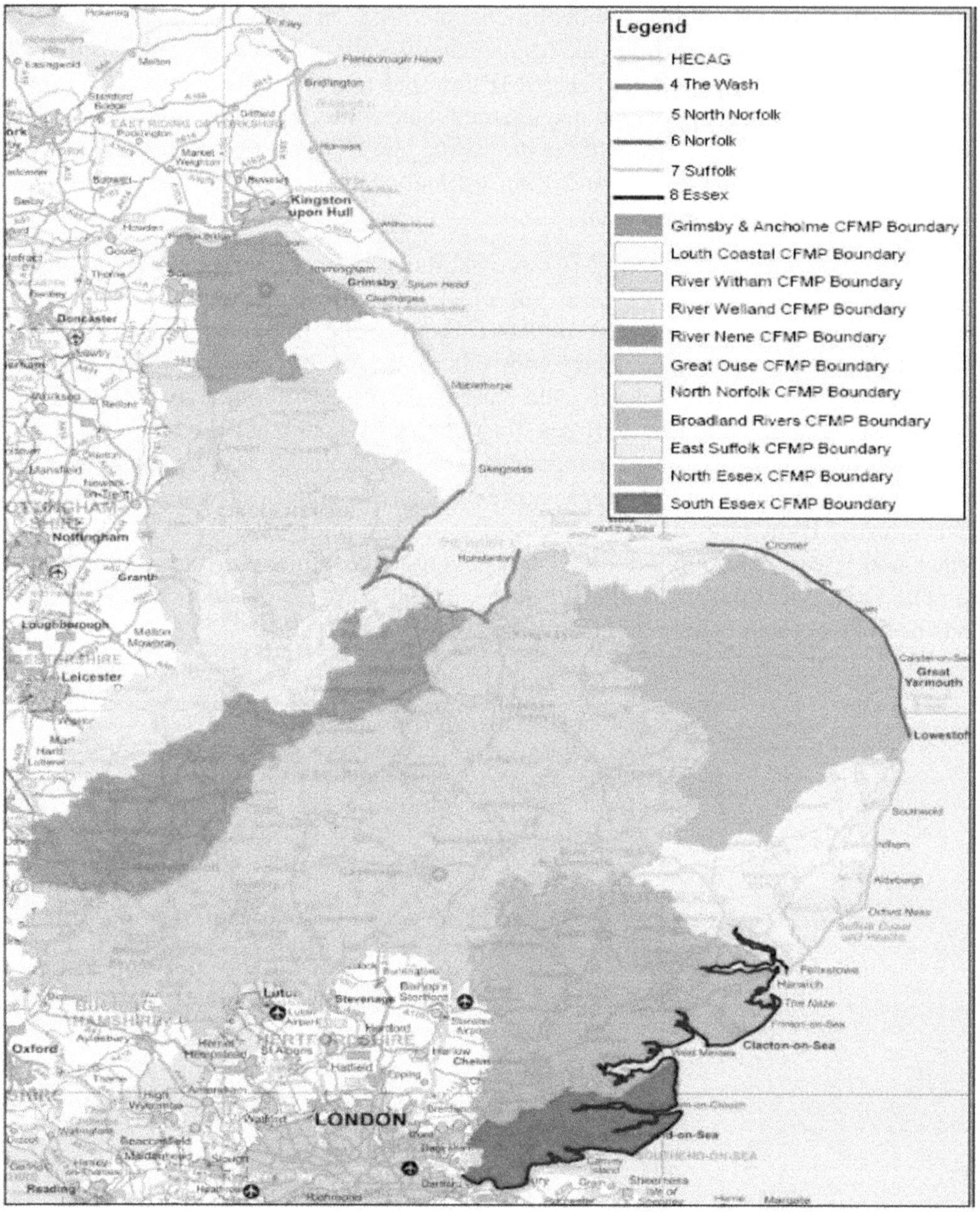

Source: Kelling to Lowestoft Ness SMP, 2012 (AECOM and East Anglian Coastal Group).

7.2.2. Shoreline Management Plan recommendations for Happisburgh

Figure 7.3 presents the assessment of risk from coastal erosion for the frontage including Happisburgh. From the mid-2000s to 2025 (purple band), an area of erosion was identified leading to the forecast loss of around 15 properties, land at a caravan (tourist) park, the coastguard station and other land. Further loss of another five or so properties and other land was identified in the period from 2025-55 (yellow band). Finally, for the last epoch of the plan (2055-2105), a further 15-20 properties was projected to be lost to erosion (red band).

Figure 7.3. Extract from Norfolk Shoreline Management Plan for Policy Unit 6.12 including Happisburgh

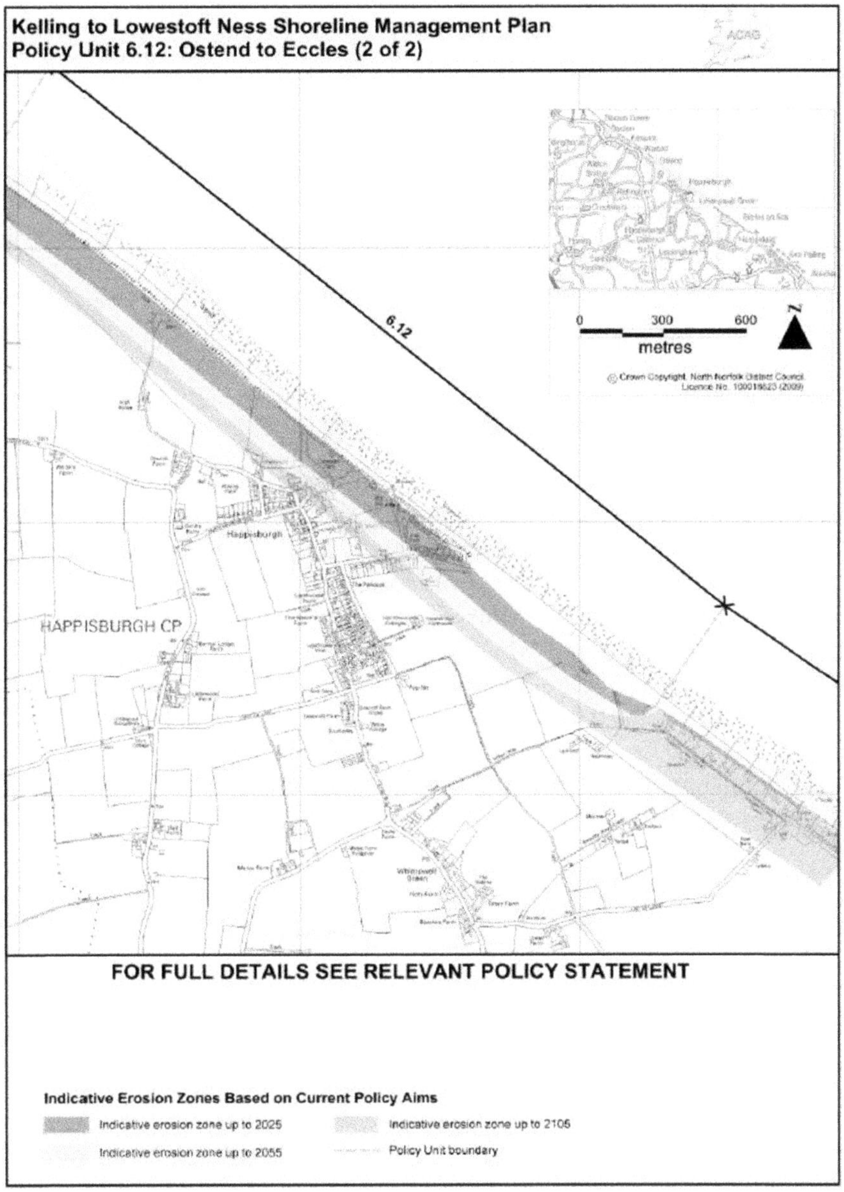

Source: Kelling to Lowestoft Ness SMP, 2012 (AECOM and East Anglian Coastal Group).

Taking account of the inherent morphology of the area and the impacts and economics of different management policies for the locality, the SMP concluded:

> *In the long term it will not be appropriate to defend Happisburgh due to the impact this would have on the SMP shoreline as a whole, as the coastal retreat either side would result in the development of this area as a promontory making it both technically difficult to sustain and impacting significantly upon the alongshore sediment transport to downdrift areas. Although there are implications, such as loss to erosion of residential properties and amenities at Happisburgh, these are not sufficient to economically justify building new defences along this frontage.*

Therefore, the long-term plan is to allow natural functioning of the coast through allowing it to retreat. However, in the short term the council will make every effort to minimise the rate of coastal erosion at this location, using appropriate temporary measures, including maintenance of the existing rock bund, with a view to allowing time for measures to be introduced to allow people to adapt to the changes in the medium and long term.[2]

7.3. The local adaptation response

Whereas in the current survey of OECD member country approaches to coastal risks, "adaptation" can often mean providing defence, in the case of Happisburgh and many areas on the English east coast, "adaptation" has a very different meaning. As highlighted in the SMP extract above, the economic and environmental justification for defence at Happisburgh was weak: the clear implication was that the affected community would need to "adapt" to coastal change in other ways. In essence, this meant using land-use planning and other mechanisms to move, over time, the community onto land out of risk.

During the first decade of this century, the SMPs being conducted around the English and Welsh coasts highlighted a growing need for some communities to explore new approaches to adapt to coastal change, where traditional defence approaches were proving economically and environmentally unsustainable. Between 2010 and 2012, the Department for Environment, Food and Rural Affairs (Defra) made available a grant scheme to local authorities to test such approaches, known as the Coastal Change Pathfinder Programme. One of the largest recipients of funding was North Norfolk District Council (NNDC), which put forward a range of innovative projects to test adaptation approaches in the real world of the Norfolk coastline, in conjunction with existing, but novel, approaches to land-use planning. In Happisburgh, this included the following projects to "roll back" important properties and features to new sites:

- nine residential properties at short-term risk of loss to erosion in Beach Road
- an important local business, a caravan park, at risk of partial short-term loss
- a car park used by visitors to the beach, and beach access.

This case study focuses on the biggest of the schemes, the Beach Road residential rollback. However, some information on other projects advanced by the NNDC as part of the Pathfinder Programme is provided towards the end of this case study. Further detail is available in Regeneris (2011[2]).

7.4. Beach Road project: Overview

This project was an attempt to pump-prime development activity which was, in principle, already enabled through a novel local land-use planning policy known as "EN12". The policy grants development opportunities to owners of properties at risk of coastal erosion, according to the risk "contours" set out in the SMP. Owners of residential properties have an opportunity to develop on land not otherwise allocated for residential use, provided their existing property is at risk of loss within 20 years. A similar opportunity is afforded to business properties; in this case, the loss period is 50 years. The development opportunity is tradable in conjunction with the property, and the idea is that those finding themselves at risk acquire a tradable value which can offset some of the financial loss associated with properties facing erosion. The value of the opportunity is enhanced through the "planning gain" associated with enabling development of land not already allocated for residential use (e.g. agricultural land). This element, in particular, should in theory make buying the development opportunity (and associated at-risk property) attractive to developers, yielding funds to help existing property owners to move. Figure 7.4 illustrates the economics of the approach.

Figure 7.4. The theoretical economics of the North Norfolk "EN12 Rollback" planning policy

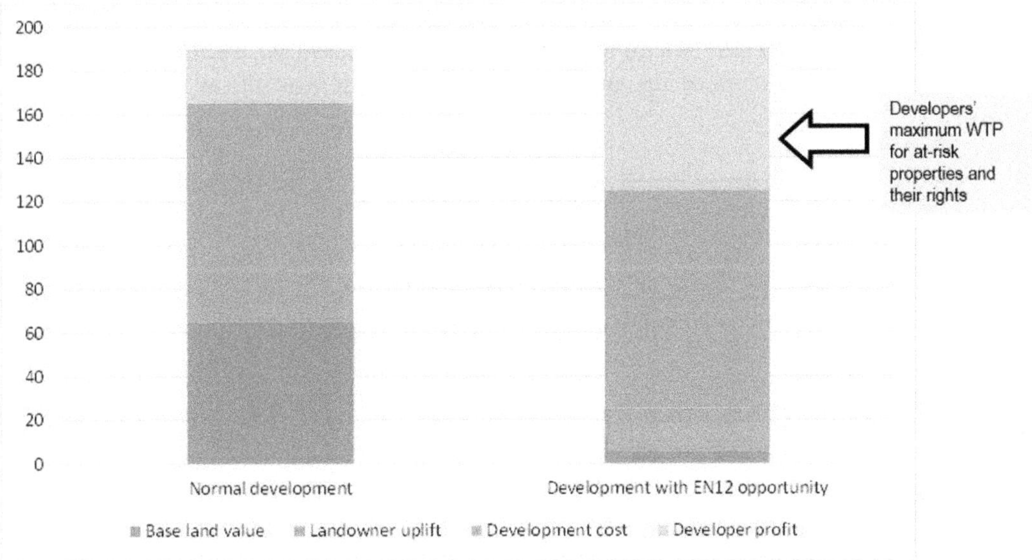

In Figure 7.4, which uses purely illustrative figures for development values albeit loosely based on local averages, the left-hand column shows land value (blue), development costs (grey) and developer profit (yellow) for a conventional development on already-designated residential land. The right-hand column shows the equivalent for a development using an EN12 Rollback opportunity. Because the latter allows development on land not currently allocated for residential use, land costs can in theory be much lower (e.g. agricultural land value – the blue bar). For the same development costs (in grey), and assuming the same end-market value for the property is achieved, the development profit element is therefore potentially much higher. In reality, this profit element will be split between the developer (yellow) and the landowner (brown) through negotiation and depending on market conditions and relative market power of the two parties. In this example, it is assumed the landowner captures a quarter of the profit that would otherwise have gone to the developer.[3]

The difference in profit (yellow bars) between the two scenarios indicates the theoretical developer's willingness to pay for an EN12 Rollback opportunity, discounting any residual value of the at-risk property to which it is attached. At first glance using these illustrative figures, this might be a little less than a third of the market value of a new property. In practice, the value passed on to the at-risk property owner will have to be less than this for the transaction to be attractive to the developer. For these reasons, on this illustration, it is clear that the value of the EN12 Rollback opportunity realisable by an at-risk property owner would not be expected fully to pay for a relocation. However, the greater the residual life of the at-risk property (say for rental[4]), the greater the potential total proceeds, indicating that early action on the part of at-risk property owners is advisable.

As "EN12" was a new arrangement in the NNDC's planning policy (now adopted on a more national basis), it was felt appropriate to use some of the Pathfinder Programme funds to test the idea, providing demonstration and "pump-priming" benefits. The first stage was to negotiate to purchase identified properties in Beach Road, Happisburgh. These properties were, in practice, at near-term risk (within 20 years), had limited remaining economic life and some were already in poor condition through understandable lack of investment (Figure 7.5). In theory, a valuation of these properties was their "at-risk" value plus the value of the EN12 Rollback opportunity (in concept, as above). In practice, because the project was breaking new ground, the NNDC ultimately paid an estimated theoretical value based on potential future rental valuations for the remaining property life, the valuation of the rollback opportunity and a disturbance payment. In reality, the NNDC paid approximately GBP 700 000 (for nine properties, in 2011). On an average per-property basis, this was around 45% of the overall average price in Norfolk at the time ((n.a.), 2018[3]).

Figure 7.5. Properties in Beach Road, Happisburgh before the rollback scheme

Source: Eastern Daily Press.

The economic analysis above does not adequately convey some of the practical challenges of rollback schemes. In the case of Beach Road, there were difficulties associated with seeking planning consent within the community for a site not in a currently designated residential area, and negotiating purchases both of at-risk properties and replacement sites. However, at the time of writing (2018), implementation of the scheme is nearing completion. Properties on Beach Road were demolished once purchased by the NNDC, with the area landscaped, and a new site for nine replacement units was eventually found. Planning consent was achieved and an agreement reached with a developer to buy the site with associated permissions. It is hoped construction will soon be complete. Receipts to the NNDC after costs totalled GBR 250 000, which went some way to offset the GBR 700 000 outlay for the original properties and the associated administrative and other costs. As such, while the scheme is not close to being self-financing,[5] it has proved an important trial with numerous research and demonstration benefits.

7.5. Cost-benefit analyses and assessment of trade-offs

The costs and benefits of the Beach Road rollback scheme have been assessed on two occasions, in 2011 and 2015. Both of these analyses were conducted before the completion of the scheme and it would perhaps be valuable to revisit these assessments now that the project has been completed. In 2011, Regeneris Consulting concluded the societal benefit-cost ratio of the Happisburgh rollback was 0.7:1. Essentially this seemingly poor result was because the scheme ultimately replaced one set of properties with a similarly beneficial set, at a cost in terms of administration, demolition, etc. Regeneris did estimate in 2011, however, that "when using an investment model and without factoring in the management costs or void rental periods, when the EN12 opportunity value is applied, the model is financially self-supporting".

Understandably, this assessment focused primarily on tangible property-related values and was not able to quantify the wider benefits of facilitating the continuation and regeneration of Happisburgh as a viable community. Such wider values remain a challenge for benefit-cost analysis and include health and stress impacts, reputational damage to the area, crime and other impacts associated with the area becoming increasingly "blighted", and a social opportunity cost to the community of focusing on erosion issues rather than wider community development.

Risk and Policy Analysts (RPA) revisited the cost-benefit assessment in 2015 as part of a further *ex post* evaluation of a number of rollback schemes facilitated by the Coastal Pathfinder programme, and drew similar conclusions. The estimated range of benefit-cost ratios for rollback schemes involving new development was 0.5-1.1:1. More generally, RPA concluded:

> *Overall evidence from the Pathfinder projects suggests that rollback, with the right policies and mechanisms in place, is a feasible adaptation option that is desirable from the perspective of the local authority and the individuals at imminent risk of coastal erosion. Rollback options may also be cost-beneficial based on the economic assessment. Buy-in at the community level can be more difficult to achieve, but effective communication can increase awareness and understanding of the situation (in terms of the options available in the wider context of coastal erosion issues) and thus increase desirability. The problems encountered in the Pathfinder projects provide valuable lessons for other local authorities in terms of expected issues and how to overcome them. The key areas to focus on when identifying the usefulness of rollback include:*
>
> - *Understanding the make-up and geographical scale of the community, including demographics*
> - *Understanding community expectations*
> - *Investigating community understanding of the inevitability of erosion*
> - *Identifying what the local authority can and should provide*
> - *Assessing the specific needs of individuals*
> - *Recognising which skills are needed*
> - *Accepting that rollback is likely to require long-term planning (2015[4]).*

7.5.1. Notes on other NNDC schemes

The Beach Road "rollback" scheme was one of several coastal adaptation schemes promoted by the NNDC in Happisburgh and elsewhere in the district as part of Defra's Coastal Change Pathfinder programme. Summary notes on other key schemes follow.

Happisburgh – Manor Caravan Park

Manor Caravan Park was identified at being at erosion risk and as a key aspect contributing to the vibrancy of Happisburgh. As part of the wider projects to assist the village, the park was included in the Pathfinder. Assistance was achieved through a grant to assist the business to develop and deliver options to enable it to adapt to coastal change. The grant assisted the owners to identify a rollback site away from the coastal erosion risk zone while still remaining in Happisburgh, thus retaining its economic input into the village.

With the discharge of Planning Conditions in 2018, the remaining element of the Pathfinder grant was provided to the park to assist with the installation of essential services as part of the wider relocation.

The new site will begin to open in spring 2019. The rollback of the park is a significant undertaking by the owners and was the first encouraged and initially facilitated rollback of an at-risk holiday park.

Trimingham Village Hall

The Trimingham coastline is identified in the adopted SMP with a policy of "managed realignment" as coastal protection is not considered technically feasible, environmentally acceptable or economically viable. Due to this, the SMP also highlights the need to develop alternative measures to assist with managing the impacts of a changing coast.

Trimingham has a number of coastal adaptation needs and the Pathfinder provided an opportunity to relocate the "Pilgrims Shelter" (village hall) away from erosion risk. An initial grant was provided to Trimingham Parish Council to assist with the purchase of land, the application for consents and to act as seed funding to assist with attracting further funding.

Following significant effort by the Parish Council and local community, the additional funds were raised for the new Village Hall culminating in the successful opening of the facility in summer 2018. Discussions are now underway with regards to the repurposing of the "Pilgrims Shelter" and guidance is being provided by the NNDC Economic Development Team as to how this building may be integrated into the Deep History Coast initiative while also continuing to provide a valuable local function.

The replacement of the Village Hall at Trimingham is a successful example of one aspect of adapting the coast and its communities to coastal change. This was only achieved through initial identification of a need, funding to kick start the project, and determination and hard work by key members of the local community.

Trimingham – Residential properties

Further coastal adaptation has occurred at Trimingham with the demolition and replacement of four dwellings which were at risk of coastal erosion (all were served with prohibition orders). The NNDC provided guidance for a private initiative to utilise the NNDC rollback planning policy and facilitated access to Defra's Coastal Erosion Assistance Grant[6] to assist with the demolition of the properties.

The four properties now have planning consent for replacement in nearby Mundesley. The original dwellings, now demolished, no longer pose a potential threat of collapse onto the adjacent cliffs (a Site of Special Scientific Interest) with the risk of future beach debris and potential environmental hazards.

This is one of only two completed examples in North Norfolk of the private use of residential rollback. This has only been achieved through provision of assistance and guidance by the NNDC, the availability of a Defra assistance grant, and significant effort and risk undertaken by a private individual.

7.6. Lessons learnt and conclusions

The Coastal Change Pathfinder programme has provided valuable lessons and helped work through the issues associated with rollback and other adaptation interventions in the real world. The Beach Road residential rollback project has been a success in terms of facilitating a new development site out of the erosion risk area – even if construction has yet to complete – removing blighted properties at short-term risk. Some of the key lessons of the Beach Road scheme in particular include:

- The rollback and replacement of properties be it residential, community or commercial, is possible and can lead to significant local benefits. However, analysis of the finances of such schemes and real-life experience suggests that it is unlikely that without support, guidance and some funding that such approaches will be delivered by the private sector alone. Against a backdrop of poor cost-benefit returns for traditional defence measures, there was interest in exploring if rollback could provide a more economically advantageous solution. However, economic assessment of rollback schemes on the same basis as defence schemes (i.e. focusing on property impacts) has fairly consistently yielded a relatively poor cost-benefit ratio. With hindsight, this is to be expected to the extent economic appraisal characterises such schemes as simply replacing existing capital assets (properties), and indeed foreshortening the lives of existing assets, but at a cost. That said, this kind of assessment has often not been able to take into account all the wider socio-economic benefits associated with maintaining and regenerating communities blighted by risk.
- In practical terms, community acceptance of rollback schemes is challenging when there remains a perception that coastal protection is a "right". Any new development, be it for rollback or otherwise, is often challenging due to the common stance in communities of "not in my back yard".

The main ongoing issues faced for relocation/rollback post-Pathfinder are primarily threefold:

1. Local authorities' planning policies (supported by the National Planning Policy Framework) usually encourage relocation/rollback only within a restricted area and the option only exists when the asset is threatened within a certain time frame (20 years). The restricted area aims to keep housing/assets within the threatened village or area. This has the effect of discouraging rollback as asset/homeowners may want to move elsewhere or there may be no suitable sites within the defined area. This leads to assets remaining within the risk zone. The fact the policy only applies when the asset is within 20 years of risk discourages early adaptation. Asset/home-owners prefer to hold onto their property until the last moment, for example, in case a defence scheme is put into place. The property then remains within the risk zone

and the rollback is not utilised. The town of Hemsby is an example of this, where properties are being demolished right on the edge of the cliff, as there is no early adaptation incentive.

2. There is no facilitative funding, and purchasing a rollback site within the restricted area is not possible. Outside of the Pathfinder programme, there has generally not been funding available for adaptation and so asset/home-owners hold onto their property until the last moment. When trying to purchase a rollback site, landowners of potential sites realise that the individual(s) with the rollback opportunity are likely to gain planning permission, and so the price of the land is increased dramatically (sometimes tenfold, in contrast to the conservative theoretical example set out earlier in Figure 7.4). Again, this leads to property remaining within the risk zone as the rollback cannot be utilised.
3. Securing planning permission is extremely challenging. Obtaining planning permission for new rollback developments in the countryside is constrained by other policies/matters (presence of Areas of Outstanding Natural Beauty and other designated areas, pressure from local groups, etc.). Again, this leads to property remaining within the risk zone as the rollback cannot be utilised.

Rollback has the potential to avoid most of the costs and impacts associated with inaction in the face of coastal erosion risk. However, experience post-Pathfinder suggests that the key to devising a successful rollback scheme is to provide incentive for early uptake and gain community support.

Notes

[1] In principle, this means the area could benefit from enhanced funding for reducing coastal erosion risk through the government's Partnership Funding scheme, though this is contingent on the SMP recommending action.

[2] Summary of plan recommendations and justification, Policy Unit 6.12, Ostend to Eccles (2012 SMP p.95)

[3] In practice this is rather conservative and landowners have sought to capture much greater value (see "lessons learnt and conclusions" section), but this example seeks to set out the theoretical "best case" for the value of the EN12 opportunity.

[4] The EN12 Rollback opportunity is only usable once, so if the property was sold on again it would be at its inherent at-risk value.

[5] Some stakeholders in the Pathfinder scheme entertained a hope that such "rollback" approaches could ultimately become self-financing, though in practice it is clear that this would only be possible with very significant value uplift for replacement properties: implying that replacement would not be like for like but involve significantly different kinds of development.

[6] This is a fund made available by the national government to contribute towards demolition costs. It is separate from the Coastal Change Pathfinder programme.

References

(n.a.) (2018), *home.co.uk.* [3]

East Anglian Coastal Group (2012), *Kelling to Lowestoft Ness Shoreline Management Plan*, http://www.aecom.com (accessed on 10 December 2018). [1]

Regeneris Consulting (2011), *Coastal Pathfinder Evaluation: An assessment of the five largest Pathfinder projects*, DEFRA. [2]

Royal Haskoning DHV, R. (2015), *Adapting to Coastal Erosion: Evaluation of rollback and leaseback schemes in Coastal Change Pathfinder projects, Final report FD2679*, Defra. [4]

Annex A. National adaptation plans

COUNTRY	Name	Year	Link
Australia	*National Climate Resilience and Adaptation Strategy*	2015	www.environment.gov.au/system/files/resources/3b44e21e-2a78-4809-87c7-a1386e350c29/files/national-climate-resilience-and-adaptation-strategy.pdf
Belgium	Belgium National Adaptation Plan	2017	www.climat.be/files/4214/9880/5755/NAP_EN.pdf
Canada	Pan-Canadian Framework on Clean Growth and Climate Change	2016	www.assembly.pe.ca/docs/pan-canadian_climatechange.pdf
Chile	Plan de Acción Nacional de Cambio Climático 2017-2022 (PANCC-II)	2017	http://portal.mma.gob.cl/wp-content/uploads/2017/07/plan_nacional_climatico_2017_2.pdf
Denmark	Danish Strategy for Adaptation to a Changing Climate	2008	http://en.klimatilpasning.dk/media/5322/klimatilpasningsstrategi_uk_web.pdf
Estonia	Climate Change Adaptation Development Plan until 2030	2017	www.envir.ee/sites/default/files/national_adaptation_strategy.pdf
Finland	Finland's National Climate Change Adaptation Plan 2022	2014	http://mmm.fi/documents/1410837/5120838/MMM-_193086-v1-Finland_s_National_climate_Change_Adaptation_Plan_2022.pdf/582041ee-3518-4a63-bf60-7133aed95a9c
France	Nouveau plan national d'adaptation au changement climatique : Premières pistes	2017	https://www.ecologique-solidaire.gouv.fr/nouveau-plan-national-dadaptation-au-changement-climatique-premieres-pistes
Germany	German Strategy for Adaptation to Climate Change	2008	hwww.preventionweb.net/files/27772_dasgesamtenbf1-63.pdf
Greece	National Strategy for Adaptation to Climate Change	2016	http://www.ypeka.gr/LinkClick.aspx?fileticket=crbjkilcLIA%3d&tabid=303&language=el-GR
Ireland	National Adaptation Framework	2018	https://www.dccae.gov.ie/documents/National%20Adaptation%20Framework.pdf
Israel	Adaptation to Climate Change in Israel Recommendations and knowledge gaps	2014	www.sviva.gov.il/InfoServices/ReservoirInfo/DocLib2/Publications/P0701-P0800/P0739.pdf
Italy	National Adaptation Plan	2016	www.minambiente.it/sites/default/files/archivio/allegati/clima/strategia_adattamentoCC.pdf
Japan	National Plan for Adaptation to the Impacts of Climate Change	2015	www.env.go.jp/en/focus/docs/files/20151127-101.pdf

Korea	2nd National Climate Change Adaptation Strategy	2015	https://www.preventionweb.net/files/58461_korearepofsummarysecondnationalclim.pdf
Latvia	*Strategy currently under development*	-	-
Mexico	Mexico's Climate Change Mid-Century Strategy	2016	https://www.gob.mx/inecc/documentos/mexico-s-climate-change-mid-century-strategy
Netherlands	Adapting with Ambition: National Climate Adaptation Strategy	2016	http://ruimtelijkeadaptatie.nl/publish/pages/125102/2016_12_02_nas_netherlands_4.pdf
New Zealand	*Strategy currently under development*	-	-
Norway	National Adaptation Strategy (White paper)	2013	https://www.regjeringen.no/contentassets/e5e7872303544ae38bdbdc82aa0446d8/en-gb/pdfs/stm201220130033000engpdfs.pdf
Poland	Polish National Strategy for Adaptation to Climate Change (NAS 2020)	2013	https://klimada.mos.gov.pl/wp-content/uploads/2014/12/ENG_SPA2020_final.pdf
Portugal	National Adaptation Strategy	2015	https://dre.pt/application/file/69906414
Slovenia	Strategic Framework for Climate Change Adaptation	2011	www.mop.gov.si/si/delovna_podrocja/podnebne_spremembe/prilagajanje_podnebnim_spremembam/
Spain	Strategy for the adaptation of the coast to the effects of climate change	2017	https://www.miteco.gob.es/es/costas/temas/proteccion-costa/estrategia-adaptacion-cambio-climatico/default.aspx
Sweden	Impacts, vulnerability and adaptation assessments	2015	www.smhi.se/polopoly_fs/1.86329!/Menu/general/extGroup/attachmentColHold/mainCol1/file/Klimatologi%20Nr%2012.pdf
Turkey	Turkey's National Adaptation Strategy and Action Plan	2012	www.dsi.gov.tr/docs/iklim-degisikligi/turkeys-national-climate-change-adaptation-strategy-and-action-plan.pdf?sfvrsn=2
United Kingdom	The National Adaptation Programme	2018	https://assets.publishing.service.gov.uk/government/uploads/system/uploads/attachment_data/file/727252/national-adaptation-programme-2018.pdf

www.ingramcontent.com/pod-product-compliance
Ingram Content Group UK Ltd.
Pitfield, Milton Keynes, MK11 3LW, UK
UKHW051503290926
15471UKWH00008B/1379

9 789264 312470